Biomedical
Engineering
Entrepreneurship

Biomedical
Engineering
Entrepreneurship

Jen-Shih Lee

Global Monitors Inc., University of California, San Diego
and University of Virginia, USA

World Scientific

NEW JERSEY · LONDON · SINGAPORE · BEIJING · SHANGHAI · HONG KONG · TAIPEI · CHENNAI

Published by

World Scientific Publishing Co. Pte. Ltd.

5 Toh Tuck Link, Singapore 596224

USA office: 27 Warren Street, Suite 401-402, Hackensack, NJ 07601

UK office: 57 Shelton Street, Covent Garden, London WC2H 9HE

British Library Cataloguing-in-Publication Data

A catalogue record for this book is available from the British Library.

BIOMEDICAL ENGINEERING ENTREPRENEURSHIP

ISBN-13 978-981-4295-60-4

ISBN-10 981-4295-60-4

Printed in Singapore.

Dedicated to the memory of my parents,
Mr. Yu-Ri Lee and Mrs. Yao-Ze Lai Lee,
for raising the Lee brothers and sisters;
To Lian-pin, my wife and dearest friend;
To our children and our grand children;
I love them all with all of my heart.

Preface

The spiraling increase in healthcare costs and the growing number of those who have no health insurance are two daunting healthcare challenges for the United States to overcome in the coming decades. In the meantime, progress in science, engineering and medicine will continue to revolutionize healthcare in America. The professionals in biomedical engineering (BME) can meet these two challenges by creating improvements in technology that will permit more efficient and higher quality healthcare to be delivered at a lower cost, as Dane Miller, CEO of Biomet, pointed out.

The US share of the world market for medical device has been held to 45~49% in recent years. Within a span of 30 years, China has grown its GDP by 30-fold. Most PCs, Notebook computers, iPhones etc., are now manufactured by the alliance of companies in America, Taiwan and China. Because of the increase in the purchasing power of their citizens, Brazil, Russia, India and China (BRIC) will become big consumers of medical devices and pharmaceutical products.

Physical disabilities, diabetes, chronic pulmonary obstructive disease, end stage renal disease, and deadly infectious diseases are too prevalent throughout the world. It is the responsibility of everyone to improve the existing medical technology and create innovations to help the billions of people in the Third World. The medical device and pharmaceutical industry must find a way to produce affordable medical technologies and products to meet the desperate need for better healthcare for the world.

As Peter Katona stated, "BME is a profession that requires knowledge in diverse areas, welcomes risk, poses major challenges, and offers substantive rewards. Thus, it is a natural home for entrepreneurship". This description of BME fits well with Robert Nerem's projection that "The future for biologically-based engineering is exceedingly bright, but one that more than likely will be much different than what any of us can today envision."

To achieve diversity, which is essential for BME students, many BME education programs in the US have already overwhelmed their undergraduates with courses in engineering, biology and medicine. A student survey of career choices indicates that BME undergraduates want to gain business and entrepreneurial experience so that, in ten to twenty years following university graduation, they can be entrepreneurs, their top career choice, building their enterprises in medical technology which can resolve or alleviate the medical problems of their friends, relatives and patients.

Judging from the enthusiasm of, and the extra effort spent by, students at the University of Virginia and University of California, San Diego, in taking the "BME Entrepreneurship" course, the author sees that many of them have already taken a giant step toward their entrepreneurial careers. They have spent a great deal of effort to work out a business plan for the course that tells their class how qualified they are as entrepreneurs, how critical the need to resolve the medical problem is, how their product uniquely resolves the problem, and how their product can generate profits for their companies. Support for these assertions is gathered from interviews by these students with many medical and engineering experts.

This book has been written for these students and others who want to become BME entrepreneurs. Sixteen of the chapters were written to address the following five questions and related issues:

- What is required to become a BME entrepreneur?
- How can innovation or improvement be demonstrated to benefit patients while generating profits for the company?
- Who are the BME entrepreneurs whose engineering and business ingenuity led them to develop successful enterprises?
- What are the unique challenges and opportunities that BME enterprises will face?
- How do you globalize your enterprise and improve your invention for the delivery of affordable healthcare to the Third World?

This book first introduces BME as an engineering profession and highlights the innovations that have contributed to the improved healthcare of the Twentieth Century. It concludes with two chapters on how to invest, after your enterprise has achieved success, in you, your company, society, the nation, the people and the world, and how to succeed in biomedical engineering entrepreneurism with really trying (by Shu Chien).

To all of you who want to become great entrepreneurs for the worldwide betterment of healthcare, the author wishes you the best.

Jen-shih Lee

Acknowledgements

This book is on Biomedical Engineering (BME) Entrepreneurship. The writing of this book, however, was made possible by the enthusiastic support of, and valuable critiques from, many contributors, who are identified below.

First, a course with the same title was taught at the University of Virginia (UVA) in 2003. The author is in debt to the stimulating lectures delivered by Dr. Howard Diamond, CEO, Diamond Electro-Tech, Inc.; Dr. Wendell Dunn, Professor of Entrepreneurship, Darden School of Graduate Business, UVA; Dr. George Gilles, Professor of Mechanical and BME, UVA; Dr. Robert Munzner, Former Chief, Neurological Device Branch, FDA; Dr. Henry Reeves, Director, JMU Small Business Development Center, SBA; Mr. Sheridan Snyder, Chairman and CEO, Upstate Biotechnology; Dr. T. Woodworth, Virginia's CIT. A significant portion of this book has been constructed from the lecture notes of these invited speakers.

In 2007, the course was shortened and taught at UCSD. Several lectures are delivered by Mr. Eric Eng, CPA, CEA, LLP; Mr. Erik Engleson, Former CEO, Target Therapeutics; Dr. Michael Heller, Professor of Bioengineering, UCSD; Dr. Duane Roth, CEO, CONNECT; Dr. John Watson, President of AIMBE (2007-2008); Dr. Jim Wang, CEO, Harmonic Tech; and Mr. Paul Wang, Senior VP of Marketing and Engineering, Spectragraphics Corp.

The author wants to express his thanks to the students of both classes for making numerous comments in class. They interviewed many experts in the field of their company developments, spent a great deal of effort to prepare their business plans, and enthusiastically presented the vision, strategy and actions necessary to develop their companies.

To learn more about the legendary Mr. U. A. Whitaker, the author was honored to interview Drs. Burtt Homes and Ruth Whitaker Holmes at The Whitaker Foundation in Arlington, Va. At the 24th NAPSE Annual Meeting in DC, the author interviewed Earl Bakken to seek his advice on writing this book. Later, the author interviewed him once more at his Big Island home in Hawaii. When asked how students should prepare themselves for a career in BME, he replied unequivocally, "Learn to speak Chinese because of the prominent role of China in global commerce." In this Hawaii visit, the author had an opportunity to see Bakken's "integrated healing center' in Waimea, Hawaii, which has turned Hawaii's Big Island into a "Healing Island" that befits the people who live or visit there. The author appreciates greatly the chance to interview Mr. Robert Capon and Dr. Joe Linden on the building-up of Adenosin Therapeutics, and Dr. Naishu Wang on Alfa Scientific Designs, Inc.

As a graduate of the CONNECT's Springboard Program, the author is indebted to the entrepreneurial coaching of Messrs. Marty Turock, John Plavan, Ruprecht von Buttlar and Charles Novitsky. He is grateful for the coaching effort of Messrs. Les Briney and Michael Lutz when Global Monitors, Inc. (GMI) participated in the 2008 Tech Coast Angels' Quick Pitch Competition.

Special thanks are due to Drs. Charles Wang, CEO and Lily Wang, President, Optodyne. Their success in patenting, manufacturing and marketing their Laser Doppler Displacement Measuring Systems serves as our role model in entrepreneurship. They are the ones convincing the author to proceed with the building-up of GMI. Mr. Paul Wang has provided many constructive critiques to Chapter 11 "Writing and Presenting the Business Plan". The author learned a great deal from his entrepreneurial experiences as he had worked at various senior management positions on engineering, marketing and sales for some seven large to small start-up companies. Charles, Lily and Paul had spent many hours in helping the author develop the business plan of GMI.

Dr. Chor Tan, initiator of the Engineering Management Certificate International of ASME and former Dean of Engineering, Cooper Union University, provided excellent critics for improving the presentations on engineering management in the chapters of the Section IV Building-up the Enterprise. Thanks are to Dr. Jackson S. N. Tung, Chief Scientist, Yunnan Health and Development Research Association and Dr. S. X. Cai, Professor of Biomechanics, Chongqing University for the improvements of the chapter on globalization. The author received considerable help from Dr. Shyhhau Wang, National Cheng-Kung University on outsourcing to and doing business in Taiwan. Thanks are to Mr. Kenneth Weitzman on his input on patenting, Mr. Dennis White on outsourcing, hardware manufacturing, and ventilator design, and Messrs. William Murphy and William Yuan on regulatory affairs.

To the author's dear BME colleagues Drs. Peter Katona, Michael Khoo, John Linehan, and Robert Nerem, the author are gratefully for their excerpts specifically written for Chapter 18 and Dr. Shu Chien who wrote the stimulating and challenging Chapter 19 on BME Entrepreneurism.

Thanks are to these friends Drs. Bill Chen, Peter Chen, Philip Chiu, Wilfred Huang, Alvin Tong, William Yuan and Richard Wang who help edit several chapters of this book. Mr. Albert Lee, VP of Production of GMI, made many valuable contributions for the author to clearly present the steps of doing the entrepreneurship in this book.

The author appreciates the help from Professors Shu Chien and Peter Chen of University of California San Diego, Professors Shasa Popel and Art Shoukas of Johns Hopkins University, and Professors Jean-Michael Maarek and Jesse Yen of University of Southern California in performing the career survey with their students.

In 2002, the author had the chance to work with a business planning team for the course "Venture Assessment" offered by Dunn at UVA. The students of Darden School of Graduate Business are Audrey Cao, Nirav Desai and Nitin Jain, who chose CardioMonitors, Inc. as their company for the due diligence study. In just one semester and with regular weekly meetings, they conducted a thorough due diligence analysis on the business aspects of a blood volume monitor. This is the first ever experience for the author in working with a group of exceptional business students and seeing their business-like pursue on due diligence. This experience convinces the author that the success of an entrepreneurial team can only be achieved by people knowledgeable in technology development and business operation working together with the least flaws and best collaborations.

The author wants to express his thanks to websites such as Google, Wikipedia and those on current news and financial analyses. These websites provide readily information for the author to present the cases and arguments in a substantial way for the book.

The author would acknowledge the helps and advices giving by Ms. Chelsea Chin of World Scientific Publishing Company and Ms. Jiin-Yun Liang for writing the book. To finalize the book for publication, the fantastic editing of the entire book done by Mr. George Robinson of WritingEnglish.com is deeply appreciated.

Contents

CHAPTER 1

INTRODUCING BIOMEDICAL ENGINEERING

1.1. Advancements in Biomedical Engineering

The past 30 years have seen an explosion of activity in the healthcare field. Medical researchers and entrepreneurs have identified and developed a range of new produc ts and processes that are intended to address an ever expanding range of medical conditions. This growth has been led by the medical device and biotechnology industry and , more recently, the expansion of the molecular diagnostics industry. Although the medical device and biotechnology industry has experienced a number of periods of boom or bust during that time, the overall growth in the number of medical products and product revenues has been dramatic.

We anticipate that the coming years will continue to see tremendous opportunities in the field of biomedical engineering. In particular, those individuals who are able to marry their clinical and engineering capabilities with an entrepreneurial mindset have the potential to become this century's Bill Gates or William Hewlett.

During the first three years of the 21st century, important and exciting developments have taken place in education and research funding in the field of biomedical imaging and bioengineering, including the following:

- The National Institutes of Health (NIH) grant ed a total of $500 million for research and development to small businesses in the United States in 2003.
- The National Institute of Biomedical Imaging and Bioengineering was established at the NIH, with a 2003 budget of $121 million, which will be used primarily to support research in the area of biomedical imaging and bioengineering. Its budget for the 2008 fiscal year is $300 million.
- The map of human genetic codes was completed by high-speed sequencing machines.

- The Whitaker Foun dation awarded more than $700 million to universities to enhance their education programs and research conducted by their biomedical engineering facult ies and students.

On the industrial front, we al so can report these exciting developments and projections:

- The Food and Drug Administration (FDA) has taken steps to streamline its approval process in order to shorten the time required for safe and effective medical devices and drugs to reach the market.
- There is a rapid increase in the use of medical devices and prescription drugs.
- The medical and healthcare industry makes up 14 percent of the 2003 gross domestic product, and the bio -based industry is projected to make up to 30 percent of the GDP in this decade.

With such tremendous progress and developments in mind, this book is written for undergraduate and graduate students who want to acquire the basic knowledge necessary for the development of biomedical engineering entrepreneurship. In writing the book, the author had the opportunity to interview many s uccessful biomedical engineering entrepreneurs, as well as visionary educators in the field of biomedical engineering. Their foresight, leadership, accomplishments, satisfaction, and positive impact on human health and our nation's economy are revealed in the text to draw attention to the subtle aspects of becoming successful BME entrepreneurs.

The materials presented in this book will also be useful for working biomedical engineers who w ish to build up their own companies or develop new ventures with the participation of their team members.

1.2. Scope of Biomedical Engineering

The Biomedical Engineering Society (BMES) describes on its website www.bmes.org a biomedical engineer as one who us es traditional engineering expertise to analyze and solve problems in biology and medicine with the objective of providing an overall enhancement of healthcare (24). Some of the well-established specialties within the field of biomedical engineering that are mentioned on the website are:

- Bioinstrumentation

- Biomaterials
- Biomechanics
- Cellular, tissue and genetic engineering
- Clinical engineering
- Medical imaging
- Orthopedic surgery
- Rehabilitation engineering
- Systems physiology.

Work done by biomedica l engineers may include a wide range of activities in the development of:

- Artificial organs
- Automated patient monitoring
- Blood chemistry sensors
- Advanced therapeutic and surgical devices
- Application of expert systems and artificial intelligence to clinical decision making
- Design of optimal clinical laboratories
- Computer modeling of physiological systems
- Biomaterials design
- Biomechanics of injury and wound healing
- Sports medicine.

As described above, biomedical engineering covers many diversified specialties. In teaching the topic of biomedical engineering entrepreneurship, we first define biomedical engineering companies as those that produce products for the diagnosis, prevention and treatment of diseases and the maintenance and improvement of health. Their products can be medical, diagnostic, or rehabilitation devices; materials for implantation; software for data or image processing; or drugs for the alleviation, treatment or cure of diseases.

1.3. Medical Device and Pharmaceutical Industry

Global medi cal device sale s in 2008 w ere estimated to be $336 billion by MX (12). In 2006, th e medical device industry employed about 411,000 workers in the United States, accounting for nearly one third of all US jobs in bioscience (18). There are an estimated 20,000 medical device companies around the world. The 2007 revenues of the top 20 companies are given in Table 1.1. As one can see , the device market is dominated by US co mpanies (1 4 of the 20 companies are U.S. -based), which received 2/3 of the revenue.   The prospect s for medical device s look robust as the revenues of these 20 companies grew by 9% from 2007 to 2008.   Only one company   had no   revenue growth , although another experienced a decrease of 1%.

Table 1.1. The world's top 20 medical device companies (18).

Company	Country of Origin	2007 Revenues ($ billion)
1. Johnson & Johnson	U.S.	$21.7
2. GE Healthcare	U.S.	$17.0
3. Siemens Medical Solutions	Germany	$14.4
4. Medtronic	U.S.	$12.9
5. Baxter International	U.S.	$11.3
6. Covidien	U.S.	$10.0
7. Philips Medical Systems	Netherlands	$8.9
8. Boston Scientific	U.S.	$8.4
9. Roche	Switzerland	$8.0
10. Becton Dickinson	U.S.	$6.5
11. Abbott Labs	U.S.	$6.3
12. Stryker	U.S.	$6.0
13. Cardinal Health	U.S.	$5.0
14. Olympus	Japan	$4.2
15. 3M Healthcare	U.S.	$4.0
16. Zimmer Holdings	U.S.	$3.9
17. St. Jude Medical	U.S.	$3.8
18. Smith & Nephew	U.K.	$3.4
19. Beckman Coulter	U.S.	$2.8
20. Synthes	Switzerland	$2.8
Total		$161.2

The medical device market   is about 50% of the world pharmaceutical market, but is growing faster than its drug counterpart.   For purposes of comparison, the revenues of the top five pharmaceutical companies and the top three biotechnology companies are listed in Table s 1.2 and 1.3 respectively. Revenues of t he top five pharmaceutical companies gr ew by 24% in 2008. The total revenues of all pharmaceutical companies in 2006 were $643 billion (22). The US accounted for 45% of world sales.

Table 1.2. Revenues of the top five pharmaceutical companies (22).

Top Five Pharmaceutical Companies	Country of Origin	2008 Revenues ($ billion)
Pfizer	U.S.	$70.8
Johnson & Johnson	U.S.	$61.1
GlaxoSmithKline	U.K.	$45.5
Hoffmann-LaRoche	Switzerland	$40.3
Sanofi-Aventis	France	$40.0
Total		**$257.7**

The 20 06 revenues for the sector biotech are estimated a t $60 billion. The revenues of the top three biotech companies are shown in Table 1.3. These three companies experienced a growth of 23% from 2007. The American biotech industry surpassed pharmaceutical com panies to become the primary source of new medicines for the years 2002 to 2005.

Table 1.3. Revenues of the top three biotech companies (21).

Top Three Biotech companies	Country of Origin	2008 Revenues ($ billion)
Amgen	U.S.	$15.0
Genentech	U.S.	$10.5
Gilead Sciences	U.S.	$5.3
Total		**$30.6**

1.4. Supporting Societies and Professional Activities

The Biomedical Engineering Society (BMES) was founded in 1968 to serve as a professional society that repre sented both biomedical and engineering interests. Its stated purpose is "To encourage the development, dissemination, integration, and utilization of knowledge in biomedical engineering" (24). Members include leading researchers from major universities, government agencies and BME corporations worldwide, as well as doctors and industry leaders in pharmaceuticals and prosthetic devices. BMES is the approved leading society for ABET accreditation of BME, bioenginee ring and technology programs. In 2008, t he BMES Annual Fall Meeting attract ed more than 2,200 practicing engineers , as well as medical specialists , from more than 20 countries. Tracks areas of recent meetings have included: Cardiovascular Engineering, Resp iratory Engineering, Orthopedic and

Rehabilitation Engineering, Neural Engineering, Cellular and Molecular Engineering, Tissue Engineering and Biomaterials, Bioinformatics and Systems Biology, Device Technologies   —from Nano to Micro, Biomedical Imaging and Optics, BME Education and New Frontiers.

In 1991,   the   American Institute for Medical and Biological Engineering (AIMBE) was established in Washington D.C.   The principal activities of AIMBE include acting as an advocate for public policy and disseminatin g information about medical and biological engineering (23). Its four components are College of Fellows, Academic Council, Council of Societies and Industry Council   . As of 2008, the College of Fellows ha d some 100 0 scientists, clinicians and engineers who ha d distinguished themselves in   the practice of medical and biological engineering. The Academic Council is made up of the programs or departments of biomedical engineering   of some 110 universities. The Council of   Societies has 14 society members (the society members who practice medical and biological engineering number more than 50,000). The fourth component, the Industry Council, comprises large and small bioengineering companies.

The year 2009 also marked the 4 0th anniversary of the Association for the Advancement of Medical Instrumentation (AAMI).   In its founding year 1969 and under the leadership of Dwight Harken, AAMI organized a National Conference on Medical Device Regulation in Bethesda, MD to address   the device safety concerns of the medical community and the government.   As John Abele, AAMI founder and Board Member, noted, "This conference was a huge event. It was the first time that the presidents of every American Medical Association   — recognized society   were present in one room   ." The taskforce recommendation on device regulation   that came from this conference formed the framework of the "Medical Device Amendments" legislation that was passed by Congress in 1976.

The Advanced Medical Technology Associatio n (AdvaMed) was formed by companies that produce medical devices, diagnostic products and health information systems. It is a trade association to promote policies that foster the highest ethical standards, rapid production approvals, appropriate reimburse   ment and a   ccess to international markets. AdvaMed's 2009 priorities are to foster continued innovation and ensure the delivery of the best possible healthcare for all Americans.

The Medical Device Manufacturers Association   (MDMA) is a national trade associ ation   that   provides   educational and advocacy assistance to innovative and entrepreneurial medical tech nology companies. It has bee n a voice for small companies and play s a proactive role in helping to shape government policies that have an impact on medical device innovators.

In addition to the professional magazines that are published by these societies, a number of prominent magazines serve the medical device industry. The premium magazines for the biomedical engineering community and medical device ind ustry include BMES' Annals of Biomedical Engineering ; AAMI's Biomedical Instrumentation & Technology; IEEE's Engineering in Medicine and Biology Magazine; MX: Business Strategies for Medical Technology Executives; MD&DI (Medical Device and Diagnostic Indus try) Magazine; Medical Device Link; Pharma Med. Device; and Nature, Biotech.

1.5. Innovations in Biomedical Engineering

"Innovation will be the single most important factor in determining America's success through the 21st century... America's challenge is to unleash its innovation capacity to drive productivity, standard of living and leadership in global markets... For the past 25 years, we have optimized our organizations for efficiency and quality. Over the next quarter century, we must optimize our so ciety for innovation." This is the opening resolution of an Innovate America report that was presented by Samuel J. Palmisano, Chairman and Chief Executive Officer of IBM Corporation and G. Wayne Clough, President of the Georgia Institute of Technology at the 2004 National Innovation Initiative Summit in Washington DC (15).

On the subject of medical innovations, three papers in the journal *Health Affairs* (vol. 20, 2001) conclude that

- Americans believe that opport unities for medical miracles are endless, and thus are willing to pay for progress.
- When cost s and benefits are weighed, technological advances have proven to be worth far more than their costs.
- The ten most important medical innovations developed during the last 25 years and ranked by a survey of physicians are:
    1. Magnetic resonance imaging (MRI) and computed tomography (CT) scanning,
    2. Angiotensin converting enzyme (ACE) inhibitors,

3. Balloon angioplasty with stents,
4. Statins,
5. Mammography,
6. Coronary artery bypass graft (CABG),
7. Proton pump inhibitors and H2 blockers,
8. Selective serotonin reuptake inhibitors (SSRIs) and non - SSRI antidepressants,
9. Cataract extraction and lens implant,
10. Hip and knee replacements.

One of AIMBE's goals is to accelerate the   growth of the na tion's economy and the improvement of healthcare by innovations in medical and biological engineering.   Promoting awareness of the contributions made by biomedical engineers and   assuring development of a public policy for a healthy environment for medical a nd biological engineering innovation led to the   selection of 24 innovations of medical and biological engineering   for induction to the AIMBE Hall of Fame. Grouped according to the decades in which   the innovations first gained wide usage, they are:

- 1950s and earlier
  - o   Artificial kidney
  - o   X-ray
  - o   Electrocardiogram
  - o   Cardiac pacemaker
  - o   Cardiopulmonary bypass
  - o   Antibiotic production technology
  - o   Defibrillator
- 1960s
  - o   Heart valve replacement
  - o   Intraocular lens
  - o   Ultrasound
  - o   Vascular grafts
  - o   Blood analysis and processing
- 1970s
  - o   Computer assisted tomography
  - o   Artificial hip and knee replacement
  - o   Balloon catheter
  - o   Endoscopy
  - o   Biological plant/food engineering

- 1980s
  - o Magnetic resonance imaging
  - o Laser surgery
  - o Vascular stents
  - o Recombinant therapeutics
- 1990s to the present
  - o Genomic sequencing and micro-arrays
  - o Positron emission tomography
  - o Image-guided surgery

The following three criteria were used by the fellows of AIMBE to make their selections from a list of 60 innovations that were nominated for entry to the AIMBE Hall of Fame:

- The innovation must represent a significant engineering achievement
- It must be in general use
- Most importantly, the innovation must save lives and improve the quality of life for a large number of people.

As described earlier in this Section, six major medical innovations that were identified by physicians are in the AIMBE's Hall of Fame. (The other four are innovative drugs.) To further contrast the significance of these two lists (one by physicians and one by biomedical engineers), we quote from the article by Fuchs and Sox (2) on th e physicians' ranked list that

"The most surprising finding of their study was the extent to which the leading innovations were an outgrowth of physical sciences (physics, engineering, and computer sc ience) rather than disciplines traditionally associated with biomedical sciences."

2009 was the 30 [th] Anniversary of the magazine MD&DI. To celebrate this occasion, the readers of MD&DI chose 30 innovative medical devices that had a significant impact on healthcare over the previous 30 years (1). They are listed below thanks to the courtesy of MD&DI. The first year that the device was used in the United States appears first.

1. 1979 Blood and Cell Separator. This device draws whole blood, keeps the desired component, and returns the

remaining blood components to the donor to eliminate   the
risk of contamination . It enables donors to give blood more
frequently and patients to receive blood from fewer donors.

2. 1980 Implanted Cardiovascular Defibrillator for patients   who are
at risk of sudden cardiac death due to ventricular
defibrillation.

3. 1980 Angioplasty Balloon
Catheter. This percutaneous
coronary intervention has
both improved and saved
the lives of patients.

4. 1980 Cochlear Implants, which give deaf people the ability to hear.

5. 1980 Intra Articular Arthroscopic
Shaver System. Its shaver is
used in orthopedic procedures
to remove bone or cartilage
and other soft tissue from   a
patient's joint.

6. 1980 Personal Glucose   Meter. This development advances
significantly the treatment of diabetes by moving glucose
testing from the hospital to the home.

7. 1981 Laryngeal Mask Airway . This assures that a patient who is
under anesthesia has an unobstructed airway.

8. 1981 Pulse Oximeter, a non -invasive way to measure continuously
the oxygen saturation level of a patient's blood.

9. 1983 EXCEL and PAB IV Containers. These simple "devices"
provide users of infusion fluid   that is free of Di(2 -
ethylhexyl)phthalate. Its leaching   from the cont ainer to the
contained fluid may be a critical concern.

10. 1985 Automated External Defibrillator. This has been instrumental
in saving lives since its introduction.

11. 1987 Digital Hearing Aid. Its introduction enables manufacturers
to enhance features and pr ovide users with more comfort and
higher-quality hearing.

12. 1988 Safety Needles and Syringes. These
inventions contribute greatly to the
reduction of needle -stick, the most
frequent cause of blood   -borne
infections in healthcare settings.

13. 1991   Demineralized Bone Matrix Gel   . This   is   an   off-the-shelf
           product used by surgeons for bone healing.
14. 1992   Ventricular Assisted Device, a pump to help a weak heart to
           pump blood through the body and a "bridge implant" to help
           patients survive until they obtain a new heart.
15. 1992   Smart Infusion System. At the time of introduction, it was the
           first infusion system to have a dose rate calculator.
16. 1994   Palmaz-Schatz Balloon Expandable Stent. This introduced a
           new wave of treatment   to solve problems that angioplasty
           alone could not.
17. 1994   Headless Cannulated Bioabsorbable
           Interference Screw. A replacement
           of   the   metal screw with the
           advantage that the body absorbs the
           polymer, replacing it with bone and
           eliminating the   need for   further
           surgery to remove the screw.

18. 1995   Medical Lasers for surgery. Their most popular application is
           LASIK to correct myopia, hyperopia and astigmatism.
19. 1996   Angio-Seal, which uses   bioabsorbable components to seal
           punctures in the femoral artery after arterial catheterization.
20. 1998   LightCycler PCR (Polymerase Chain Reaction). This is one
           of the best known device   s in point-of-care diagnoses for
           infectious diseases. The quick disease identification enables
           immediate treatment and protection for those at risk.
21. 1999   da Vinci Surgical System. Its microchip technology and 3 -D
           optics enable surgeons to perform complex procedures by
           making tiny incisions to treat in minimally invasive fashion a
           broad range of pathological conditions.
22. 1999   Cyber-Knife Robotic Radiosurgery System. A miniature
           linear acceler ator t hat delivers non-invasively concentrated
           beams of radiation to a targeted tumor. A cumulative dose of
           radiation kill s the tumor cells while minimizing radiation
           exposure to the surrounding healthy tissue.
23. 2001   PillCam, a capsule that houses a miniature
           video camera, lights, a transmitter, and
           batteries. As it is swallowed for passage
           through the intestine,   the device   takes
           photos and sends them to a small recorder

that is affixed to the patient's belt.

24. 2002   OraQuick Advance Rapid HIV -1/2 Antibody Te st. The test correctly identified 99.6% of people who were infected with HIV-1 and 100% of people who were not infected.

25. 2003   Drug Eluting Stent. The use of medication with the stent has reduced restenosis rates and provided significantly better clinical outcomes for patients. Its introduction ushered in the era of combination products.

26. 2003   LifePort Organ Transporter. This system pumps a cold solution through the organ to reduce tissue damage while the organ is in transport.

27. 2003   Sidne (Stryker Integrated Device Network) Voice Activation System, which uses voice recognition to give   the surgeon control over endoscopy equipment in the operation room without touching a button.

28. 2005   OxyMask. Its open oxygen design eliminates CO_2 rebreathing and avoids   mucosal drying, nose bleeding, facial sores and the claustrophobic feeling that the mask can give . It also enables a patient to communicate more easily and to drink through a straw.

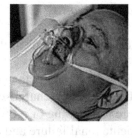

29. 2007   Pinncle TPN (Total Parenteral Nutrition) Management System, which provid es a safe and easy way to check, compound, and deliver TPN to patients.

30. 2008   Impella 2.5 Circulatory Support System.   This is a catheter that can be   inserted into the femoral artery   and on into the heart. The 12F motor and impeller inside the catheter pump blood at a rate up to 2.5 liter per minute.

The readers of MD&DI also chose the following five "older   " technologies:

1.   1800-1970s   Hemodialyzers and Dialysis Machines
2.   1960s-1970   Artificial Pacemakers
3.   1972   Computed Tomography Scanner

4.   1973   Vena Cava Filter. This filter has the same basic shape
                  as that used in oil refining to trap sludge and debris,
                  but is used to prevent life   -threatening pulmonary
                  embolisms.
5.   1977 Magnetic Resonance Imaging
   The following excerpts from the MD&DI article on 30 Years/30
Devices say it the best about the innovations coming out of the medical
device industry:
   *"Some of the devices nominated by our readers are small enough to
travel through a blood vessel. Some are so large they fill an entire room.
Some cost thousands of dollars but will stay in the body for 10 years,
and some cost pennies and are designed to be thrown away after one
use. This industry is characterized by innovators looking for the best
way to engineer a solution to a problem. And device designers are noted
for their ability to borrow ideas from other industries.*

   *In the last 30 years, we have witnessed the industry's coming of age,
with its first blockbuster device and its shift from individual   inventors
and small start -ups to globally recognized brand names. Here   (the
above list) is a look back at the devices that have changed the industry
and the world."*

1.6. Hemodialysis and its Innovators

Today 400,000 patients with chronic kidney failure,   which is known as
the end stage renal disease (ESRD), in the US and 3.5 million worldwide
are undergoing or requiring chronic dialysis (19). If left untreated, both
acute renal failure and end-stage renal disease produce uremia and death.
Here are excerpts from a speech that was given at the ceremony of the
2002 Lasker Award for Clinical Research. It celebrates the achievements
of the two scientists who made hemodialysis possible: Willem Kolff
(who is acknowledged as the "Pioneer of Artificial Organs") and Belding
Scribner (3).
   *"Our story begins in 1938 at a small medical ward at the
University of Groningen Hospital in the Netherlands. The physician in
charge was Willem Kolff, who had just graduated from medical school.
One of his first patients was a 22   -year-old man in uremic coma. The
young Dr. Kolff, then only 28 years old, watched helplessly   for four
days as the young man died in front of his eyes. He had no treatment to
offer — if only he could find a way   to remove the toxic metabolic*

wastes that accumulate in blood   when the kidney fail s...Despite the difficult circumstances of Nazi   -occupied   Netherlands, Kolff miraculously cajoled an enamel manufacturing   company to help him obtain scarce materials in order to construct the first artificial kidney. This machine, which came to be   known as the "rotating   -drum hemodializer," consisted of 130   feet of cellophane tubing made from sausage casing, wrapped 30 times around a horizontal drum made out of aluminum strips. As the drum rotated through a bath of salt solution contained in an enamel tank, the patient's blood was exposed to   the dialysis bath, allowing rapid and efficient removal of the toxic wastes.

When World War II end ed, Kolff donated all five of his artificial kidneys to hospitals in London, Poland, The Hague, Montreal, and Mt. Sinai Hospital here in New York City. This extraordinary   act of generosity enabled physicians throughout the world to   become familiar with the   new technique of dialysis. He also   provided blueprints of his "rotating -drum hemodializer" to George Thorn at the Peter Bent Brigham Hospital in Boston. This led to the manufacture of the Kolff -Brigham kidney, which was an   improved stainless steel version of the original...

The Kolff kidney solved the problem of acute renal failure, but what about the hundreds of thousands of patients with chronic   end-stage renal disease for whom prolongation of life requires   repeated dialysis three times a week forever? In the late 1950s, the conventional wisdom among kidney experts was that chronic   intermittent dialysis would never be possible because of two   insurmountable problems, one technical and one psychological.   The technical problem was one of circulatory access; whenever a patient was hooked up to a dialysis machine, veins and arteries   were damaged, and after six or seven treatments, physicians would run out of places to connect the machine. The psychological   problem stemmed from the widely held mystical belief tha t a   cellophane dialyzer outside the body could never permanently replace the complex functions of a normal organ. After all, according to the experts, the kidney was a sacred organ. Above and beyond its excretory function, it produces three essential hormones: erythropoietin for forming red blood cells, renin   for maintaining blood volume and blood pressure, and hydroxylated vitamin D for preventing breakdown of the bones.

In 1960, the impossible suddenly became possible. The psychological and technical barriers to chronic dialysis came crashing down through the research of Belding Scribner, a young professor of medicine at the University of Washington in Seattle...His idea was elegant in its simplicity: sew plastic tubes into an artery and a vein in the patie nt's arm for connection to the artificial kidney. When the dialysis treatment was over, keep the access to the circulation open by hooking the two tubes together outside the patient's body via a small U-shaped device, made of Teflon. This U -shaped Teflon device, which came to be known as the Scribner Shunt, served as a permanently installed extension of the patient's own circulatory system, shunting the blood from the tube in the artery back to the tube in the vein. Whenever the patient needed to be dialyze d again, no new incisions in the blood vessels had to be made. The Shunt was simply disconnected from the tubes in the patient's arm, and the patient was hooked up again to the machine...

The contributions of Willem Kolff and Belding Scribner revolutionized the treatment of kidney disease, saving and prolonging the useful lives of millions of people...."

As the US Renal Data System indicates, the population of patients who have chronic kidney disease increases by 8% a year. The healthcare cost incurred by th ese US patients c ame to $20 billion in 2001 (19). The annual mortality rate of hemodialysis patients is about 18%.

The patients go to dialysis clinics three times a week. In e ach hemodialysis treatment the pati ent is hooked up to the dialyzer for three to five hours. 30% of the patients experience symptoms, such as cramps, headaches, nausea or dizziness. Although t hese symptoms usually develop before a measurable decrease in blood pressure is detected, they are commonly referred as intradialytic hypotension (ID). In severe cases, shock or death can occur. ID is the key reason why these patients suffer such a high mortality rate.

The close association of hemodialysis to the development of ID indicates that ID is caused by the blood flow reduction to the brain resulted from the lowering of cardiac output . Since the patient's heart still functions normally, Starling's principle characterizes the development of low cardiac output as a result of low venous return. The low blood volume (i.e. , hypovolemia) and pooling of blood in the microcirculation are two factors that lead to low venous return (9). If hypotension results from hypovolemia, one treatment is to replenish the low blood volume with fluid infusion in the circulation. On the other hand, if blood is pooled in the microcirculation of the liver, fluid infusion may not increas e the venous return. At present, physicians do not have a technique that can determine whether the symptoms and ID result from hypovolemia or vascular pooling. Typically, the counter measure chosen is not effective in alleviating the hypotensive symptoms.

In the US about 0.4% of patients undertake hemodialysis at home while 14% of the patients in New Zealand d id in 2003 (19). Because patients can undertake home hemodialysis more often and more readily than travel to a hospital for service, the patient experiences smaller fluctuations in blood pressure a nd hypotensive symptoms are less likely to develop. An increase in the use of home hemodialysis requires better assurance of patient safety. There still are c hallenges and opportunities for biomedical engineers to further improve the monitoring technique s that can lead to the selection of countermeasures and/or adjustment of the hemodialysis process for the alleviation of hypotensive symptoms and the assurance of a safe hemodialysis for the patient.

In this book, some work undertaken to develop Global Mon itors, Inc. and its anti -pooling vest are used to exemplify the processes that you will us e to assess, launch and build your own venture. The mission of the company is to improve the delivery of hemodialysis care to millions of patients. The overview of he modialysis in this book , the reason why GMI is working on its R&D and the commercialization of anti-pooling vest and blood volume monitor (11), and the impact that the vest and monitor have on the quality of life of hemodialysis patients and operating cost s of dialysis clinics are presented as a n example for the readers develop the justifications for their own venture products.

1.7. The Impact of Medical Device Innovations on Healthcare

When you review the list of innovations described in Section 1.5, you will probably be impressed by how these innovations save lives and improve the patients' quality of life . On the other hand, you will also read news items that contain these messages:

- The high cost of medical t echnology: who's to blame? In most industries, technology tends to lower costs. Not healthcare. Why is medical technology out of control and is there any way to curb its cost and spread? Technology and its associated costs account for as much as 50 percent of medical inflation (4).

- Technology could increase   healthcare costs without markedly improving quality, according to experts at Wharton (7).
- Propelled by the incre   asing use of new drugs, imaging technologies and other wildly expensive innovations, (health) insurance premiums are rising fast (20).

The table below   was used in Congressional testimony by Peter Orszag, Direct or of the Congressional Budget Office to illustrate the factors that contribute to the growth of healthcare spending (14). The contributions from technology-related changes in medical practice range from 38% to 65%. A technical review panel that was formed to advise the Center for Medicare and Medicaid Services on future healthcare cost trends used similar information to conclude that about half of health expenditure growth is attributable to technology change. H   owever, the research quoted in Table 1.4 merely suggests that the change in medical practice due to technology advancement contributes to about one half of health expenditure s. In no way does it support the three news messages that were given previously.

Table 1. 4. The e stimated contributions of selected factors to   long-term growth of healthcare spending per capita, 1940 to 1990 (Source: Congressional Budget Office 14)

	Smith, Heffler & Freeland (2002)	Cutler (1995)	Newhouse (1992)
Aging of the Population	2%	2%	2%
Changes in Third-Party Payment	10%	13%	10%
Personal Income Growth	11-18%	5%	<23%
Prices in the Healthcare Sector	11-22%	19%	Not Estimated
Administrative Costs	3-10%	13%	NE
Defensive Medicine and Supplier-Induced Demand	0	NE	0%
Technology-Related Changes in Medical Practice	38-62%	49%	65%

Let us examine the meaning of the large percentage (i.e., 38% to 65% in Table 1.4) by analyzing how an invention is likely to change the medical practice, increase expenditures, save lives and produce higher productivity. The study selected would be the implantation of pacemakers in patients done by Moss and Rivers (13) and with the implantation expenses listed by Rinfret et al (16). For all living patients their productivity would be $50,000 per year. Table 1.5 lists the total

medical expenditures, total productivity, productivity/expenditures and
device cost/total expenditures.

Table 1.5. A comparison of a hypothetical expenditures and productivity for 50 patients
with pacemaker implantation and historic heart operation

	With pacemaker implantation*	With the historic operation**
Total Medical Expenditures	$1,975,029	$400,000
Total Productivity	$19,500,000	$4,000,000
Productivity/Expenditures	9.9	10
Device Cost/Total Expenditures	20%	NA

* 11 patients died during the 10-year study of Moss and River. For simplicity, we
assume that these patients were not produc tive since day one and that their cost of
operation was $18,000 per patient. There were implantation costs and follow-up costs
for living patients at a total expenditure of $45,452 per patient . 39 patients lived
beyond the study period. The pacemaker would be dual -chamber at a unit cost of
$7,720. The age of the patients was 68 ±8 years. For a younger group, the total
productivity would be higher.
** For purposes of comparison, we assume that 80% of 50 patients would receive an
open heart surgery to correct the abnormal heart rhythm at a lower cost of $10,000 (in
2008 dollar s) per operation. 50% of the patients with this "historic" surgery were
assumed to have a productive life of four years as the surgery might not enable the
patient to regain fully his or her normal heart function.

These hypothetical calculations certainly indicate that the total
health expenditures increase significantly because of the change in
medical practice. However, the continuation of the lives of these
patients contributes a prod uctivity that is 10 times the expenditures. This
benefit is an add -on to the fact that there are 39 patients living beyond
10 years as shown by the study of Moss and Rivers on pacemaker
implantation. Even though the price of the pacemaker is much higher
than that of the pacemakers for most current uses, the total cost for
pacemakers is estimated to constitute only a small fraction (20%) of the
total expenditures.

The introduction of expensive medical technology has led to some
increases in healthcare cost while the effectiveness of the technology is
still under evaluation. Blaming technology innovations as the reason for
run-away healthcare expenditures is not justified and does not satisfy
our desire to have quality healthcare at an affordable price . As
concluded in Chapter 18, it is the responsibility of all constituents,
citizens, engineers, physicians, hospitals, industry, professional
societies, trade organizations and education al institutions, to work

together to utilize innovations and improvements for the good of the nation and the people of the world.

1.8. Career Interests of Biomedical Engineering Students

The top career choice o   f 401   biomedical engineering (BME) undergraduates 10 to 20 years after their university graduation is entrepreneurship (10). It is time to not only recognize this, but also to modify our curriculum so that it can prepare students to meet their career interest and expand the biomedical engineering industry.

Advances in electro nics, computers and materials have contributed greatly to the development of   the medical devices and diagnostic industry. The growth in this industry leads to not only   a better understanding of biology and medicine , but also to better healthcare. This industry differs from a consumer-oriented industry.

First, most of the products of the biomedical industry serve a smaller subset of people , as exemplified by the use of   the glucose sensor for people who have   diabetes. However, a s we   acquire a   better understanding of health and disease, this industry   will be ready to produce many new devices, diagnostic methods and treatments for the prevention and alleviation of a wide array of diseases. Thus, the BME industry is fertile ground for BME graduates   who wish to assume a leadership role in the development and growth of BME ventures.

Many of the brightest university students have chosen to study BME. This is certainly an exciting field in which to carry out leading research. They will be well rewarded as their work can save lives and improve the health of patients. The author believes that , for the new discipline of BME to mature into a full -blown engineering discipline, it needs more entrepreneurs and jobs for our graduates. For this reason, I undertook a survey of the career choices of 401 BME undergraduates studying at the University of California San Diego, Johns Hopkins University and the University of Southern California. I wanted to learn whether these undergraduates were interested in becoming BME entrepreneu   rs immediately after graduation or 10 to 20 years after they ha   d gained more professional experience and education.

As an introduction to the career survey, a brief lecture entitled "Challenges and Opportunities in BME Entrepreneurship" was presented to s tudents who were   taking BENG 1 "Introduction to Bioengineering" (UCSD, Instructors: Shu Chien and Peter Chen), BME

202 "BME in the Real World" (JHU, Instructors: Sasha Popel and Art Shoukas), and BME 101 "Introduction to BME" (USC, Instructors: Jean-Michael Maarek and Jesse Yen).   63% of respondents were freshmen. Sophomores, juniors, seniors and others made up 9%, 12%, 11% and 5% respectively.

In the lecture, I highlighted the challenges and opportunities in BME entrepreneurship by quoting from an article that appeared in the January, 2006 issue of MD&DI magazine.   It says that *the implantable medical device industry has grown exponentially over the last thirty years*   . When a large number of patients are using a medical device, the industry has large revenues and employs many engineers. On the other hand, this quote also implies that a much longer time is required for patients to accept medical devices for example, than for consumers to accept a new type of television. Should the medical device cause even a few patients to experience a serious incident, it may mean the end of that device company.

Several medical devices were discussed to further highlight the challenges and opportunities. For example, total knee replacement has enabled patients to regain motion without pain. However, about 10% of implanted total knee replacements may become defective in 10 years. The annual Medicare cost for defective knee replacements came to $208 million for the year 2005. One of every 200 patients dies during the day following the replacement. The message to the students is that there   is still a great need for them to improve the engineering of total knee replacement and its implant procedure.

In 2005, one million cardiac pacemakers were implanted in patients worldwide. Medtronic and Guidant (now part of Boston Scientific) are major companies   that produce many pacemakers . They had   2005 revenues of $10 billion and $3.8 billion respectively.   Medtronic was founded as a two -person company in 1949 . The precursor of Guidant began as a three -person company in 1972.   The message is that many large medical device companies   had humble beginnings and required many years to succeed.

At the end of the lecture, 3   "x5" index cards were handed out   to students during the discussion period for the   ir use in recording their names, class years, majors, and minors. The following six career choices for the students to prioritize were listed on PowerPoint:
1. Industry
2. Government

3. Graduate or Professional School
4. University or Research Laboratory
5. Entrepreneurship
6. MD or LLD.

I advised the students   that,   if they choose Category 5 Entrepreneurship, it would mean that they will work on an entrepreneur team to build, organize and manage a business venture. The selection of Category 6 MD or LLD   would mean that they w ill be clinicians who work with patients or attorneys who work with clients. If they obtain an MD and want to teach at a university or do research in a research institute, then they should choose Category 4.

I also reminded the students that employees in industry can form an entrepreneur team within to work on projects that are an extension of the company's work . Further, t he industrial jobs are more stable.   Many small ventures will fail during their first three to five years. On the other hand, the entrepreneurs own the compan   ies and employees of a   large company may only own a small share.

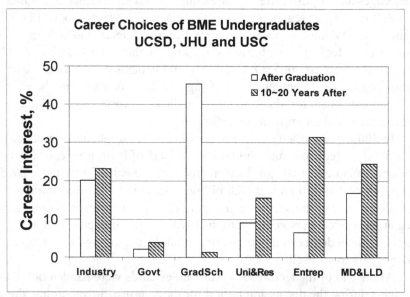

Fig. 1.1. Career choice s of BME undergraduates of the University of California San Diego, Johns Hopkins University andthe University of Southern California.

The first question asked the students to identify their first and second choices from the six categories of career choices to pursue upon graduation from university. By appropriately ranking the first and second choices, I obtained the distribution of their career choices that are depicted by the open bars in Fig. 1.1 of the previous page. One can see that 45% of these students indicated that they would choose to attend graduate or professional school. Many of them then wanted to go on to teach at a university or to practice as clinicians or attorneys. 20% chose to be employed in industry right after graduation. Only 6.5% thought that they might work as entrepreneurs.

Similar two-choice answers for their career interests 10 to 20 years after graduation were obtained and appear as shaded bars in Fig. 1.1. By that time, few would be thinking of going to university. Instead, the top choice is entrepreneurship at 32%. The second is the MD or LLD category (25%) and the third is the Industry (23%).

These distributions are quite similar for each of the three universities, as the standard errors for the distributions are less than 2%. The response seems to indicate that the students had given considerable thought to their future career well before my lecture presentation and understood the challenges and opportunities in BME entrepreneurship. Based on my informal discussions with the students, I believe the students who chose an entrepreneur career really want to translate their BME knowledge into inventions and then commercialization for the benefit of people.

1.9. Three Development Phases to Success

Most medical device enterprises are started by persons who have a desire to solve medical problems and a good idea that promises to do so. Unfortunately, desire and ideas alone do not guarantee success. A great deal of hard work and critical thinking is required to get any venture off the ground. In this book, the development of a company is addressed in chapters written for the following three development phases:

Phase I.   Assessing your invention
Phase II.   Launching your venture
Phase III.   Building up your enterprise.

Section II of this book will help working and would-be biomedical engineers **assess** how well their ideas will succeed. The three chapters in Section II provide guidelines for potential entrepreneurs to work on the following issues of Phase I development:

- Evaluating what they have and   need in order to prepare themselves to become successful entrepreneurs,
- Designing a creditable medical-device invention that will appeal to patients, physicians, hospitals, medical device makers, and drug manufacturers, and
- Carrying out meaningful research on the marke ting potential of the invention
- Raising funds to do a feasibility study with the goal of showing that you can use state-of-the-art technology to build your device. A feasibility study may be interpreted as synonymous with proof of the concept.

Section III will guide the entrepreneurs in **launching** their ventures to the point where pre   -production models are produced. The sev   en chapters in the Section   are written to help you deal with the following issues:

- Describing the financial preparations needed to start a company, as well as building the entrepreneurial team,
- Patenting the invention and maximizing its   profit generation potential,
- Advancing the company with governmental and community support,
- Winning grant money and investment from an angel to carry out the research and development of the medical invention,
- Understanding FDA device regulations,
- Preparing for FDA 510(k) submission of a new medical device,
- Presenting the business plan to attract more capital.

With the tasks of Part II accomplished, we assume that by now your company has demonstrated the efficacy of your product and raised sufficient fund s to proceed to the manufacturing and   sales phases. To provide guidelines for **building up** your enterprise, the six   chapters of Part III address the following issues:

- How to manage the company's finance and to price the product.
- How to negotiate employment   and licensing deals, mergers, acquisitions and the sale of a company.
- How to lead the company with effective management of people, time and resources.
- How to get the product manufactured.
- How to establish a market niche for your product.

- How to globalize the company once you   have established a strong US market.

The book conclude s with two chapters on   what to invest in the future and how to succeed in biomedical engineering entrepreneurism with really trying.   The former is a collection of   bits of wisdoms from prominent academic ians, community leaders, government officials, entrepreneurs and philant hropists. The latter is written by Shu Chien of UCSD.

1.10. About the Author

Jen-shih Lee, Ph.D., was professor and former chairman of   the Department of Biomedical Engineering at the University of Virginia, as well as Director of the University's Institute for Technology in Medicine. He served as President of the Biomedical Engineering Society in 1994/1995 and as Chair of the Council of Societies of AIMBE from 1995-1997. Lee received the Distinguished Lectureship Award from the Biomedical Engineering Society in 1998 in recognition of his research contribution to the biomechanics of microcirculation and its therapeutic impact on blood volume control,   as well as   the Distinguished Service Award in 2002. He is also a scientific consultant to CardioResearch Inc., which his wife, Lian-pin Lee, Ph.D., founded to build on their academic research in the field of fluid mechanics and blood flow and   to develop state-of-the-art medical devices and t   herapy for better diagnos es and treatment of cardiovascular disease. Following their move to San Diego in 2004, L. P. and J. S. Lee merged CardioResearch Inc. into a newly founded Global Monitors, Inc. (GMI) to work on the manufacturing and marketing of tw o products - the Lee Monitor and anti -pooling vest for the improvement of hemodialysis care.

   In preparing this book, Jen   -shih Lee consulted more than 100 experts on how best to   motivate students and biomedical engineering entrepreneurs so that they   will build successful enterprises for better healthcare delivery and improvement of the nation's economy. These experts are educators   in leading academic biomedical engineering departments, founders of biomedical engineering enterprises, authorities on business and administration, attorneys and certified public accounts, inventors of medical devices, government officials, and visionaries in the field of biomedical engineering. Their ideas, experiences, thoughts, and advice are woven throughout the text and were drawn from personal interviews, telephone conversations, and lectures   given to students of Lee's "Biomedical Engineering Entrepreneurship" class, which was offered at the University of Virginia in the spring semester of 2003 and at the University of Califo   rnia San Diego in the spring of 2007.   In addition to the contributions made to the course and book by   lecturers and consultants, my students of the class made valuable suggestions that helped improve the book's presentations.

References

1.   30 Breakthrough Medical Devices of the Past 30 Years, *MD&DI*, **31:6**, p25 (2009).
2.   Fuchs, V. R. and H. C. Sox, Jr. Health Affairs, **20**:30 (2001).
3.   Goldstein, J. L., *J. Am. Soc. Nephrol*, 13:3027-3030 (2002).
4.   Ham, F. L.,   *Business & Health*   ,   Nov. (1989) findarticles.com /p/articles/mi_m0903/is_n11_v7/ai_8540359/
5.   Hawkins, B., *MD&DI*, **31:6**, p32 (2009).
6.   Industry Statistics, *PharmaMedDevice* (2009).
7.   Knowledge.wharton.upenn.edu/article.cfm?aricleid=2260, June 10 (2009).
8.   Lähteenmäki R., and S. Lawrence, *Nature, Biotech*, **25**:729 (2007).
9.   Lee, J. S., *Annals of Biomed. Eng.*, 28:1 (2000).
10.   Lee, J. S., *Bulletin Biomed. Eng. Soc.*, 30: 4, p17 (2006).
11.   Lee, J. S., in Biomechanics, from Molecules to Man,   "Tributes to Yuan -Cheng Fung on His 90th Birthday", (eds.) S. Chien, P. Chen, G. Schmidt-Schonbein, P. Tong and S. Woo, World Scientific (2010), pp. 219-230.
12.   Medtech's Top -25 Firms Post Strong Revenue Gains in 2007,   *MX*, May/June (2008).
13.   Moss, A. J. and R. J. Rivers, *Circulation*, 57: 103 (1978).
14.   Orszag, P. R., ww.cbo.gov/ftpdocs/89xx/doc8948/01-31-HealthTestimony.pdf Jan. (2008).
15.   Palmisano S. J. and G. W. Clough, National Innovation Initiative,   (2004) http://www.ibm.com/ibm/governmentalprograms/NII%20Final%20Report.pdf
16.   Rinfret, S., D. J. Cohen, G.A. Lamas, K. E. Fleischmann, M. C. Weinstein, J. Orav, E. Schron, K. L. Lee and L. Goldman,*Circulation*, 111:165 (2005).
17.   Rosen, M. *WTN News*, June 2 (2008).
18.   Top Companies Report,   www.mpo-mag.com/articles/2007/07/top-companies-report, *Medical Product Outsourcing (MPO) Magazine*, July/Aug (2007).
19.   US Renal Data system.   *USRDS 2003 Annual Report* , NIDDK, at www.usrds.org (2003).
20.   Weinstein, M. M, New York Times, July 29 (2001), www.nytimes.com/2001/07/29/weekinreview/thenation-curbing-the-high-cost-of-health
21.   *Wikipedia*, List of biotechnology companies
22.   *Wikipedia*, List of pharmaceutical companies
23.   www.aimbe.org
24.   www.bmes.org

CHAPTER 2

EVALUATING YOUR
ENTREPRENEURSHIP

2.1. An Entrepreneurial Team

Webster's dictionary defines an entrepreneur as someone who organizes, operates, and takes risks in a business venture in   the expectation of gaining a profit. Do not interpret this d   efinition to be the lone -wolf model in which the person goes out and does all that is required to start a business in relative isolation.   For high -tech businesses, very little is accomplished without a team effort and no one can master of all the skills required to establish and operate a biomedical engineering venture. The person who is in charge of the team must have <u>leadership</u> qualities.

   Leadership differs from managership. The former attempts to instill a vision, trust and self   -confidence in the team   while the latter   puts emphasis on the management and control of the team.

   If you want to become a successful entrepreneur, you must possess another critical attribute - <u>perseverance</u>. The ability to stick with a task for as long as it takes to complete i   t is essential if you hope to raise venture capital, move your product to the manufacturing and marketing phase, and make the first few sales.

   You will seldom get a chance to present your business plan to a venture capitalist as the result of a single pho   ne call or an introduction from an acquaintance. In fact, the venture capitalist may intentionally put you off for a while precisely to see how well you persevere in the face of delays or an initially lukewarm reception. Perseverance is a trait that the venture capitalist will want to see you demonstrate before he or she grants you an appointment to make a 10 to 20 minute presentation of your business plan.

   Similarly, making the first sale of your product, which is an equ ally challenging task, can be done only with perseverance. The perseverance of an entire entrepreneurial team that is committed to developing and selling a high -quality product is essential if you want your product to penetrate the market significantly, particularly in the face of competition.

What additional trait does it take to be come an entrepreneur in the medical device industry? One thing that's essential is commitment and desire, - a <u>passion</u>, if you will, to explore unknowns for the improvement of the quality life of patients. This is not unlike the passion and curiosity that drives researchers to engage in scientific endeavors. Since it is easy to become discouraged by set-backs and the belief that most ventures will fail, the ability to pick yourself up from a setback, dust yourse lf off, and begin all over again with <u>courage</u> is vitally important for the entrepreneur's eventual success.

In essence, the entrepreneurial team needs a leader, who has:

- Leadership
  - o Builds up the team with qualified and motivated individuals,
  - o Inspires and orients all with the vision and goals for the company,
  - o Generate the team's trust and self-confidence,
  - o Manages the team for timely task execution and device development,
  - o Gears up sales and marketing of the products,
- Perseverance
  - o Remains persistent despite an expectation that 80% of ideas or proposals will be rejected,
  - o Raises funds to establish and operate the company,
  - o Getting the product developed to its utmost level in performance, safety and effectiveness,
- Courage and Passion
  - o Takes calculated risks as t he company develops and markets its product,
  - o Makes changes in the company direction when warranted,
  - o Does things ethically and professionally with the goal of benefiting people.

These traits in a team leader are summarized in Fig. 2.1.

One popular myth about entrepreneurs is that they are basically risk-takers. This is not true. Entrepreneurs are risk *managers*. They are very good at figuring out the minimum essential risks that they will have to take to get the company off the ground, and they cleverly devi se ways to share these risks with other people.

For example, entrepreneurs may start a company with their own money, but as soon as they can, they will borrow money from banks and investors so that they don't have to use more of their own money than is necessary.   They will develop contracts and enter into business arrangements that require customers, vendors, and other people to bear some of the risks.

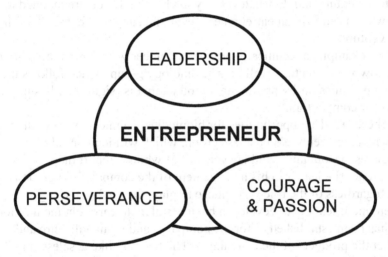

Fig. 2.1. Three major attributes   that the leader of   a biomedical enginee ring entrepreneur team must have.

Entrepreneurs who perceive themselves to be risk-takers are actually gamblers, and in the long term, the house always wins.

Something else that entrepreneurs do well is figuring out what might appear to be a risk, but really isn't. They will dig around to discover that the venture is really quite different than what one might have perceived from the outside. By cutting right to the heart of the venture, they can figure out the minimum essential work to do and the minimum essential risks to take in order to make the venture a success.

Entrepreneurship is an art that can be learned. Think about it in this way: In medical school, professors teach their students the best scientific practices for   use in healing sick patie nts, as well as more subjective things like an appropriate bedside manner. However, there are limits to what any professor can teach.   To develop into a capable physician and provide the best possible patient care, a medical student must develop the art of getting to the heart of an issue.

The same is true for the entrepreneur. An entrepreneur can be taught the best business practices and develop more subjective attributes like strong interpersonal skills, but he or she must also develop the ability to get to the heart of an issue.

Since entrepreneurship is a team effort, you have two options in an entrepreneur team - lead or follow. If you are inclined to lead, you can create a venture and do whatever you choose. If you are inclined to follow, you can jo in an entrepreneur team and support the growth of the new venture.

For example, a technically oriented engineer w ho has an inclination to follow will function well in a technology group, which follows the company's mission by producing a product that is significantly superior to that of competitors.

There are also opportunities for biomedical engineers who wish to work in a new venture's business group, which will include sale associates, accountants, and lawyers, all of whom support the entrepreneurial leader in his management of the company's operations.

Regardless of the role you choose to play, the goal of the entrepreneur team is to develop a business plan, to carry out the mission that has been established for the company, and to manufacture and market the products of the company. The team is like a salesman who has the vision, perseverance, passion, courage, arrogance, and assertion that they can run the company and sell the products.

2.2. John Abele, Pete Nicholas, Medi-Tech, and Boston Scientific

A partnership arrangement, which operates by consensus, seldom works for a developing company. However, the complexity of running a high - tech business may require a team of technology and business experts to work together. A good example is the partn ership of John Abele and Peter Nicholas, they formed Boston Scientific to acquire Medi-Tech, a company making steerable catheters for percutaneous transluminal angioplasty and cytology brush for lung sample collection, in 1979 (2). As described in "The Ship in the Balloon" a book by Jeffrey Rodengen (2), each of these two partners br ought something unique to the company. *Nicholas, with extensive managerial and financ e experience, would be responsible for the business decisions.* *Abele, with his enduring interest in the medical technology that was slowly gaining ground, would enhance the cause of minimally invasive therapy and guard the soul of the enterprise.*

Here are three excerpts from Nicholas on this partnership:

"We are simply going to run our business on the basis of what we agreed to agree about and what we agreed to disagree about, and that's it."

"We are going to develop a partnership. We are going to create a 50/50 enterprise. We made a commitment to make this little enterprise the sole focus of our careers."

"I was thinking about ownership from a control point of view only because I didn't know him (Abele). As I got to know him, it became clear to me that comp any control was not the issue. We were so close in philosophy that he would almost always agree with what I wanted to do."

In April, 1979, Cook Inc. expressed an interest in acquiring Medi - Tech for $400,000 in cash with the condition that Abele would stay on as President for two years. To make a bid for the company, Abele wrote a letter to Cooper Laboratories, the owner of Medi -Tech who wanted to sell the company, in which there was this statement:

"Until now, the only other parties who are interested in M edi-Tech were interested in it only with me, and only if it were operated as a development group. I am not interested in that arrangement......

The only reason I am in a position to make any offer is that a gentleman by the name Pete Nicholas has agreed to wor k with me on a partnership basis. He brings not only financial backing and expertise, but the critically needed administrative, strategic and people skills that complement my technical and market strengths. He is motivated by the same desire for equity and independence as I am. He is not interested in working for Cooper. "

At that time, Medi -Tech's annual revenue was $2 million. According to Rodengen's book, a sale price of $800,000 was reached by negotiations that were long and complex. Nicholas persuaded some bankers to put up $500,000 and the partners indebted themselves to the maximum to scrape up an additional $300,000. They turned away several investors and investment firms in order to keep Boston Scientific a private company. Immediately after the takeover, they reorganized the company for long term success by aligning the company's efforts with these company's strategic intents: increasing R&D spending, expanding sales coverage, acquiring new business units, and creat ing a company in which culture, m ission and values reigned supreme. In 1992, Boston Scientific went public and Abele and Nicholas sold 25% of the company for $450 million. As a result of their effort and many more acquisitions, Boston Scientific's 2007 revenue was $8.4 billion.

2.3. Nature of Entrepreneurship

Is an entrepreneurial venture an independent venture? In some cases, yes. In others, no.

Some entrepreneurial ventures are launched within large existing corporations. A big corporation can set up a new partially-independent ventures division to investigate new market opportunities, as well as new businesses developments. The corporation may provide internal funding for its employees to explore the potential of a venture. Encouraging results may lead to more company support to car ry out the research and development of this partially-independent venture.

Another type of entrepreneurial venture is known as an acquisition. In this situation, the entrepreneur buy s an existing small business, often a young start -up. The entrepreneur then decides how to add substantial value to the acquisition well in excess of what the previous owner had dreamed of, or incorporate s the acquisition into a product that he or she is already developing in order to significantly expand th at product's function.

Regardless of the form that a new venture takes—independent, part of a large corporation, or an acquisition, entrepreneurship involves innovation. Innovation has not only a technical side, but also a business side. As an entrepreneur, you will be cal led on to manufacture new products, open up new markets, generate new customers, and develop new ways of thinking about and operating a business. The venture usually starts small and grows rapidly to become large. So, high-tech entrepreneurship is about new business, rather than small business.

As a biomedical engineer, are you in the right profession to become an entrepreneur? There are many traditional industries that are involved in mechanical, civil, chemical, and electrical engineering. New industries in computer engineering and information technology have grown rapidly over the last 30 years. Now the time is ripe for industries that are based on biomedical engineering to be launched and developed. So, yes, you are in the right profession.

Will it be easy? Not necessarily. Just like the stock market, it can be very difficult to pick marketable innovations that will become winners— the kinds of exceptional and useful products on which a biomedical engineer might hope to build an entrepreneurial career.

Even so, the field of biomedical engineering offers its practitioners the opportunity to engage in a high   -quality career with many professional options, rather than a low-quality career with few options at all. In the opinion of   both the author and Wende ll E. Dunn III, an entrepreneurial education expert who previously served on the faculty of the University of Virginia's Darden School of Graduate Business and   is now Foundation Chair in Entrepreneurship at the Business School of the University of Auckland , the nice thing about medical device   s and biotechnology is that they will have a significant impact on healthcare for our society and the world —during the remain der of our lives, in much the same way that information technology has had on society over the last three decades and will continue to do for long into the future.

We're coming now to the era of medical device s and biotechnology. With the tremendous progress   that has been made in basic biological research, medicine and engineering, we will see absolutely extraordinary development in the field of medical device and biotechnology in the next 50 years, particularly   in biomedical engineering innovations, clinical implications, spin-outs, commercial opportunities, and everything else that accompanies biotechnology and biomedical engineering.

2.4. Wanting To Be an Entrepreneur

Is entrepreneurship equivalent to small business or self   -employment? Yes and no.

Yes, all entrepreneurial ventures begin as small businesses, but whether they have the potenti al to grow into large businesses like other small businesses do depends on a variety of interesting factors.

And, yes, most entrepreneurs are self   -employed in so far as they work exclusively for themselves, manage their own time and resources, set goals , etc. However,   self-employment for the biomedical engineering entrepreneur is often more challenging than it is for other entrepreneurs.   Among other things, biomedical engineering entrepreneurs must deal with highly technical content, sophisticated equipment, huge capital costs for the development of their products, and the FDA codes and regulations that regulate the marketing of medical products.

Often, pe rsons want to become entrepreneurs because they don't want to work for some one else. They view entrepreneurship as a way in which to gain some control over their lives, to be come their own boss and to achieve a level of independence. Certainly, becoming an entrepreneur can brings all of this- to some extent.

However, entrepreneurship also can be as co nstraining as it is liberating. For example, w hen you own an d operate an entrepreneurial venture, you cannot just resign your job and change employment if you become frustrated or bored or discouraged. To succeed, you often must tough out the day-to-day gr ind, see difficult tasks through to completion, live with disappointing outcomes, and find the stamina to try again tomorrow.

Entrepreneurs spend a lot of time thinking through issues. How can I develop a new product, or significantly improve an old one? How can I create a new market, or penetrate an existing one? How can I generate new customers?

Sometimes these questions are easier to answer than at other times. On the one hand, if you are going to create something new, you have the ability to determine, at least to some extent, how to develop the product and how to find or create a market for it. On the other hand, if you're going to charge ahead into an existing market, you must be absolutely certain that your device is so superior to that of your co mpetitors that you can set the rules for dividing up the playing field. A product that offers only a minimal improvement over that of a competitor will often limit you to playing by the rules that have already been set by other people.

It is very difficu lt to come out on top when you have to play by someone else's rules. This is not to suggest that the rules in place are unfair, but it is always preferable to create your own rules, to build your own game, and to define your own basis for competition than to have to buy into someone else's well-established game.

2.5. Career Entries to Entrepreneurship

The best entrepreneurs come in one of two forms. The first type of entrepreneur has a feeling and an affinity for people . H e or she recognizes that there a re many opportunities to exploit and seeks th em out. The second type of entrepreneur is more technically oriented . He or she has a new or different way of solving a problem or making use of a platform (or enabling) technology.   By solving a whole class of problems with a certain technical approach, this second type of entrepreneur seeks out ways of implementing this technical approach commercially.

While business schools attract and graduate numerous entrepreneurs, they are not the largest source of entre preneurs. Business schools provide them with extensive knowledge   of running a business with great efficiency. Consequently, business schools are great places to find chief financial officers, marketing experts, operation managers and strategy planners for your entrepreneurial team, but not necessarily   for people who will take or manage risks.

The traits or skills   are necessary to be come an entrepreneur are leadership, perseverance,   passion and   courage—attributes that are widely distributed throughout society. Schooling is not necessarily a requirement. Anyone possess these attributes has the potential to become a successful entrepreneur, as long as he or she also has a great idea, a way to raise   the operational capital, and a means to sell the product.

As an alter native to going to business school, several universities offer a Master of Engineering Management program for engineers who want to manage and operate   a complex business in this new Century. Courses are offered in marketing, management and financ   e and accounting of high tech companies. To enhance their management skills and careers, engineers can choose to   participate in the program offered by Engineering Management Certification International of ASME.

Students can learn about the entrepreneuria l game while they are still in school by participating in fund raising activities for their colleges and universities, or by helping existing firms   to market their product lines. Hands-on experiences like these are great ways   to pick up basic skills and gain credibility within a specific organization—credibility that may lead to an invitation to continue full time after graduation.

An enterprising student can always find an alumnus, or alumna, who owns his or her own business and ask   him or her to be put to work. Using such old -school ties is a great way to get one's foot in the door and gain industry experience.

Most cities have local technical councils or organizations   that actively promot e entrepreneurship and help people   to develop and prepare business-plan presentations. Becoming involved with these councils or organizations is another good way for students to study new ventures or participate in a small three - or four -person technical team and learn how to write a business plan or business concept.

Another entry point to entrepreneurship is by gaining employment with a family business. If you have no prior business experience, look around for business people who know you, or who know someone you know, because these are the people who are most likel y to give you the greatest break. If you like the ir business, you could offer to work for them or volunteer your services for the summer, or part -time during a school term, or for a year or two after you graduate.

Students who want to gain some business experience can also seek out academic entrepreneurial ventures —new businesses that have been built on the research of one or more professors. These days, a growing number of professors have businesses on the side that are sanctioned and supported by the un iversity where the professor works. Most of these business activities are licensed by the university. However, very few professors have much ex tra time on their hands with which to fully develop their ventures into commercial successes, and would welcome any additional help that they can get. Students specifically could look for opportunities to work on the development of a new or improved technology, while learning something about the business aspects of the venture at the same time.

Resourceful students may find other career entries to entrepreneurship beyond those just mentioned. The important thing to remember is that there are many ways for would -be entrepreneurs to gain business experience without actually having to attend business school or to commit to working in a particular industry.

2.6. Practicing Entrepreneurship

What do you really need to start a venture? Your product must have customers who are willing to trade resources with you, whether or not they are in cash, in exchange for value. Thi s is the starting point of the business. If you have enough customers, you may not need to invest any personal cash, as the banks may be willing to lend you their money. On the other hand, if a lot of research and development is required before you can drum up customers, you will need to fully commit your personal resources and bear all of the risk up front.

A safe strategy for accomplishing this is to break the business development down into manageable pieces and   then do them one at a time. If the first piece works, then do the second one. If that works, then do the third!   As mentioned at the beginning of the chapter, the successful entrepreneur is one who can figure out how to carve the entire project   up into digestible pieces and get each one done with minimum financial risk.

Many universities   offer   courses on innovation, design, and entrepreneurship. Students who are interested in biotechnology and biomedical engineering could actually generate a venture idea from class activities.

However, take not e: not all courses in innovation, design, and entrepreneurship are created equal.   Look for those in which the curriculum is not shaped around a very specific idea, but rather provides some breadth in the coursework , so that you can follow your specific passion or focus of interest and still learn something relevant.

When do you want to   begin your entrepreneurship? There is a temptation to put it off, to think of it as a long   -term proposition — something to consider in 10 years, or maybe 15, when you're most likely to be in a position, professionally and financially, to do what you really want to do.

However, during those 10 to 15 years, you will probably marry, start a family, and buy a house. Before you know it, the freedom to do what you want will be gone.

Consider this observation   of Professor Wendell Dunn. Years ago, Dunn was an emergency medic. He saw a lot of patients who, according to their families, died before ever having accomplished what they really wanted to do. They had continued to defer thei r dreams for a variety of reasons, and had borne the pain of never   reaching where they   had wanted to go.

So when it comes to deciding when to start your entrepreneurial venture, we say, "Do it now"!   At least make the commitment and get started. If you put it off, it probably won't get done.

One way to think about beginning your entrepreneurship is for you to start with the industry. Pick a high -promise industry, like biomedical engineering, and say, "I am going to learn about the structure, conduct, and people of this industry." Learn who the big players are and who the small players are. Learn who will fail and who will succeed, and why. Learn what the rules are by which these businesses compete. Learn how well the winners perform in comparison to the l osers. Learn who is making money and why patients want their products. Learn about the technical content of successful products by their practices in science, engineering and medicine. Finally, learn whether or not the industry is poised to have extraordin ary growth—so that you will know if you want to pursue your entrepreneurship within it.

If you do all of these things, you will find that biomedical engineering is a profession that is worthy of your entrepreneurial commitment and devotion. Biomedical en gineering is *the* industry to pursue in this Medical Device and Biotech Century.

2.7. Entrepreneurship and Visions of Uncas A. Whitaker

Mr. Whitaker had built up the AMP Inc. to become the world's leading manufacturer of electrical, electronic, and fib er- optic connector and interconnecting systems (1). In addition to his legacy of entrepreneurship, Whitaker and his wife, Helen, left their wealth to The Whitaker Foundation to promote the growth of a new engineering discipline — biomedical engineering (3). Whitaker is a true role model for all who work in biomedical engineering. His career path is summarized below to illustrate how he prepared himself in becoming an entrepreneur and a visionary.

U. A. Whitaker

Education Pursue and Career Development Whitaker obtained his B.S. in Mechanical Engineering from MIT in 1923. He took courses in political economy in which MIT had earned a reputation for providing first-rate training, not on ly for engineers, but also for future business administrators. His thesis, "The Design of a Rubber Heel Testing Machine," gave him an opportunity to develop a practical approach to problem formulation, problem solving and, most importantly, a belief that a n engineer needs to fully understand the requirements of his customers and then design the best machine in order to serve them well. This viewpoint is a major tenet of Whitaker's engineering and business philosophy in building his career and company.

He went to Westinghouse Air Brake to work as an assistant foreman in the engineering division. In this environment, he was encouraged to concentrate on original development. During his final two years with the Westinghouse Company, he filed some twenty -seven o f his patentable ideas. In the meantime, he earned a B.S. in electrical engineering in five semesters from the night school of Carnegie Institute of Technology (now Carnegie-Mellon University). The attraction of a job that combined engineering development and management responsibility led Whitaker to accept the position of division head of Development and Design in the Hoover Company. One of the major challenges that Whitaker took on was the design and production of an electric cleaner that could be offered for sale at a price that people during the depression era would buy. Although this had been tried without success, Whitaker developed in five years the Model 150 vacuum cleaner that had a selling price of $79.50. This was 30% lower than the price of the previous model made by the Hoover Company and credit terms of $1.50 weekly, payable monthly, made this new vacuum cleaner a hot seller. In the nine years (a depression period) of his employment at Hoover, the patents that were filed under his name and the doubling of his salary from $3,000 to $6,441 from 1929 to 1938 attest to his remarkable accomplishments. During this period, Whitaker also completed law school and passed the Ohio bar examination in 1935.

American Machine & Foundry Company was looking fo r a n engineering business type of person to reorganize its entire engineering function and they decided that Whitaker was the man they needed. As Director of Research and Standards and having assignments of a rather broad nature, he described his job as:

- Reorganization of the design and cost -estimating activities so that the cost of any particular machine can be established before design work ha s started , rather than after the design has been completed. The reduction of manufacturing costs will be part of this assignment.

- A study of all technical activities of the company with a view to working out a long -term plan for the future development of the engineering and other technical divisions.
- A study of the patent activities of the company in cooperation with the Patent Department.

This job enabled him to gain valuable experience and insights in decision making at the highest corporate level. He built a reputation as not merely a successful engineer , but a brilliant businessman. During the interview to fill an executive position, he so impressed the important business management firm of Booz, Fry, Allen and Hamilton that it produced a future opportunity for Whitaker to run his own "little firm" that he could build into something big. His theory of building a business was to out -engineer all others, which evolve d into the semi -official slogan, "Engineering the hell out of a product ," of AMP Inc ., which he founded in 1941.

His friend and associate , George Hastings, described Whitaker as always being profit-minded. He did not just want to design things; he wanted to design things for a profit. The people who came to work for him paid a lot of attention to what things cost. Hastings further stated that Whitaker was always able to develop a good deal of loyalty in his engineers. When he had his own company, many of them were determined to go with him.

Acquisition of AMP In the fall of 1941, Whitaker along with a handful of associates and investors took over a small firm that was producing solderless electrical termi nals for the aircraft and marine industries. Whitaker, as Vice President and General Manager of AMP , oversaw the activities of six divisions: Financial, Sales, Engineering, Patent and Legal, Production, and Inspection. He also headed the Engineering Divisi on, which was composed of three departments – Production Engineering, Experimental Engineering, and Research. In the first three years, Whitaker discovered that solderless electrical terminals, despite their excellence in concept and saving in labor cost, did not sell themselves. It was a formidable task to convince the aircraft and marine industries to switch from the well-established practice connecting wires by twisting and soldering to the more cost effective method of using solderless connections. Fortunately, Whitaker was able to reorganize the company by replacing the previous owner of the firm with G. Earle Walker, who buil t a powerful and successful sales organization for the firm. With patience and a lot of hard work, the Sales Division gained such important new accounts with familiar names as IBM and Douglas Aircraft. With the introduction of the Diamond Grip Insulation Support Terminal, which immediately became a best - seller in mid -1942 because of its superior electrical and mechanical properties and its lightweight and compact form, AMP developed into a real factor in the competitive field of solderless connectors.

Whitaker always made a point of finding the best men and then giving them a free hand to carry out their responsibilities. This pol icy applied not only to key management personnel and engineers, but also to those who sat on the company's board of directors. Many of these persons were former associates of Whitaker at Westinghouse Air Brake, Hoover, and American Machine & Foundry Compan y. Whitaker understood the need to be particularly careful in leading his engineering talent, both in protecting them from distraction s and in managing their activities to mitigate frustration. He knew that creativity had to be nurtured, as well as watched over.

He had frequent patent meetings with engineers during which he asked them what they had accomplished. In Whitaker's view, the primary purpose of patents was to create the spirit of competition in his engineers and to spur them on to "engineering th e hell out of a product." In these meetings, Whitaker not only was an outstanding source of encouragement, but also the boss who put the emphasis on finding ingenious solutions to problems . This not only made solution s patentable, but also provided a great commercial advantage.

In 1940s, the annual sales of AMP grew from $2 million to $3 million. The average profit after tax was in the range of 1 to 4% of the sales. However, the next decade would prove that Whitaker's optimism about the electrical terminat ion business was correct. In advance of many other American industries, Whitaker led AMP into international markets with the establishment of many wholly -owned subsidiaries overseas. As a result of engineering development and sale effort s, Whitaker built the company into a Fortune 500 company by 1965. Less than 25 years after its founding, AMP had become a multinational enterprise with subsidiaries all over the world and annual sales well in excess of $100 million. In the 1960s, AMP experienced an annual growth rate of 20%, twice the growth rate of the entire electronics industry. By now, AMP had grown to become the world's leading

manufacturer of electrical, electronic and fiber -optic connectors and interconnection systems with annual sales in the range of $10 billion.
Successes and Growth In receiving the 1960 Growth Company Award from the National Association of Investment Clubs, Whitaker stated:

"There are two basic reasons for AMP's continued success and growth -- accomplished, incidentally, without be nefit of mergers or acquisitions. The first of these reasons -- the engineering approach, the second -- our direct sales method.

At the outset, AMP adopted a very broad engineering approach and applied it to a confined product area. This approach was appli ed to the wire termination field and to this day is very appropriately described as "Precision Engineering Applied to the End of a Wire." This field has been the backbone of the company, our bread and butter items, and will continue to be so during the nex t few years. As a result of this precision engineering, AMP produces complete terminations that usually reduce termination costs through speed, simplicity and uniform quality of application.

An engineering approach such as this is no small task as eviden ced by our present customer list which numbers in the thousand s, by our 15,000 product items, and by some 2,000 patents issued both here and abroad. It requires spending some 13 or 14% of our sale dollars to maintain a staff of over 500 persons in research, development, and engineering activities, the majority of whom are graduate scientists or graduate engineers or engineers specially trained in the areas of physics, electronics, chemistry, electro -mechanics, atomic energy or other related fields.

The foundation of this (direct selling) program is a force of highly trained District Sales Engineers exceptionally qualified to work with the customer's own engineering and other technical personnel. At staff level, we have both industry sales sections concentra ting on individual industries and their changing technology and product sales managers promoting our newer lines of products."

Whitaker believed in competition and the associated notion that the business that did things better than its competitors would s urvive. Whitaker expressed this business philosophy in the following statement:

"The success of a business venture depends much more on the intelligence, ability and drive of its employees than on low taxes, low interest rates, or low labor rates. For instance, the wages in our plants

in the United States are the highest of any in the world, yet we produce most of our products at a lower cost than anywhere else. "

Legacy of Mr. Whitaker   All the se entrepreneurial accomplishments and his endowment to and vision for the biomedical engineering discipline will always be remembered   by all of us . The contribution to healthcare that he envisioned for biomedical engineers is best summarized by the following excerpt written by Ruth Whitaker Holms, Ph.D., Foundat ion Committee Chair, Whitaker Foundation in 1992 (3):

"My father Uncas A. Whitaker had two distinct visions, and he pursued both during his lifetime. The first involved the creation of an engineering-based manufacturing company, and he lived to see AMP Incorporated become the world's leading producer of electrical connecting devices. His second vision was to expand significantly the use of engineering techniques and principles in biomedical research. During his lifetime, he initiated and supported biomedical research programs that encouraged the interaction of engineers with scientists and physicians. Biomedical engineering research, however, was only in its infancy when he died in 1975. The full development of b   iomedical engineering as a research discipline is the mission of The Whitaker Foundation.

After my father's death, a biography was written of his life with the title 'The End Is Just the Beginning'.   The reference is to the end of a wire where the AMP conn ectors were attached and also to the future of his company after his death. It is our hope that the title also will appropriately describe the conclusion of The Whitaker Foundation in 2006.   If the Foundation programs are successful, biomedical engineering programs will have superbly trained faculty investigators and the supportive environment needed to make even greater contributions to the prevention and treatment of disease and injury. When this occurs, my father's vision will be realized, and The Whitake r Foundation will have completed its mission. "

References
1.   Cohn, W. H., *The End is Just the Beginning*, Carnegie Mellon Univ., (1980).
2.   Rodengen, J. L., *The Ship in the Balloon*, Write Stuff Enterprise, (2001).
3.   The Whitaker Foundation, 1992 Report.

CHAPTER 3

ESTABLISHING YOUR VENTURE INVENTION

3.1. How an Entrepreneur Acquires a Venture Idea?

The success of Whitaker in building AMP Inc. (described in Section 2.7) illustrates that one way to acquire a venture idea is by acquisition. However, before you do that, you will need to have built up a reputation as someone who can run a successful business and knows the market potential of your venture. Both are important when obtaining venture-capital investment or a bank loan for your acquisition. An example of the importance of the team in an acquisition is provided by Abele and Nicholas of Boston Scientific (Section 2.2). Finally, to put your business on a growing path as Whitaker did, you must follow his lead and hire outstanding engineers and business professionals—perhaps people whom you already know through established networks or previous contacts —and make a firm investment in engineering innovation, marketing and sales.

As a middle ground between the de novo creation of a new entity or the acquisition of an existing business, there is the establishment of a partnership with other like minded entrepreneurs. For an example, we can look at Adenosine Therapeutics, LLC (ATL), which was founded by Robert Capon and Joel Linden in 1999.

Capon earned his Bachelor of Science degree in mechanical engineering from the University of Virginia and then worked in marketing for Hewlett-Packard for six years. He next earned a Master of Business Administration degree from Harvard University and then worked in General Electric (GE) for three years , eventually serving as manager of a venture development team within GE. After his tenure at GE, he successfully built up three biotech companies. Two were sold to private owners and one, a pioneer in antiviral drug resistance testing known as Virologic, successfully completed its Initial Public Offering (IPO) and is now traded on the NASDAQ exchange.

Meanwhile, Linden was working as a professor of medicine at the University of Virginia. His research interest is cardiovascular physiology. Over the years, Linden worked with a number of colleagues to successfully construct a series of novel synthetic adenosine derivatives.[1] With this success behind him, Linden began looking for a partner to create a company that would investigate the therapeutic potential of the derivatives in treating inflammation, heart disease, asthma, chronic obstructive pulmonary disease (COPD), diabetes, and Parkinson's, and then commercialize the adenosine derivatives for use in therapy.

In late 1990s, Capon made it known to the technology community that he was looking for a new biotechnology company to develop. After a period of investigation and mutual due diligence, Linden established that Capon was, in fact, a world-class business person, Capon verified that Linden was a well-established researcher in adenosine and the two joined forces to form ATL. With these two exceptional individuals at the helm, Bristol-Myers Squibb, a global pharmaceutical company, had sufficient confidence in ATL to offer it a fee for the right to license the firm's adenosine derivatives for the treatment of digestive disease. This funding added capital to support the company's operation. The combination of the Capon's business savvy and Linden's research excellence also enabled ATL to win numerous Small Business Innovation Research (SBIR) grants to carry out the company's R&D goals. Currently, the company works with some twenty laboratories on the clinical evaluation of adenosine derivatives.

Ventures can be developed not only as a result of acquisitions and partnerships, but also from ideas generated from your education or work experience. There are unlimited opportunities for the cross pollination of ideas in discussions with colleagues in different fields of expertise. Once the concept for a new business idea has been identified, it is important to solicit feedback by means of your connections with physicians, biomedical engineers, and other health professionals. After the idea has been initially validated, you can use your expertise—the knowledge and skills you acquired at the university you attended and at

---

[1] Adenosine is a naturally occurring substance in the body. It is produced by cells under stress. Linden's lab had used advanced technologies to identify the adenosine-specific receptors on cells that were responsible for regulating inflammation. The synthetic adenosine derivatives were then developed to see whether these receptors could be turned off in order to turn down (or even reverse) the inflammatory responses of diseases.

the places where you have worked—to create a biomedical-engineering solution.

Most new business ideas germinate in one of two forms. The first form consists of newly dev eloped technologies or processes that are applied to existing problems. The second form consists of an existing problem that lacks an acceptable solution or creative individuals who are looking to reach out for new and creative solutions. Many of the venture ideas that were responsible for the successes of Medtronic Inc., a medical technology company that was founded in 1949 , fall into this "from problem to solution" category. The following section, condensed from *One Man's Full Life* the autobiography of Earl E. Bakken (1), describes three Medtronic successes. The first involves the development of an external pacemaker as a venture idea that arose from the "blue baby" problem. The second concerns the opportunity t hat led to the invention of the Hunter -Roth electrode, which expanded the use of the pacemaker to Stokes -Adam disease. The third success entails the acquisition of someone else's venture idea through licensing , an arrangement that gave Medtronic the right to commercialize the Chardack-Greatbatch implantable pacemaker.

3.2. Three Inventions of Medtronic Inc.

When Bakken, co -founder of Medtronic Inc., graduated from high school, he wanted to work with electricity. Because of films like *Frankenstein,* the unforgettable story of the learned doctor who, through the power of electricity, brings to life a man who was assembled from the body parts of corpses , Bakken became intrigued with the idea of using electricity to restore life. From a very young age, Bakken had read *Popular Mechanics* and *Popular Science* magazine voraciously. Despite the excellent instruction he received at school, he considered many of the most important lessons he had learned to have been self-taught.

After working as a radio instructor in the U.S. Army for three years, Bakken returned to Minneapolis to earn a BS degree in electrical engineering from the University of Minnesota's Institute of Technology. During this period and then later, while working on his master's degree there, he became acquainted with s everal people who worked in the University Hospital, which was located across Washington Avenue from the Institute, and provided them , on an ad hoc basis, with an on-the-spot repair service for malfunctioning medical equipment.

At a fami ly birthday party, he talked to Palmer J. Hermundslie , his brother-in-law, about the occasional work he was doing at the hospital. A few days later, on April 29, 1949, Bakken and Hermundslie formed a partnership to service medical electronic equipment, giv ing birth to Medtronic Inc. They set up shop in a garage in Minneapolis. As told by Bakken, they grossed a grand total of $8 (about $72 in 2008 dollars) for the repair of a centrifuge during their first month in business.

They supplemented their modest r epair- and equipment -building activities for doctors in the following year by selling medical equipment for other companies. The increased activities not only kept them in business, but also provided an entrée to the labs and offices of doctors, nurses, an d technicians whose needs, knowledge, and encouragement would prove to be critical to Medtronic's growth and success.

The "Blue Baby Problem"   In 1954, Dr. C. Walton Lillehei [2] of the University of Minnesota Hospital began to operate on infants who had congenital heart disorders that robbed their blood of oxygen and caused a bluish, or "cyanotic," cast to their skin , giving rise to the use of the term "blue babies" to describe them. The operation, while effective, often interfered with the ability of the he art to conduct electrical impulses to produce a regular heart beat, resulting in a condition known as "heart blocks."

To remedy this problem, Lillehei used AC -powered external pacemakers to stimulate the tiny hearts to beat following surgery. Built on vac uum-tube technology, the pacemaker was bulky , but could be wheeled around and plugged into a wall socket. On October 31 st, 1957, a three-hour electrical-power outage in Minneapolis threatened the lives of the babies who had undergone surgery and depended o n use of the pacemaker. Tragically, one baby died that night. The next day, Lillehei asked Bakken if Medtronic could come up with something better.

Bakken's first approach was to convert the DC voltage of an automobile battery to AC, and use the battery to run the pacemaker. It was quickly deemed to be an inefficient way to resolve the problem since only a 10-volt pulse was required to stimulate a baby's heart.

Bakken then recalled having seen a circuit for an electronic transistorized metronome in *Popular Electronics* magazine that transmitted clicks through a loud speaker with an adjustable rate to adapt

[2] Dr. C. Walton Lillehei is frequently acknowledged as being the "Father of Open -Heart Surgery" and the surgeon who was first to correct most cardiac defects.

to the music. He dug up the back issue and built that circuit in a four-inch square, one-and-a-half-inch thick metal box with terminals for connection to the battery and wires to carry the pulses to the heart. In four weeks, he had designed, constructed, and tested in his garage shop the first small, self-contained, battery-powered, transistorized, external pacemaker that could be taped to a patient's chest wall. When pacing was no longer needed, the wires could be withdrawn without having to reopen the chest.

Bakken took the device to the University's animal lab and tested it on a dog. "Of course, it works," Bakken remembered having stated on completion of his test. The next day, as Bakken returned to the Hospital to work on another project, he spotted a little girl who was wearing the prototype that he had delivered only the day before. Lillehei explained that his lab had told him that the pacemaker worked and that he had wanted to use the best technology available to save the child's life.

Bakken later wrote of this event: "We [Medtronic] were struggling to survive. When a customer asked for something, we provided it as quickly as we could—and only then hoped it might somehow earn us a few bucks. We were operating—not by design, but by necessity—according to a principle that has since been popularized by the statement: *Ready, fire, aim!* We got the order, built the product, and only after rushing it to the customer, debated its long-term possibilities for the company. As it turned out, of course, that battery-powered pacemaker put us in the cardiac pacing business."

Because of the response of the medical community to the success of Lillehei's operations on blue babies, the general press soon picked up the story of the little Medtronic box that kept children's hearts beating after surgery. People were calling it a "miracle." By the end of 1958, some 60 orders for the pacemaker came into Medtronic from all over the country. (To put this figure and the company's subsequent success with this product in perspective, consider the fact that, in 2003, a Medtronic-manufactured pacemaker or electrical stimulating device is implanted into a patient every seven seconds!)

The experience and knowledge of Bakken, as well as his network of physicians, put Medtronic *"Ready"* in coming up with a solution to the problem of cardiac pacing. They *"Fired"* the prototypical device in four weeks with the enthusiastic support of Lillehei. However, they immediately found an imperfection in the design of the prototype pacemaker—the children on whom it was used thought that it was a toy and pulled at its knobs and switches. The model was immediately modified with the knobs and switches moved into a recess, reflecting the "*Aiming*" part of the popular statement that Bakken had quoted. In other words, once an idea is ready, and the prototype is fired, the successful entrepreneur will always fine -tune his or her product so that its aim is right on target. Since that time, the proven wisdom of "Ready, fire, aim!" has inspired Medtronic to continuously improve the functionalities of its products.

Treating Stokes-Adams Disease   The confluence of transistor, battery, materials, and cardiac surgery created a fast -moving stream of new therapeutic possibilities. In 1959, Dr. Samuel Hunter of St. Joseph's Hospital in St. Paul, Minnesota,   decided that Medtronic's battery - powered pacemakers might be used to good effect on patients with Stokes-Adams dis ease, a chronic, progressive condition   that results in long-term heart blockage in older patients. Consequently, Hunter and Norman Roth, a Medtronic engineer, developed a new type of bipolar electrode that could be sutured to the patient's heart to more ef fectively concentrate the pacemaker's current to the location where it was needed. This concentration reduced the current by 70 percent with   the electrode technology that was available . Soon, they had good clinical results, as demonstrated by a 72-year-old patient who lived for another seven years with the help of his Hunter-Roth electrode and pacemaker.

Implantable Pacemakers   Dr. William Chardack, a heart surgeon, and Wilson Greatbatch, an engineer, began the development of an implantable pacemaker in la te 1950. This pacemaker was powered by batteries that had been newly developed by Greatbatch to work inside the human body for a long period of time. They carried out testing of the implantable pacemaker with animal studies. By early 1960,   they had obtained encouraging results on the performance of this pacemaker when implanted in a human patient.

Chardack and Greatbatch became acquainted with Bakken after they expressed their interest in using the Hunter   -Roth electrode for their implantable pacemaker. Re cognizing the scientific and commercial opportunities of collaboration, Bakken signed a licens   ing agreement with them that gave Medtronic the exclusive right to manufacture and market the patented Chardack   -Greatbatch implantable pacemakers in exchange for a royalty of 10 percent o f sales. By the end of 1960, Medtronic production in Minneapolis had received 50 orders for this new device at $375 each, the equivalence of about $2,725 in 2008 dollars.

These three examples of Medtronic's success reflect the importance of networking in entrepreneurship. As summarized by Bakken: "*I truly believe that those personal connections have been at least as important to our success as our products. To my eyes, high tech has always depended on high touch to be effective.*" The image of a happy Bakken and Koch on their first meeting that appears in Fig. 3.1 clearly illustrates one successful result of personal connections and a high touch.

Fig. 3.1. A 1986 Florida meeting of Earl Bakken with a happy 5-year-old Lyla J. Koch who received a Medtronic pacemaker when she was only a month old.

The Medtronic examples also illustrate the importance of building up your reputation as someone who can provide engineering solutions to medical problems and one who will diversify his or her product line when the opportunity to acquire an exclusive license on appropriate patented technology becomes available.

3.3. Evaluating Your Invention

Each step in the creation of your new venture raises the cost and commitment required to move to the next step. Therefore, it is prudent to evaluate any new business idea against a standard battery of marketability questions. Ten questions, grouped in three categories, are listed next for your consideration:

Patient Needs

1. <u>Do physicians and patients want your device</u>? It is important to meet the needs of customers, meaning th ose physicians, patients, biomedical engineers, or health professionals who are most likely to use your product. Engineering a device and then looking f or its medical applications will not, in most cases, produce a product that can precisely fit the needs of the physician and patient. After a device has been developed, these customers should be continuously solicited for feedback on ways to improve your product.

2. <u>Does your device solve an important medical problem</u>? The importance of the medical problem may be closely related to the size of the market and patient demand for your device. Inventing a device or developing a new molecule that can improve or tre at many clinical conditions or diseases may imply that you have a potentially large market for your product.

Superiority of Functions or Competitive Advantages Intertwined closely with patients' needs, this category of superior functions will help physicians to improve their ability to care for their patients and enhance patients' quality of life.

3. <u>What technological advantage does your invention have over that of its competitors</u>? In the case of device development, an improvement in sensitivity by a fact or of 10 will be extremely desirable for you to successively market your device. Also, you will have an overwhelming edge if your device is non -invasive while the products of your competitors are invasive. Better performance of the device and robustness t hat make the device easier to operate by health practitioners are two other factors that would add to the superior functions of your invention.

4. <u>Do you have the capital and technology to build the device or to develop the drug</u>? The more complex your device or drug is, the more capital you will need for its research and development. Whether the activity is R&D, clinical trials, or marketing, each takes time to complete. I n many instances, R&D and clinical trials may yield a conclusion that the drug or device i s ineffective, and you'll need to begin again. Because of the extensive effort involved, and the chance for failure, the conventional wisdom is that between $300 million and $1 billion is required to produce an effective drug that

becomes widely used. To b   e successful, an entrepreneur must develop a realistic estimate of the time required to complete the technology development to enable the company to set a timetable for raising the capital to complete the technology and proceed ing to the manufacturing and marketing phases.

5. <u>Is the timing right?</u>   Bakken's success with his portable external pacemaker provides an example of good timing. First, transistors had already been invented. The transistors enabled Bakken to miniaturize the pacemaker that previously had been constructed with vacuum-tube technology. Secondly, open   -heart surgery had progressed to the point   where it opened up the opportunity for Bakken to develop a pacing device that would help return the heart's function to normal.

6. <u>What is your long -term plan to enable you to   remain competitive and diversify your product line?</u>   In this high-tech era, you need a plan to continuously improve all aspects of your device to assure that you can maintain your company's viability. Make sure that your company can p   roduce more than one successful product. For example, the value of ATL, the bio -tech startup described earlier in this chapter, is high   because the adenosine derivatives   that it produces have potential therapeutic values for many diseases.

Overall Costs and Benefits   The spiraling increase in   healthcare expenditures has been blamed on the introduction of expensive medical technology. In such a   climate, the overall cost s and benefits o f introducing your device must be addressed.

7. <u>How will the FDA regulate your device?</u>   In the opinion of many, working out a favorable FDA classification is a task that requires your utmost attention. The topics covered in Chapter s 7 and 8 will help you get a feel for the complexity and uncertainty involved in navigating FDA rul es and regulations and how these rules and regulations will dictate the level of work that   is necessary to get your product to market. Suffice to say that the more justification for your product that the FDA demands, the more capital you will need to get y our device or drug to the marketplace, if ever.   Thus, this question is placed in the cost category.

8. <u>Is your price competitive?</u>   In some cases, the price of the medical device is of little concern once it is regarded as cost effective by insurance companie s and the government. In all cases, the price is much less important than the device's clinical power and its quality

and your service. As evidence-based pricing becomes a requirement, you need to conduct a comparative cost analysis with the products of your competitors so that health insurance w ill pay for the use of your device or product.

9. Will your device qualify for insurance reimbursement?   If your competitor's device s are already in use with a medical procedure approved by the Center for Medicare and Medicaid Services (CMS) and the American Medical Association (AMA), your new device can be considered as an improved use so that the existing reimbursement applies. If the procedure that uses your device is new, you need to apply for its listing and rei mbursement in a time consuming and expensive process as described in Section 16.1.

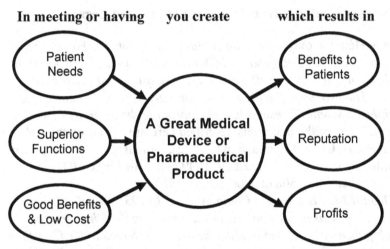

Fig. 3.2. Three key factors for generating a great product that provides benefits to patients and increases your company's reputation and profits.

10. What are the overall cost and benefits of your device to patients and hospitals?   The overall cost of your device includes the cost to purchase the device and the cost of additional labor in the hospital to use the device. Use of the device lead to a   shortening of hospital stays, a shorter use s of the intensive care unit, a faster recovery outside of the hospital, a better quality of life of patients, and a quicker recovery of the patients' productivity. It is still uncertain how these benefits are   to be considered by the government and public as part of the   reduction of the overall cost.   New

methodologies to assess the effectiveness of medical therapies and technologies are on the way as a result of the initiatives on Heath Technology Assessment and Va lue Based Purchasing described in Section 16.1. The costs and benefits o f the device 's use can be a factor that you have to examine in order to minimize its impact   on the marketability of your device or product.

For each of the companies that we examined previously, the answers to the questions above are definitely affirmative.   Thus, each of these companies create d a great product that led to benefits   for patients, the company's reputation and the company's profit, as illustrated in Fig. 3.2.

A few more examples will be cited later to further elaborate on the answers to these ten questions.

3.4. Wallace Coulter's Invention, His Venture and Legacy

Wallace Henry Coulter *was an engineer, inventor, entrepreneur and visionary. He was co -founder and Chairman of Coulter* ® *Corporation, a worldwide medical diagnostics company headquartered in Miami, Florida. The two great passions of his life were applying engineering principles to scientific research, and embracing the diversity of world cultures.* Most of the mat erials described here are given on the website of Wallace H. Coulter Foundation (2), including   the first patent submitted by Coulter on August 27, 1949 and issued by USPTO as patent number 2,656,508 on October 20, 1953.

An Elegant Idea Becomes a Company   *In 1935, he joined General Electric X -Ray as a sales and service engineer in the Chicago area servicing medical equipment. Later he was transferred to the GE office in Manila to make sales and service calls to t he entire Far East. After the War, Wallace came back and worked for several electronics companies, including Raytheon and Mittleman Electronics in Chicago. He maintained a laboratory at home to work on promising ideas and projects. One such project was for the Department of Naval Research, where Coulter was trying to standardize the size of solid particles in the paint used on US battleships in order to improve its adherence to the hull.*

He began tinkering in his garage laboratory in his spare time, experimenting with different applications of optics and electronics. Upon returning to the garage one cold, blustery evening, Wallace was faced with a challenge. The supply of paint for the experiment had frozen while he was out. Not wanting to go back out in the cold, he asked himself, "What substance has a viscosity similar to paint and is readily available?" Using his own blood, a needle and some cellophane, the principle of using electronic impedance to count and size microscopic particles suspended in a flui d was invented - the Coulter Principle.

Remembering his visits to hospitals, where he observed lab workers hunched over microscopes manually counting blood cells smeared on glass, Coulter focused the first application on counting red blood cells. This ins trument became known as the Coulter Counter™. This simple device increased the sample size of the blood test by 100 times tha t of the usual microscope method , counting in excess of 6 ,000 cells per second. Additionally, it decreased the time it took to quantify cell counts of blood from 30 minutes to fifteen seconds and reduced the error by a factor of approximately 10 times.

US Patent 2,656,508   The following is quoted from his 1953 patent describing how and why he invented the Coulter Counter.

"This inven tion relates to means for detecting and counting particles suspended in a fluid medium.

In the counting of particles of the type contemplated by my invention, heretofore it has been difficult to obtain accurate results because of the limitations inherent i n methods used and in the associated apparatus required. Some previous methods have been based upon colorimetry, that is the utilization of color density of a given sample to obtain a measure of the number of particles suspended, when compared with other k nown standards. In certain other methods, the sample is placed in a counting chamber and the particles are actually counted under a microscope, or the sample may be placed between microscope slides for counting.

Information of the type obtainable by deter mining particles concentration is especially valuable to the medical profession. Blood cell counts as well as the counts of other particles in the body fluids serve for many diagnostic purposes and as well to evidence of physical and pathological condition s of different parts and organs of the body. Obviously such information, in order to be of great value, must be obtained quickly and must also be accurate. The previous methods alluded to were not only subject to great inaccuracies and required considerable time to be accomplished properly, but as well required the

*services of highly skilled technicians and hence were not readily
available to all who required the same. ... ...*

*A further object of my invention is to provide new means for
detecting and counting particles whereby a sample of the concentration
to be measured is caused to pass through a constricted path and the
presence or absence of a particle in the constriction gives rise to a
detectable change in the electrical characteristics of the path. "*

Early Developments *That same year, two prototypes were sent
to the National Institutes of Health for evaluation. Shortly after,   NIH
published its findings in two key papers, citing improved accuracy and
convenience of the Coulter method of counting blood cells   . That same
year, Wallace publicly disclosed his invention in his one and only
technical paper at the National Electronics Conference, "High Speed
Automatic Blood Cell Counter and Cell Size Analyzer".*

*In 1958, Wallace and his brother, Joseph Coulter, Jr.,   founded
Coulter Electronics to manufacture, market and distribute their Coulter
Counters. From the beginning, this was a family company, with Joseph,
Sr. serving as secretary -treasurer. Wallace and Joe, Jr. built the early
models, loaded them in their car   s and personally sold each unit. In
1959, to protect the patent rights in Europe, subsidiaries in the United
Kingdom and France were established. The Coulter brothers relocated
their growing company to the Miami area in 1961, where they remained
for the rest of their lives.*

Coulter Corporation *Under his tenure as chairman of the
Corporation, the company developed into the industry leader in blood
cell analysis equipment, employing almost 6,000 people, with over
50,000 instrument installations. The company   has spawned entire
families of instruments, reagents and controls not just in hematology,
but also in flow cytometry, industrial fine particle analysis, and other
laboratory diagnostics.*

*Coulter insisted that the company control the entire supply chain:
research and development, manufacturing, distribution, sales, financing,
training and after -market service and support. In fact, Wallace's vision
is illustrated by the fact that Coulter Corporation was the only
diagnostics company to support its instrument   ation with the required
reagents and quality control materials to operate the full system. His
own personal field experience in sales and service helped formulate
Coulter's "Rule of a good salesman   — List the positives and
concentrate on them and after yo   u make the sale, service the needs of*

*your customer the best you can. Do this and you will build a loyal
customer base that will stay with you in the hard times."*
Landmarks in Hematology   The following   appeared in   the article
"Fifty years of Hematology Inn   ovations" written by Berend Houwen
MD, Ph.D., Medical Director of Beckman Coulter Inc.

   *"The Coulter Principle—and Coulter Counter—were landmarks in
the field of hematology," says John A. Koepke, MD, professor emeritus
at Duke University in Durham, NC, a nd one of the first to purchase the
Coulter Counter Model A when he worked for the University of
Kentucky Medical Center in Lexington, KY.*

   *Before this technology existed, lab technologists had no choice but
to do all their blood counts by hand. The Coulte   r Counter literally
brought automation to hematology labs for the first time."*

   *The Coulter Counter "essentially changed the face of medicine by
turning hematology guesswork into accuracy," Dr. Jones says.*

   *"While the previous technology provided a standard   precision
deviation of ±10%, the Coulter Counter reduced this deviation to ±1%,"
says Jones. "This made a significant difference in clinicians' ability to
make accurate diagnoses and, more importantly, exact measurements of
change in patients undergoing treatment."*

Wallace. H. Coulter

*Initially, the original
Coulter Counter helped
clinicians count and measure
only red blood cells. Later, as
the technology and
instrumentation evolved, it
enabled clinicians to also count
and measure white blood cells.
In the 1970s, it progre   ssed
again, enabling technologists to
separate platelets   —particles
that are less than one -tenth the
size of red blood cells. The
Coulters thus demonstrated that
rare hybrid of business foresight
and scientific exploration in
developing their products.*

The Legacy of Coulter   His deepest passion was to improve healthcare and make the improvements available and affordable to every one. He dedicated his wealth to the Wallace H. Coulter Foundation to continue the improvement of healthcare thr ough medical research and engineering. The Foundation has funded   translational research partnerships of many universities to promote   collaborations between biomedical engineers and clinicians, support the movement of promising technologies to clinical appl ication, and develop sustainable processes. The ultimate goal of these partnerships is to generate outcomes that will save, extend, and improve   the lives of patients, who suffer from any disease or condition, in any size market, in any discipline, in any c ountry throughout the world. This goal of the Foundation   reflects Coulter's values: e ndless curiosity, continuous learning, teamwork, consideration and respect for the individual, ethics and integrity.

3.5. The Venture of Howard Diamond

After receiving his doctoral degree in physics and electrical engineering, Howard Diamond became a professor of electrical engineering at the University of Michigan. Wishing to concentrate on the development of a venture idea, he left his university position after 10 years   and formed Transidyne General Corporation to build and market his patented microelectrode technology as chemical sensors.

While exhibiting at an instrumentation convention, Diamond met a physician who asked about the use of the company's technology to monitor blood parameters for open   -heart surgery. At that time, blood samples were collected and delivered to a clinical chemistry lab for cumbersome and   on-line, non -real-time measurement. Some of the measurements were being made with Diamond's microelectrode systems in the lab.

Although various people had tried to place an array sensors into an extra-corporeal circuit to monitor blood parameters during open   -heart surgery in real time, the idea had never   been successfully marketed for two key reasons. First, the FDA considers direct contact with a patient's blood as invasive. Therefore, the FDA   had required that extensive clinical studies be conducted to demonstrate the safety and effectiveness of the sensor array. Secondly, because sensor outputs drift over   time, they must be calibrated in real time—an impossible task with the sensors in situ.

Diamond came up an ingenious design that avoided the invasive classification and the calibration problem. His utility patent (Number 4,798,655: "Multiparameter Analytical Electrode Structure and Method of Measurement") was obtained in 1990, and a new company, Diamond Electro-Tech Inc., was founded to develop the blood-gas monitor for use in the emergency room and for critical surgery in the operating room.

Diamond's design included an array of sensors that provide a surgeon with real-time measurements of oxygen tension PO_2, PCO_2, pH, hematocrit, and concentration of K^+ and Ca^{++} of blood from the venous line (i.e., blood coming from the vein of the patient), as well as those measurements for blood flowing to the arterial line (i.e., blood oxygenated for return to the artery). As designed, a minute amount of blood was withdrawn to flow past a microchamber, which contained an array of six blood gas and electrolyte sensors. The filling volume of the chamber was about 80 µl, and the blood was discarded after its passage through the sensors. Then, a standard calibration solution was switched on and flowed past the sensors for calibration. Because only blood withdrawn from an extra-corporeal circuit was used and then discarded, the FDA considered the monitor to be non-invasive and approved it in within two years as a Class II device (see Chapter 7 for more information on FDA device classifications).

In 1988, Diamond Electro-Tech was sold by acquisition to Mallinckrodt, a global manufacturer and marketer of healthcare products in the fields of respiratory care, diagnostic imaging, and analgesic pharmaceuticals, for the handsome sum of $30 million.

From his experience in developing medical and dental devices, Diamond formulated the following six design criteria:

- The KISS Principle: Keep It Simple, Stupid! The operation of the system must be simple and robust for usage by common people. Extensive training, tedious data interpretation, and multi-step preparation need to be avoided at all cost.
- Do not require the operator to calibrate the system. It must be self-calibrating. You want the operator and the physician to deal with the problem of the patient, not of your system.
- Never tell the doctor how to run his business. Present your new system as a much better improvement in the way that the doctor does things.

- Design for the minimum possible regulatory category (e.g., non - invasive versus invasive).
- If sterility is important in the clinical use of your device, it will lead to the opportunity to develop a sterile disposable sensor.
- Design for marketability and for distribution and service requirements.

3.6. Magnetic Guidance System for Less Invasive Surgery

On December 23, 1998, BBC News reported the following:

The first magnetically controlled brain surgery has been performed in St. Louis, Missouri. It was announced on Wednesday.

In the operation, a catheter was moved by superconducting magnets through a patient's brain in order to retrieve a biop sy sample of a tumor. The path was plotted on a brain scan by a surgeon using a computer mouse.

On January 7, 2003, the CNN website posted this news:

Dr. Demetrius Lopes snaked a thin wire with a tiny magnet on its tip into an artery in Paul Kelsey's groi n and threaded it all the way up into his brain.

Aided by a helmet -shaped magnet hung over Kelsey's head, Lopes guided the wire through twists and turns deep in the brain, finally reaching swollen blood vessels that were giving the Chicago man double vision. A few squirts of glue to seal off the excess blood flow, and Lopes pulled the wires back out—surgery done.

Normally, curing Kelsey's disorder would require operating through a hole drilled in his skull. But doctors now are creating ways to treat brain aneurisms and other disorders in a less invasive procedure of magnet guidance than traditional surgery.

The concept of the magnetic navigating system was the brainchild of two doctors and one professor at the University of Virginia in 1984: Mathew A. How ard III, a 4 [th] year medical student ; Rogers C. Ritter, a professor of physics; and M. Sean Grady, a resident at the Department of Neurological Surgery. Their first patent (Number 4,869,247: "Video Tumor Fighting System") was granted in 1989 and Stereotaxis Inc. was formed in 1990 to bring their pioneering work to clinical fruition. On its website (www.stereotaxis.com), Stereotaxis describes its technology as one that "fuses real -time imaging and image -guidance techniques with digital workstations, to bring computer-integrated surgical automation to the catheter lab addressing clinical needs in interventional medicine."

Through the dedicated effort of George Gillies, a professor of mechanical and biomedical engineering at the University of Virginia, and man y other professionals, the early R&D was carried out and a prototype was completed in 1994 that had one fixed cryostat containing three pairs of super -conducting coil s. By controlling the currents in the coils, instead of their placement around the head, the change in magnetic field permits the catheter tip to be steered in three dimensions.

Since its founding, Stereotaxis has received several rounds of venture capital investment and private placements of stocks for a total of about $150 million.

In May 2002, the company received something just as good . It was notification from the FDA that its Telstar ^{TM} Magnetic Navigating System had been categorized as a Class II device, because it is largely equivalent to other legally categorized Class II devices. Th e FDA letter further stated that Stereotaxis therefore can market the device, subject to the general-control provisions of the FDA Act.

After some twenty years of research and development, the company had succeeded in receiving FDA approval for the medical use of this marvelous and powerful magnetic technique. Reaching this stage required hard work and the commitment of many devoted individuals and investors , all of whom are convinced that their technology will elevate interventional procedures to an unprecedented level.

3.7. Innovations and Improvements

Revolutionary Products vs. Improvements The tools and technology required to build Stereotaxis Inc.'s magnetic guidance system are new and revolutionary. Extensive research and development went into bu ilding magnets that have no moving parts and can guide the catheter tip through the brain's circulatory labyrinth. Carrying out this level of R&D within a small business tests the limits of entrepreneurs who must raise significant sums of venture capital a nd build up innovative technology long before marketing. Consequently, the price of the magnetic guidance system, like the price of a magnetic resonance imaging (MRI) system, will be considerable.

In contrast, when a new device represents an improvement o n existing technology, the likelihood of it being developed successfully will be higher, the company's investment in R&D will be lower, and the manpower necessary to do the job will be less. This tradeoff in risk often must be made at the expense of a decr ease in the total potential market share for the new product, and a risk of a shorter period of market exclusivity. The differences between these two categories of technology are highlighted in Fig. 3.3.

Between these two scenarios is disruptive technology. It may require less capital than a revolutionary product to develop . A disruptive technology will involve higher risk and a better reward than a product that offers only a significant improvement.

Impact of Improvements on Growth Webster's Dictionary defines "new" as "never existing before" and "innovation" as "something newly introduced". Although external pacemakers were already available in 1940s, the drastically improved patient care due to the introduction of the implantable pacemaker by Greatbat ch and Chardack certainly makes their pacemaker an innovation. Since then, Medtronic has made numerous improvements to the pacemaker for better cardiac rhythm disease management (CRDM). The improvements include adaptive pacing, use of wireless technology a nd internet, and expansion of diagnostic and monitoring capabilities.

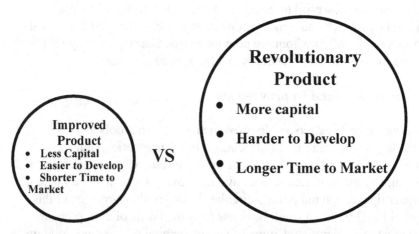

Fig. 3.3. Some key differences between improved and revolutionary products.

Since the introduction of implantable pacemaker in late 1960 , the revenues of Medtronic in CRDM have grown to $4.9 billion in 2008 (which is 37% of Medtronic 's total revenues). With the original patents of pacemakers already having expired, the growth in pacemaker sales clearly demonstrates the importance of improvements to the financial success of today's Medtronic.

Improvement is essential for the continuous growth of a company. On the other hand, if you are a competitor, your financial success can be achieved easier when you come up an innovation to solve an important medical problem or an improvement that is revolutionary or disruptive.

References
1. Bakken E.E., *The Man's Full Life*, Medtronic Inc., p. 45-54, (1999).
2. www.whcf.org/WHCF_WallaceHCoulter.htm

CHAPTER 4

RESEARCHING THE MARKET FOR YOUR INVENTION

In this chapter, we first discuss the purpose of market research and then review the websites you can use to collect market information that is relevant to the medical problem that you intend your device to resolve. Consult also Section 16.1 and 16.2 , which help you to set the direction of your market research because of the special roles your customers will have in making the purchasing decision and the unique market characteristics of the medical device and pharmaceutical industr y. This chapter conclude s with stories of two biotech ventures that were founded by Sheridan Snyder to illustrate his views on marketing and his thoughts and advice about entrepreneurship, company building and market research.

4.1. The Purpose of Market Research

Market research is necessary for you to obtain answers to the following three questions:
- What is the size and opportunity of the market that you are targeting?
- What differentiates your product from those of your competitors?
- What resources (time, personnel, and capital) will be required to get you through the R&D and manufacturing phase and to achieve your goals in marketing, sales and profitability?

The second question is synonymous to competitive advantages over your competitors. Getting positive answer to these questions , which are highlighted in Fig. 4.1 , will hopefully lead to positive market research results with the conclusion that it is worthwhile and feasible to develop your product.

To gather answers to the questions above you need:
- To interview people about the prospect of your product,

- To check with literature on science , engineering and medicine about your invention,
  - To surf websites about disease and patient needs,
  - To attend scientific, engineering, and   medical meetings to identify your competitors, visit their exhibit booths and learn about development trends and any state-of-the-art research that is already underway.

Fig. 4.1. Positive market research   results generated wit h positive information   about market size, competitive advantages and resources required.

In addition, you should also be able   to use similar search technique s to answer the following, related questions:

- On technology and competition:
  1. Will your product be functional and cost effective?
  2. Who are your current and future competitors?
  3. Will your product offer better performance than competitors' products?
  4. What is your invention's intellectual property position?
- On the clinical impact of your product:
  5. What is the disease or medical condition that your product addresses?
  6. What is the size of the potential population of patients who could use your product?

7. What cannot be accomplished clinically without your product?
- On financing:
    8. How long will it take to get to market?
    9. Are your competitors well -capitalized firms or small businesses?
    10. What are the resource requirements for development?
    11. Global vs. domestic marketing?
    12. How will you finance your operation in both the short-term and the long-term?
- On reimbursement and regulatory issues:
    13. Are there any comparable existing products that are already approved and available in the market?
    14. What regulatory approval processes do you anticipate your product will require?
    15. Once approved by FDA, what reimbursement mechanisms will be utilized for your product?

By doing research to obtain answers to these questions during the Assessing Phase you will also get some ideas about the number of devices that you can sell and what would be a competitive price so that you will know whether your company can become profitable. With the feasibility study at the Assessing Phase done, you will also have an estimate o f the manufacturing cost of your product. With more marketing research, you will obtain more data with which to prepare a financial projection for your company. Once you get to the Launching Phase, you may obtain additional marketing information to enable you to develop an attractive business plan and then raise the funding needed to manufacture and market your product.

4.2. Websites and Literature on Medicine and Engineering

There are many nonprofit organizations that provide information about diseases or the body's organs, including the following:
- American Diabetes Association (www.diabetes.org)
- American Heart Association (www.americanheart.org)
- American Liver Foundation (www.liverfoundation.org)
- National Kidney Foundation. (www.kidney.org)
- National Brain Tumor Foundation (www.braintumor.org).

The AMA (www.ama-assn.org) is another powerful resource. It lists on one website the names of some 105 medical specialty societies, such as the American College of Cardiology, the American Academy of Orthopedic Surgeons, and the American College of Anesthesiology, all of which can help you to acquire more information.

In addition to medical sp ecialty societies and the societies of medical and biological engineering (listed in Chapter 1), there are many professional societies that have a specific focus on the fields of medicine and engineering. One example is the North American Society of Pacin g and Electrophysiology (NASPE), which hosts annual scientific sessions in various U.S. cities.

At NASPE's 24 [th] annual scientific session, which was held in May, 2003, in Washington D.C., 111 companies exhibited their pacing and electrophysiology products. Their names can be found on the society's website (www.naspe.org), along with a brief description of what they do. Guidant Inc., for example, exhibited at the 24 [th] annual session and described itself as "a world leader in the design and development of cardiovascular medical products. Our devices help patients with heart disease return to active and productive lives."

Another exhibitor at the NASPE 24 [th] annual scientific session was Medtronic Inc. (discussed in Chapter 3). The author was amazed to learn that Earl E. Bakken, who co -founded Medtronic Inc. in 1949 (and has served as its emeritus chairman since 1989), attends NASPE meetings regularly and was manning the Medtronic exhibit, where the author had an opportunity to interview him for this book.

In addition to being able to meet company representatives and size up the competition, entrepreneurs who attended the NASPE event had an opportunity to sit in on educational sessions involving cardiac resynchronization therapy, sudden cardiac death prevention trials, and patient selection and technique s for atrial ablation. Clearly, involvement with organizations like NASPE can provide the resourceful entrepreneur with a wealth of useful information.

Consider this additional example. The National Kidney Foundation website (www.kidney.org) provides the following statistical information:

- More than 20 million Americans —one in nine adults —have chronic kidney disease. More than 20 million others live at increased risk. K idney disease is one of the costliest illnesses in the U.S. today.

- More than 400,000 Americans suffer from chronic kidney failure and need an artificial kidney machine to stay alive.
- Diabetes is the leading cause of chronic kidney failure . It accounts for approximately 44% of new cases of chronic kidney failure in the United States each year.
- Uncontrolled or poorly controlled high blood pressure is the second leading cause of chronic kidney failure in the United States. It accounts for about 35% of all cases.

With statistics like these, an entrepreneur can readily estimate the size of the patient population that would potentially benefit from the use of a new device that will alleviate a certain kidney disease or better diagnose the cause of kidney failure.

The following government -wide websites will be of interest to the biomedical engineering entrepreneur:

- National Institutes of Health (www.nih.gov). The NIH is the steward of medical and behavioral research for the nation.
- Small Business Administration (www.sba.gov). One of the SBA's goals is to maintain and strengthen the nation's economy by aiding, counseling, assisting, and protecting the interests of small businesses.
- U.S. Patent and Trademark Office (www.uspto.gov). The USPTO promotes industrial and technological progress in the United States and strengthens the national economy.
- Food and Drug Administration (www.fda.gov). The FDA promotes and protects the public health by helping safe and effective products reach the market in a timely way, and by monitoring products for continued safety after they are in use.
- Global Network of Environment & Technology (www.gnet.org). This site links interested parties to technology programs and agencies in all 50 States. Some of the listed agencies provide financial assistance to small businesses and start-up companies.

More information on how these three agencies —USPTO, SBA and NIH—can help your venture development is provided in Chapters 6 to 9.

Following web links and doing Google searches will also yield useful information for your market study. Additional source s of market information are the research reports published by Wall Street research analysts. Analysts frequently publish industry overview reports for targeted markets (i.e., breast cancer or implantable orthopedic devices).

These reports typically include statistics quantif   ying the size of a
market,   giving   assessments of competitors, and   providing in-depth
analyses of publicly traded companies within that market segment.

4.3. Two Biotech Ventures Founded by Sheridan Snyder

Many people acknowledged Snyder as a legendary entrepreneurial figure
in the biotechnology industry because of the enormous success that has
been enjoyed by the biotechnology firms   that he established. Sh eridan
Snyder graduated from the University of Virginia in 1958 with a degree
in French and Linguis tics. Two years after   his graduation, his father
died, and he learned that the family business had been far less successful
than he had   believed. Determined to turn the family's fortune around,
Snyder launched his own career in business at the age of 24. Since then,
he has founded 17 companies.

In this section, we look at two of his companies   , Genzyme and
Upstate Biotechnology, to help you gain some knowledge of how Snyder
worked to resolve the special marketing opportunities   offered by these
two ventures.

Genzyme   Gaucher's disease is a very specialized disease that is
prevalent among Jewish people   of Eastern European ancestry. It is an
enzyme-deficiency disease.   Without the metabolizing enzyme called
glucocerebrosidase, the body's organs become enlarged   and, in severe
cases, can stop functioning properly, causing death , Gaucher's disease
kills thousands every year.

After many years of research, scientists at the National Institutes of
Health finally obtained a purified glucocerebrosidase enzyme that c ould
potentially be used to replace the deficient enzyme in people with
Gaucher's disease and restore them to good health. Unfortunately, no
pharmaceutical company was interested in producing the purified
enzyme as a therapy because the market for it was t   oo small —the
disease affects fewer than 10,000 people worldwide.

NIH asked Snyder if he had an interest in developing the therapeutic
enzyme for treating Type 1 Gaucher 's disease,[1] the most prevalent form
of the disease. In 1981, he co -founded Genzyme and ten years later the
company received FDA approval for Ceredase® (alglucerase injection),

---

[1] Type 1 Gaucher's disease does not involve the central nervous system. Types II and III are rarer
forms of the disease and symptoms often include problems of the central nervous system.

the first effective therapy for Type 1 Gaucher's disease. It represented a scientific breakthrough, because it was shown in clinical trials to not only relieve sy mptoms, but also to reverse the disease. In 1994, Genzyme received FDA approval for Cerezyme® (imiglucerase for injection), an improved therapy for Type 1 Gaucher 's disease, which is now used to treat 95 percent of patients and is available in 60 countrie s.

While the development of the original therapy, Ceredase®, was good news to people who were suffering from Gaucher's disease, it also presented Snyder's young company with a difficult question: How much money could Genzyme charge each patient for the drug?

Because of the high costs to develop the therapy and produc e the enzyme, and the limited number of patients who needed it, Genzyme had to charge $140,000 per patient per year in orde r to make even a small profit. However, a cost that high raised i mportant ethical questions: What if a patient couldn't afford the therapy? Should he or she be denied it? At the time, no insurer was prepared to reimburse that amount of money to a patient who had to take the therapy, although Genzyme had the proof necessary to justify its fee. Recognizing the benefit to patients, the U.S. Congress through Medicare and many non - profit organizations stepped in, and the therapy for Gaucher 's disease, despite its high price, was approved for reimbursement —although not without a lengthy battle first.

Genzyme has since broadened its biotechnology to develop therapies for patients with many dif ficult, debilitating diseases. It is now a company of 6,000 employees in Boston and has annual revenues of $1.3 billion.

What is the lesson? You don't need to have a huge market in order to have a hugely successful idea. If your product is the only one that is capable of treating or curing a rare disease, you can still find a way to improve health and make a profit. As a case in po int, the FDA has a specific provision entitled the Orphan Drug Act , which is designed to promote the development of drugs targeted at rare serious conditions. It is intended to promote the development of new drugs in clinical areas far outside of the blockbuster market segments.

Upstate Biotechnology Snyder became involved with Upstate Inc. in 1998 as a result of the company's attempt to sell out to a non -profit foundation. After a careful market analysis, Snyder decided to merge his company, Argonex, into Upstate and served as the Chairman and CEO of the new company.

In the years since, Upstate has obtained licenses   from 220 institutions to manufacture novel , leading-edge proteins and reagents that are used to gain a better understanding of protein   -to-protein interactions, the function of proteins within the development of disease, and the role of protein in cell signaling. Discoveries in cell signaling and advances in drug discovery may revolutionize medicine in the coming years. The company employs about 220 people and is headquartered in Charlottesville.

Upstate has developed a method to attach different proteins to one microscopic sphere (appropriately known as a "microsphere") and then screen the various reactions of the proteins with laser -based technology. This method has transformed the way in which   people are tested for allergies. When you tested someone for allergies in the past, you needed a different test for each allergen. Now, with this Upstate technology, you can put all of those scr eening proteins on one microsphere, and test for all of those allergens in one pass with one drop of blood. In essence , Upstate's new test method will be used by everyone   who has allergies and at a much lower price than afforded by other systems. With 55% of people in the US having at least one or two allergies, it is not difficult to estimate the likely market size for such a screening device.

Before too long, there will be biochips with test sites in microarrays that enable many tests to be performed at the same time. They will have more screening power than what is possible with microspheres. Twenty-five years from now, Snyder predicts, you'll be able to go down to the drugstore and   purchase a $10 bag of vitamins   , each of which will contain its own bi ochip so that will permit the   screening of large numbers of biological and chemical compounds   for disease diagnosis to the detection of bioterrorism agents   . Microarray development is certainly within the domain of biomedical engineering. With such a high-potential idea, it is an exciting time to be in biomedical engineering.

Snyder believes that his primary responsibility to shareholders is to create value for them. This is the only   criterion by which he evaluate s himself as a company's CEO. The fact t hat Upstate, which was valued at $5 million in 1998, was sold in 2004 for $205 million to Serologicals Corporation means that he is doing his job very well.

The sale of Upstate resulted in a gift of $45 million to the University of Virginia Health Cente r to build a new children's hospital, the Emily

Couric Cancer Center and the Sheridan G. Snyder Translational Research Center.

4.4. Entrepreneurial Advice and Thoughts from Snyder

According to Sheridan Snyder, entrepreneurship is simply the translation of science and engineering to commercial application. In the lecture that he delivered to the class in biomedical engineering entrepreneurship at the University of Virginia in February , 2003, he addressed many interesting questions: How does a venture dev elop? What forms the basis of it? Who are the parties involved? What is venture capital? How does someone get involved in a venture? Should you think of yourself as an entrepreneur? Some highlights from his talk are given here.

Snyder admitted that, despite his advancing age, he couldn't get over the habit of building biotechnology companies. He enjoyed developing and expanding new things. It was especially fun to be able to " *get up in the morning, knowing that you will be developing a new cancer therap y using a kinase to block the mutation of a certain breast cancer gene* ," he said.

He encouraged students to follow his lead in creating biotech companies. " *There's no law that says you can't be an entrepreneur* ," Snyder said. "*There's nothing that says you can't raise money. There's nothing that says you can't create a business plan. The only thing that will stop you is a straight line between your two ears. The only thing you need is the conviction that you, indeed, can do it.*"

Snyder recalled a tim e when a bright MBA student from the University of Virginia asked whether he stood a better chance of becoming a successful entrepreneur if he first went to work for the management consulting firm of McKinsey & Company or another consulting firm. Snyder's advice to him was this: " *Go to either company.*" Once a would -be entrepreneur learns everything possible about running a business from working for a good company, " *the entrepreneur, by instinct, will go straight from there to file incorporation papers and set up his or her business* ," he said. " *You'll find your way, you'll survive, and you'll succeed.*"

According to Snyder, there are only two reasons to fail in developing a company. " *One of them is if you die* ," he said. " *The only other reason is incarce ration. If they put you away for 45 years, you're not going to be able to develop your company .*" Except for these two reasons, there is no reason for failure. " *Don't say, I can't get money, or I can't do this or that.*"

Here's another tip that Snyder gave to the class. If you want to start a biotech company, then building up a solid reputation as a successful entrepreneur is important. As an example, he cited the friendship that he has developed through the years with Sydney Brenner, a molecular researcher who received the 2002 Nobel Prize in Physiology or Medicine for his discovery of the RNA messenger, and who has worked with James D. Watson and Francis H. C. Crick, the two scientists who discovered the structure of DNA at Cambridge University. The b rilliant Brenner was the first person to recommend Snyder to a venture capitalist when Snyder was starting up Genzyme. It was "the funniest thing," Snyder said, *"to hear a future Nobel Prize winner telling the Rothschild Fund to invest in Sherry Snyder —someone without an advanced degree, any science background, and who had never invented anything in biotech in his life —simply because Brenner thought that I would succeed in developing a biotech company,"* Snyder said.

Snyder expressed his hope that the students would one day latch on to some interesting biomedical engineering idea, such as biochips that float in your bloodstream and emit therapies. " *Just let your imagination go,*" he said. " *The world already has all sorts of information that you can use to de   velop your idea for biomedical engineering entrepreneurship. Think of biomedical imaging. Some of the images are cell-based and some are molecular-based. They are just incredible. Soon you'll be able to connect biomedical imaging with therapies.*"[2]

However, imagination will carry you only so far. " *It's important to understand your market before you go too far down the development track,*" he added. " *For those working in the world of science, you're emotionally excited about the science, and you are att   ached to the science. You feel you are going to re -do the world. That makes you a little bit blind. Sooner or later, the market is the judge of whether or not your product is going to succeed.*"

"Why wait for the judge ?" he asked. " *Understand the judge at the front end, and your chances for success are going to be a lot better. The judges for a company are the investors. They're going to vote for what*

---

[2] The magnetic guidance system for less invasive surgery that is described in Chapter 3 is such an example.

you're doing, especially if you have done a thorough job o f the market study."

As a venture capita list, Snyder wants to see a market study that reflects a minimum of 50 interviews with relevant experts —half conducted by telephone and half in person. Such extensive interviewing helps ensure that accurate assumptions will be made about the competitive environment for a particular technology. " *No matter what you think your science is, it's going to have to move out into the world and compete against others ,*" he said. " *The sooner you know what the competition is, the better off your company will be.*"

Another thing that creates value for a new company in the eyes of investors is the attainment of milestones. "*Science is nebulous and fuzzy during its development period, especially in academic research,*" Snyder said. "*Even though you think you have achieved a great advance in science, its value may stay within the university. Don't ever think that you can make a business merely by selling or licensing technology. A lot of people have tried to do that and have actually failed. If you can't put your product in a box and send it out with an invoice and sell it, you haven't got a business.*"

Snyder reminded students that , in biotechnology, the market pulls and the science pushes. " *This is something you've heard many times ,*" he said. " *It is a big temptatio n when you're involved in science, when you're involved in biomedical engineering, or when you're involved in protein chemistry* " to get involved in the science push without considering the market pull.

Two weeks prior to delivering his lecture to student s at the University of Virginia, Snyder had been at University College in London, where ten of the leading researchers there talked with him about the regulatory role of nitric oxide. While he admits that getting his mind around the science can sometimes be challenging for a former French major like himself, he has no trouble in understanding the market for cell-signaling proteins. Because he knows that a market exists, he was willing to make a 10 -year agreement with University College in London to produc e the cell -signaling proteins that had been invented there.

"*The worst time to figure out your market is when your time for research and development has run out,*" Snyder says. "*If you understand what market you're aiming for from the beginning, then your science is going to push and the market will pull you to the right direction.*"

What makes a company succeed? It requires more than a good idea or a scientific discovery. *"You've got to have a product, and you've got to have enough science behind the pr oduct that you can leverage it to build the company,"* he said. *" You have to ask yourself: Do you have a product broad enough to create a whole company? Don't get sucked into building a company when really what you have is a relatively narrow piece of science."*

A strong intellectual property position will help improve a company's chances for success. *"It's very difficult in the early stage to try to develop a company without an intellectual property or a patent ,"* Snyder said. *" Patenting your invention c an be done with a small investment. But it's not easy."*

"This is why entrepreneurship in biomedical engineering calls for partnership between business people and engineers. They've got to work together to understand the market, not merely the science," he said.

Snyder likes to work with small companies, which often have the feel of a family as employees grow close to one another. *" The whole team is trying to accomplish something ,"* he said. *" It's the same type of pioneering that mountain climbers ge t by going out together to the peak of Mount Everest."*

After starting up 17 companies, Snyder still has a hard time to let them go, precisely because he becomes attached to each company and the people who work for it. Nevertheless, if you've do ne your job well, he believes, eventually a time will come to exit. Usually that time comes when the company's value has become so high that there is a risk of someone attempting a takeover. *"You go public. You sell. You merge ,"* he said of the exit strategies available to the entrepreneur.

BioCatalyst International is the most recent of Mr. Snyder's business enterprise. In partnership with leading scientists, BioCatalyst forms a series of start -ups to move the scientists' ideas beyond the boundaries of science into profitable biotech companies.

"If you keep looking around, you'll start to find that all of a sudden, something will make sense to you," said Snyder, who added that most of the ideas for his ventures have come from his associations with venture capitalists and renowned scientists.

"If you like to take risk, like the chance to succeed, and don't want to be bored, a career in building companies will be the right place for you, although it will scare the pants off you at one time or another ," he concluded.

CHAPTER 5

FORMING THE COMPANY

5.1. Rationale for the Corporation

When tax and liability are taken into account, you may decide to establish your company as an S Corporation . Before recei ving any venture capital or going public, you may change it to a C Corporation.

Although the cost to establish a sole proprietorship, partnership or limited partnership is relatively low and the operation of each is simple, they are bad entities for most business operation s as they do not offer any liability protection fo r the owners, meaning that your business, house, and personal property can be lost in legal liability suits. A Limited Liability Company (LLC) does not have a problem of liability. As an LLC does not issue stock, the IRS treats an LLC as a partnership. If your LLC is registered in Nevada and you are a resident of California, you must be cautious because you might be liable for payment of the same onerous fees as a California LLC . The LLC is a relatively new entity. Many legal issues concerning LLCs have not been fully tested in the courts yet. Some venture capitalists do not like to invest in LLCs.

An S Corporation operates under flow -through taxation, meaning that any gain or loss is passed on to the shareholders of the corporation . There is no income tax payable by an S Corporation. Within certain limits, a company loss flows through as a loss of the shareholders when they determine their taxable incomes. In contrast to a C Corporation, an S Corporation is subject to the following four restrictions:

- The sh areholders can be only individuals, estates and certain trusts,
- The total number of shareholders of an S Corporation may not exceed 75,
- The S corporation may have only one class of stock. Differences in voting rights are allowed,
- No shareholder may be a non-resident alien.

If your S Corporation violates any of these restrictions, the IRS will notify you of the termination of your S Corporation status and convert it to a C Corporation.

A C Corporation is required to pay income tax. Its loss can no longer flow through to its shareholders. The C Corporation can use any after-tax gain for future growth and expansion. It can also distribute the gain as a dividend to shareholders. The dividend distribution to shareholders must be included in their taxable incomes for income tax payment.

To fully understand the consequence of this so called double taxation (i.e., the corporation pays tax once on its profit and the shareholders pay individual tax on the dividends they received from the C corporation), we will examine the case of a corporation that has a taxable income of $50,000. At this income or profit, the corporation tax rate is 15%. When the shareholders received their dividends, they will pay individual income tax at the rate of 28%. For C Corporation, one scenario considered is the case (shown in the second column of Table 5.1) in which no dividends are distributed to the shareholders. In the other scenario (the third column), all after-tax profit is distributed to the shareholders as dividends. The fourth column describes the case of an S corporation. In the last two cases, the individuals reinvested their after-tax cash in the company. The final amount that the company has, either because there was no dividend distribution or because the dividends were reinvested in the company, is termed the "amount remaining" in the company to enhance the capital that the company is holding for growth, acquisition, loan pay-back, and investor buy-out. The corporate tax, the dividend distribution to shareholders, and the tax on individuals are listed in sequence as the second to the fifth row of Table 5.1.

Table 5.1. Amount remaining in a C or S Corporation with a profit of $50,000

	C Corp. with no dividend distribution	C Corp. with full dividend distribution	S Corp.
Corporate profit	$50,000	$50,000	$50,000
Corporate tax	$7,500	$7,500	0
Distribution to shareholders	0	$42,500	$50,000
Individual tax*	--	$11,900	$14,000
Amount remaining	$42,500	$30,600**	$36,000**
Difference (%)		-28%	-15%

*At an individual tax rate of 28%.
**Reinvested in the corporation.

As seen in the last row of Table 5.1, the first scenario of a C Corporation with no dividends declared or distributed   has retained the greatest amount of amount remaining. The amount remaining is 28%   lower for the C Corporation that distributes   all of its profit as   dividends to the shareholders and then receives the after-tax amount back as reinvestment in the company . The S corporation   that received reinvestment of all profits had an amount (of profit) remaining that was 15% lower than that of the C Corporation that declared and distributed no dividends.

In Table 5.2, we show the impact of double taxation for a company that has a profit or taxable income of $10 million . According to the tax rate schedule for corporation s, the tax is $3.4 million . For the dividends distributed to the share holders , we use an individual tax rate of 35% for the calculations. As seen   in the last row of the table, the amount remaining for   a C Corporation   that distri buted all of its profit as dividends distribution is 67% lower than the case of the C Corporation that had no   dividend distribution . On the other hand, the amount remaining in the S C orporation is only a negligible percentage lower than the case of C Corporation that distributed no dividends.

Table 5.2 Amount remaining in   a C or S Corporation   from a pre-tax profit of $10,000,000

	C Corp. with no dividend distribution	C Corp. with all profit distributed as dividends	S Corp.
Corporate profit	$10,000,000	$10,000,000	$10,000,000
Corporate tax	$3,400,000	$3,400,000	0
Distribution to shareholders	0	$6,600,000	$10,000,000
Individual tax*	--	$1,190,000	$3,500,000
Amount remaining	$6,600,000	$2,210,000	$6,500,000
Difference in %		-67%	-2%

*At an individual tax rate of 35%.

After any investment in capital assets (buildings, machinery) and acquisitions, the cash remaining in the company is termed the accumulated earnings or retained earnings. Tax complications may arise if your C Corporation has too   much accum ulated earnings. Although your company may claim that the accumulated earning is kept as working capital or as a reserve for an economic downturn, it may be up to the IRS and then the court to decide if your company is at risk will be taxed an additional 4 0% in excess of   the company's regular tax rate .

The reason behind such a penalty is that IRS wants your C Corporation to distribute dividends so that IRS will have an opportunity to tax the "profits" again. Although the tax courts have the final say on such an issue, it is much better for you to consult your CPA and attorney to protect your company on the subject of how you distribute dividends and handle your accumulated earnings.

If the operating capital of the company comes from individual angel investors, your company can remain as an S Corporation. If you need capital infusion from venture capital firms and/or other companies in exchange for shares in the company, these firms will become owners of the company and the restriction on shareholders will require your company to become a C Corporation.

If any large company owns more than 50% of your company's shares, your company (even if it has fewer than 500 employees) may no longer qualify to receive government assistance as a small business.

The owners of an S or C Corporation are the shareholders. Some shares have voting right and others do not. Only C Corporations can have more than one class of stocks, such as common shares and preferred shares. Preferred shares often have priority over common shares in the payment of dividends or the distribution of assets on liquidation of the company.

The corporation files an article of incorporation with the state and has by-laws that govern its operation. The by-laws stipulate, for example, the choice of bank and auditor that the company will use, who have signing authority (the authority to make financial commitments on behalf of the company), who are the Directors of the Board and who has been elected to the positions of Chairman of the Board, Chief Executive Officer, and President.

In summary, the filing of a corporation may be a simple technicality, but operating the company for optimal taxation is complex. In this section, we cover only a few operational features of a C or S Corporation. To set up a corporation that is right for you, to run it in accordance with federal and state laws, and to protect and advance your business interests, it is important that you work with advisors who are knowledgeable in legal, tax and accounting matters of a corporation.

5.2. Organizational Structure

You may start your company as a two -person company with a CEO and a chief technology Officer (C TO). The CEO is responsible for the business development of the company and the CTO is responsible for product R&D. They work together to map out the vision , strategy and plan to grow the company. Depending on the situation, the CEO and CTO can be the same individual.

As the company moves into the Assessing Phase, an entrepreneurial team is established to carry out the items described in Chapter 2 to 4 and also the feasibility study, which will demonstrate that the device can be built with current technology . The management may change to reflect the state of the company at the Assessing Phase.

As the company proceeds to the Lau nching Phase, you hire more people to do the jobs listed in Chapter s 6 to 11 . You may invite th ose entrepreneurs, BME experts and physicians whom you interviewed previously to serve on your Advisory Board. Because this Board is advisory, the liability of its directors is much less than the directors of a regular Board of Directors, which has the sole authority to hire (and fire) the CEO of the company and oversee all activities of the company . As more funds are required to operate the company, it may be des irable to hire a CFO to manage the company 's finances. The R&D activities also need to expand to include work on patent and regulatory affairs. You may consider having a semi-formal organization as depicted in Fig. 5.1.

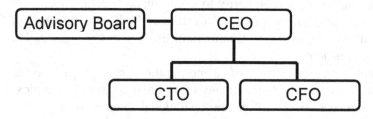

Fig. 5.1. Organization chart of a company in itsLaunching Phase.

When the company reaches the Building -up Phase, the company will add a VP o f Manufacturing with responsibility also for quality control and regulatory affair s and a VP o f Marketing and Sales to promote the product and manage the company's sale activities. A Board of Directors that reflects the interest of stockholders and investors in the company should be established. The company's organization may have a structure like that as shown in Fig. 5.2.

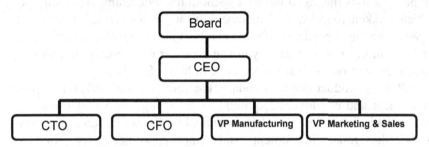

Fig. 5.2. Organization chart of a company in its Buildingup phase.

5.3. Capital Required for the Company's Operation

Phases in Development   As described in Chapter 7, your company can apply for SBIR Grants to fund its o   peration. NIH will fund your Phase I feasibility study   with up to $100,000 for six months and the Phase II research and development work   with up to $750,000 for two years. In this book, Phase I corresponds closely to the Assessing Phase and Phase II corresponds to the Launching Phase.

In view of the NIH funding levels for Phase I and II, we suggest that you may need to raise $50,000 to $150,000 to accomplish the tasks in the Assessing Phase and $750,000 to $1,500,000 for the Launching Phase. If you can raise this much money for the company's operation, it is likely that your entrepreneur team in the Assessing Phase will have two to four team members at most. The officers and staff of the company may grow to five to ten members   during the Launching Phase . In the Building-up Phase, the complexity of manufacturing and marketing the product may require that you   raise $2 to $4 million and hir e 15 to 20 staff members. These development   requirements are summarized in Table 5.3.

Table 5.3. The time required, the investment sought and the employees hiredduring three phases of company development . The values listed are   only suggested and you can expect large variations, depending on the complexity of the development.

	Assessing Phase	Launching Phase	Building-up Phase
Time Required	6 months to 1 year	2 to 3 years	3 to 5 years
Investment Sought	$0.05M to $0.15M	$0.75M to $1.5M	$2M to $4M
Employees Hired	2~4	5~10	15~20

Raising money is not only challenging, but also time consuming. A CEO must be careful in managing the money, find other revenues, and employ various means to reduce expenditures. For example, Medtronic, which Bakken founded, had income from its repair service and selling other companies' products. If a job can be done by a part-time employee or for a short period of time, you can consider outsourcing the job to a competent contractor, instead someone in-house full time.

If your product is revolutionary, the complexity of R&D, the time, investment and employees required can be as high as 5 to 10 times of that listed in Table 5.3. For pharmaceutical products that require clinical trials, the time, investment and employees necessary for the development may be 50 to 100 times more than those in Table 5.3. In any case, the development of a good business plan may help you to generate a more realistic estimate of the time, money and people needed for the Assessing, Launching and Building-up Phase.

Sources of Funding   The first source of funding may come from the entrepreneurial team that founded the company. They can use their own savings, borrow from the family, secure loans from banks or obtain cash from credit cards. Bank loans will require collateral whereas credit cards do not. However, the interest rate of credit cards is much higher than the interest rate of bank loans. The funds that are obtained by the founders of the company will be termed the founder investment.

The second sources of funds are the family, friends or angel investors who want to invest in your company. We assume that all of these investors qualify as individuals for tax purpose and that the invested money is used to acquire stock at their market value (the nominal value that was agreed upon as the market value at the time of investment). The funds so obtained will be termed "angel investment." Venture capital firms are the third source of funds. Shares are acquired by the venture capital firms at the same or different market value or price that was offered to angel investors.

When the company achieves a certain status defined by the stock market, your company can be listed on a stock exchange and sold in that market. The first time your company's shares are sold in a securities market is termed your company's initial public offering (IPO). Your company can also sell bonds in a bond market to raise operating cash. These two methods of raising money are not available to start-ups, because they are unlikely to meet the listing requirements of the securities or bond market.

Chapter 1 2 provides a more detailed description o   f obtaining financing from angel investors and VC's, what they are looking for, and the due diligence they undertake to evaluate your funding request.

5.4. Company Registration, Share Distribution and Exit Strategy

Registering the Company   To get the company registered, the first step is the selection of the company 's name. Make sure that the name does not infringe upon the trademark of another company and has not been used as a corporation name in the state in which you are going to register and/or work . Next, obtain an employer-identification number from the Internal Revenue Service (IRS). For a small company that is owned by a few founders, the   founders can serve as the various officer s (e.g., president, secretary, treasurer) of the company . If it is to your benefi t to have the income and loss of the corporation flow through to the owners (i.e., the shareholders), you will set up your company as an S corporation.

Discuss your   plan to   form the corporation with a competent attorney before registering your company in the state where you plan to operate. As an alternative, you may register your company in Delaware or Nevada in which there is no state corporation tax for out   -of-state companies. After registration, you will receive a corporation certificate from that stat e. Your attorney will provide you a corporate seal, stock certificates, the by-laws of your company, and sample forms for recording the minutes of directors' meetings . The by-laws describe the way in which your company does business and how to elect and re move officers and directors of the corporation . Finally, you must designate an agent and register him or her with the state as this agent 's service is an important aspect of protecting your corporation status.

Company Location   The location selected to establish and build up the company is an important decision . First, it determines the challenge that you will encounter in recruiting the right workers. If your company is a high-tech or biotech company, San Diego, Boston and San Francisco are places to consider. This is because many similar companies   have been established in these metropolitan areas. Community support, cost of living, local tax incentives, and the environment are other factors that you need to consider as you decide where to locate your company.

Investment and Stock Distribution We use the XYZ Company at some hypothetical settings to illustrate the relationship between investment and stock distribution. Assume that the company's Board of Directors authorizes the issuing of 5 million shares and that the founders will invest $100,000 in the company. Soon after the Assessing Phase begins, the team convinces several angel investors to invest $300,000. With these two investments, the team is also able to win a Phase I grant of $100,000 for the Assessing Phase and later a Phase II grant of $750,000 during the Launching Phase. Suppose that the progress in R&D and the NIH funding convince a few venture firms to invest $2,000,000 to move the company to the Building-up and Commercialization Phase. This venture investment will normally be made in several installments as certain milestones are reached during the Building-up Phase. Over this course, the company's employees also invested $40,000. In sum, the company will have total funding of $3,290,000 with which to take the company to the stage of marketing its product for a profit.

In recognition of the work performed by the founders, the market value at which they will acquire their shares in the company will be set at $0.1. Thus the founders will receive 1 million shares for their investment of $100,000. After the company demonstrates the invention's potential, the market value of the share may increase to $1. Thus, the angel investors will receive 300,000 shares for their investment of $300,000. Following this investment, the company will remain as an S Corporation if the angel investors are individuals and the total number of shareholders is less than 75. Equally important for the entrepreneur team, the company will remain in their hands because they own the majority of the company shares.

With more work accomplished by the company as it moves to the Building-up Phase, the market value may rise to $2.00 per share. The $2 million investment by the venture capital firms will enable the angel investors to purchase 1 million shares. In order to obtain the VC funding, you may have an agreement that states that the VCs have preferred shares and majority control of the Board of Directors. (What should be agreed upon in the agreement will be reviewed in Chapter 13.) At this time, the company needs to be converted to a C Corporation, because some shareholders are now corporations. As the company advances through the three phases, employees will be making a substantial contribution to the company's development and deserve to be rewarded with stock option s. 200,000 shares of the option pool are reserved for the employees at a favorable   option price to reward their contribution.

The   market value/share assigned and the number of shares allocated for the founders, ange l investors, venture   capital firms and employees are listed in the third and fourth column s of Table 5.4. With 2.5 million shares already allocated, the company will have another 2.5 million shares for an IPO or later rounds of venture financing.

In case a second round of venture funding becomes necessary, the board may authorize the issuance of additional   shares so that   the company can raise additional operating funds. In so doing, the shares that the founders and early investors own will suffer dilution. They will represent a proportionately smaller share of the ownership of the company. Dilution of the founders' holding as a result of several rounds of financing is significant for the company   that is   developing the magnetic guidance system (Section 3.6).

Table 5.4. Distribution of XYZ   Company shares to founders, angel investors, and venture capital firms

	Cash received	Market value/share	Shares
Founders	$100,000	$0.1	1,000,000
Angel Investors	$300,000	$1.00	300,000
Venture Firms	$2,000,000	$2.00	1,000,000
Option Pool*	$40,000	$0.2	200,000
SBIR Grants	$850,000		0
Total	$3,290,000		2,500,000

* An additional 2.5 million shares are reserved for IPO.

Demands and Traps in Financial Transactions   The a ctual closing of financial transactions between   the company and investors and the demands from angel investors and venture   capital firms are much more elaborate and extensive than the simple transaction of stocks   illustrated here. Demands from investors can include the appointment of certain directors to the board and creation of many classes of stocks other than common and preferred stocks . Some demand s can even be   a trap in disguise that would enable investors to take over your company without due compensation. Chapter 13 explains what those demands ma y be and how to negotiate terms that are mutually acceptable and beneficial.
Valuation and Control   The Market value per share is the value of the company divided by the outstanding shares at that time. How does

one put a "value" on a proposed business or a start-up? One way is to determine by accounting the value of tangible properties , such as land, buildings, equipment and patents that the company owns.

Another conventional approach is to set a price -to-earnings ratio and then use the earning s of the last fiscal year to calculate the value of the company. However, it is hard to determine the value of the company before the company has had any earning s or only has the potential to make money in the future . The use of price -to-earnings ratio applies mainly to well -established companies. Consequently, assigning a value to a company that has just been formed becomes a matter of sheer salesmanship by the entrepreneurs and the credibility of the business plan. Just like buying a house, the value of the company or the market value per share is whatever investors are willing to pay and the company owners are willing to accept.

Who holds control of the XYZ Company in Table 5. 4? Although the venture firms only have about 43% of the shares, it is likely that their shares are preferred shares. However, they may have been able to succeed in negotiating an arrangement by which they will have four seats on the Board of Directors (i.e., select four of the Directors) , with two seats for the founders and angel investors, and one independent seat (Director). In effect, they have legal control of the company.

In high tech businesses, the founders often bring to the table expertise that is essential to the operation of the business . T hus, the founders exert "control" even th ough they may own only a small fraction of the company and occupy at most two seats on the Board.

Exit Strategy As previously agreed by the founders and the investors, angel investors and venture capital firms may want at some future time to recover their investment and take their profit . The first thing to do is to ask a professional or CPA firm to estimate the value of the company based on its stock market performance . Suppose the value of the company is estimated to be a total of $ 25 million. This valu ation implies that the 2.5 million shares, which the founders, investors and employees own, are worth $10 per share.

One way by which the company can repay the investors is by using some of its cash reserves and obtain a bank loan using the company as collateral. If the investors and the company agree that the share price is $10 per share, th e value of the investments of the four categories of share holders, which appear in Table 5.4, are shown below in Table 5.5. The angel investors' payback is $3 million . T he venture capital firms' payback is $10 million. After the se two groups "cash out," the founders and employees   retain the company as an employee-owned private company. In this   exercise, the founders and employees   receive the greatest gains because of t   heir extraordinary effort in getting the company to a point at which its share price is $10.

Table 5.5. Increases in value of holdings at a price of $10/share in the XYZ Company

	Value of Initial Investment	Shares Owned	Final Value of Investment
Founders	$10,000	1,000,000	$10,000,000
Angel Investors	$300,000	300,000	$3,000,000
Venture Firms	$2,000,000	1,000,000	$10,000,000
Employees' Options	$40,000	200,000	$2,000,000

Suppose the angel investors made th eir investment seven years ago and the VC   invested five years ago . Then, the annual rate of return would be 39% for angel investors and 38% for VC.

If you have a good valuation for your company, it is time to pursue an IPO to obtain more cash for the company to repay the angel investors and ventu re capital firms. Then, your company will become a public company. Of course, there are many regulations for a public company to comply with.

As the third exit strategy, hopefully you can sell the company for $25 million. In th at case, the venture capital firms will recover their investment and a 500% return and the angel investors   will recoup their investments and   a 1,000% return. Please note that the hypothetical amounts used for the calculation are the net proceed generated from   a bank loan, IPO or sale of the company. Make sure that you have a team of qualified advisors to carry out ethically and legally   the stock distribution and the exit arrangement.

CHAPTER 6

PATENTING YOUR INVENTION

6.1. The U.S. Patent and Trademark Office

The basic role of the U.S. Patent and Trademark Office (USPTO) is to promote the progress of science and useful arts by granting patents to protect inventions over limited periods of time. Primarily, patents prevent public disclosure of your invention from reducing your opportunity to achieve economic gain from its development and sale. Secondly, patents inherently encourage public disclosure by safeguarding the inventor's rights to economic gain. Thus, they support the free exchange of new ideas, so that other inventors can build on the patented device or process to promote further advances of technology. Congress believes that the patent disclosure process is very important for expansion of the nation's economy.

A booklet that explains patents and the USPTO's operation is available at its website at www.USPTO.gov. In this chapter, we review the basics of patenting and examine a number of patent issues of interest to entrepreneurs.

6.2. Utility, Design, and Plant Patents

There are three types of patents: utility, design, and plant.
Utility Patents   A utility patent is granted to someone who invents a new and useful process, machine, article of manufacture or composition of matter, or any new useful improvement. Since a new medical monitoring device is a machine, its patent will fall into this category.

When you invent a new process to measure a medical parameter, such as blood pressure, hematocrit, or glucose concentration in blood, you can elect to register the process as a utility patent. This type of patent also covers new drugs, new man-made materials that are suitable for implantation, and new ways to produce materials with biological compatibility.

Here's an example of a highly successful utility patent . Two years after forming The ALZA Corporation, Dr. Alejandro Zaffaroni filed a patent application that was entitled "Drug -Delivery System" in June, 1970. The application comprises a porous reservoir that contains a drug for delivery to a host environment at *a controlled rate for a prolonged period* of time in order to produce a local or systemic physiological or pharmacological effect. As the first one of many such patents issued to ALZA, the USPTO granted the patent in December , 1974. Built on the development and marketing of this and many other   drug delivery systems, the ALZA Corporation   has become a billion -dollar company and a leader of drug delivery solutions by oral, transdermal, implantable, and liposomal technologies . The corporation has some 3,000 active or pending U.S. and foreign patents . It is also of interest to   note that Zaffaroni is   the inventor or co -inventor of more than one hundred patents, the latest of which was granted in 2008.

Design Patents   Design patents, in essence, are given to new, original, and ornamental designs   of an article of manufacture . Design patents protect only the   *appearance* of a manufactured article, not its structural or functional features.

For example, when you manufacture the central processing unit (CPU) of a computer, you lay out the semi -conductors or transistors in a particular design that processes and transmits various binary signals. The circuit design of your CPU is patentable   . That i s why whenever Intel came up with a new Pentium CPU, the company would apply for a design patent . However, if Intel invented a new way of packing transistors into a CPU to achieve a much higher processing speed,   it would file a utility patent, which covers   matters concerning the functionality of the CPU.

Plant Patents   Plant patents may be granted to anyone who invents or discovers and asexually reproduces a distinct and new variety of plant. If you insert a gene into a plant so that it   will produce some special chemical or pharmaceutical substance, you may have a patentable plant.

Plant patents also apply to innovations involving cells, animals, or other biological entities.

Additional Patenting Considerations Each of these three patent types is screened according to three criteria: new, useful, and non-obvious. For example, if you come up with an invention, design, or plant, but patents for similar inventions, designs, or plants already exist, you cannot patent your invention. An idea becomes patentable only when you generate or produce *new* versions of existing inventions. Similarly, if a medical device is not deemed useful, you cannot patent it. For example, a thermometer that does not perform its intended purpose, the measurement of temperature, is not patentable. Also, you cannot patent a process or device if it is obvious that everyone already knows about it. The term "non-obvious" or "sufficiently different" is determined by a "person" who possesses skill in an area of technology related to the process or device.

Patent requirements and the impact of being granted a patent are illustrated in Fig. 6.1.

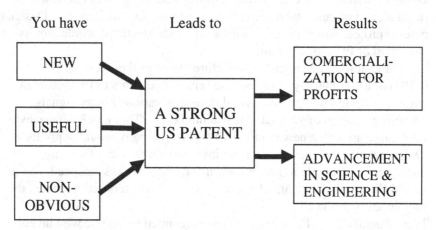

Fig. 6.1. The features of a strong US patent and the impact on the commercialization of the product and the advancement of science and engineering.

If your patentable (but currently unpatented) invention is published in public media, such as newspapers and journals, or presented in public forums, such as conferences or classrooms, it can no longer be patented. If you want to publish your results before a patent has been filed, you can file a provisional patent with the USPTO. The provisional patent allows you to publish your results after the filing while you still have a year in which to submit your patent application.

Within a year of receiving a patent approval, you   may submit a continuation-in-part for any new invention   that is an improvement or redesign of the original patent   . The a ttorney costs   of filing a continuation-in-part are lower than the costs of the initial patent, which provides sufficient reason to file one, when appropriate . Another reason to file a continuation-in-part within the first year is that applications that are submitted *after* the first year of the initial patent approval may be denied by the U SPTO, due to similarities between the original patented product and the one for which an application for the continuation-in-part was submitted.

Patents have 20-year lifespans. Even if you file a provisional patent application before the non -provisional application, the 20 -year term of the patent begins on the date on which the non-provisional was received by USPTO . If it takes two years for USPTO approval of   your non - provisional patent application, you will have 18 years remaining on your patent in which   to complete the development of your invention and manufacture and sell it without competition in the United States.

Until your patent expires, you must pay an annual fee to the USPTO to maintain the active status of your patent   . Fees are l ower for paten ts granted to small businesses.

6.3. Trademarks and Copyrights

Trademarks and copyrights are two other types of legal protection   that the federal government   grants to intellectual properties . Trademarks protect words, names, symbols, sounds, or colors t hat distinguish goods and services. If the words used in your trademark describe a general class of goods or one with a specific , but general, function, the USPTO may not grant you the trademark.

Copyrights protect works of authorship that have been tangib   ly expressed. They apply to books, music CDs, movies and software.

Although all patents, trademarks, and copyrights have a defined period of protection, Congress has voted on occasion to extend the period for some trademarks and copyrights   . In general,   however, trademarks that are registered after November, 16, 1989, are effective for ten years, but unlike patents, can be renewed forever by the USPTO as long as the trademark continues to be used in business   . Copyrights are registered by the U.S. Library of Congress and last for the lifetime of the author, plus 70 years.

It is worthwhile to note that there is a major difference between the copyright of a book and that of a piece of computer software . A book can be lent to many readers without violating it s copyright, but software cannot. Computer software can be loaded onto one computer for use by one or more persons, but not onto several computers for use by many people. This practice extends to the health care industry in that one copyrighted software c an only be installed in one particular machine for diagnosis and treatment . However, t his machine can be used by many users for many patients.

A software licensing agreement can arrange for the rental of the software. In other words , the user will pay a r ental fee whenever the software is used.

Your software should be copyrighted . You can upgrade the software to increase its power in processing, diagnosis or treatment. This is another avenue for your company to continuously generate new revenues and profits.

6.4. The Importance of Patenting Your Intellectual Property

The disclosure of your invention can lead to advancement in science and technology for the nation . It is equally important for the prosperity of your company that you file a patent applic ation so that you can obtain patent protection f or your invention to maximize its profitability. The first concern is the expense in obtaining patent protection, e specially for a start -up that has limited capital . The second concern is that y our disclosure may enable your competitor to invent an even more efficient and cost-effective product that can put your company out of business . In the following pages, we will consider a number of issues t o help you decide whether patent protection will overcome these two concerns.

An alternative to patenting is to decide not to disclose your invention, but to protect it as proprietary information . You need to ensure that your invention cannot be duplicated by reverse engineering. Date all documents related to your pro prietary information for use in a court of law in case your ownership of the proprietary information is challenged by your patent-holding competitors.

Suppose someone filed a patent at the USPTO well before yours or obtained a patent for an invention that is similar to yours. As you introduce your product to the market, they can bring suit in the US Courts for an injunction to stop the sale of your product because it infringes on their patent . When you begin to make lots of money in the sale of your product, they can also start an infringement suit and request damages and a punitive payment. Long before the c ase ends, you will face large legal fees for your attorney to defend your case.

In such a legal proceeding, whether your competitor has its product on the market is not relevant if it is diligently developing the product. See the discussion on patent troll in Section 13.1 . Your competitor's patent readily put s it in a position to sue you for patent infringement. If you were to lose the suit, you could no longer sell your product and your company might be obligated to pay huge punitive damage s. Such a legal challenge, whether successful or not, w ould impact your company financially.

It is a well know n fact that the Coca -Cola Company owns the world's most famous commercial trade secret, the formula used to make Coca-Cola, a product invented in 1886 . Asa Candler bought the formula and brand in 1886 and incorporated The Coca -Cola Company in 1 889. The company's 2007 revenue was about $29 billion and its net income was $6 billion. No patent was ever filed for the formula. The company's current policy is still to keep most of i ts product formulations trade secrets. Don't use this as an excuse to not file your own patent application as your medical invention is very different from a beverage formula. Your invention may be easily produced with the "same" function, whereas a new beverage can only be imitated because the "taste" may still differ. Secondly, please note that the patent position of Coca-Cola in beverag e technologies is strong . The Coca-Cola Company has approximately 800 US patents and 1,800 international patents (1).

During the development of your company, you will approach venture capitalists for funding. The question of your patent situation and barrier to prevent competitors from entering the market will always come up in meetings with them. A poor response to the question about patent protection will often mean that you will receive no venture capital funding.

There are many successful companies that have strong patent portfolios. In 1997, Boston Scientific acquired Target Therapeutics in a tax-free stock swap for approximately $1.1 billion (3). This was more than 10 times Target's total sales, in contrast to the usual formula of ten times earning s. The reason for this high price is that Target had pioneered the field of interventional neuroradiology and neuroendovascular therapy and had dominant patent posi tions in this area by having been the first mover in certain stent development s. Their Guglielmi Detachable Coil for the treatment of inoperable or high risk brain aneurysms was the first device in that category to be approved by the FDA. Guido Guglielmi a nd Ivan Sepetka are the inventors listed in the USPTO patent #5,122,136, which was filed in March 1990 and granted in June 1992, entitled "Endovascular Electrolytically Detachable Guidewire Tip for the Electroformation of Thrombus in Arteries, Veins, Aneurysms, Vascular Malformations and Arteriovenous Fistulas" . At the time of acquisition by Boston Scientific, Target was the plaintiff in litigation with Scimed (a company acquired by Boston Scientific in 1995) and Cordis (a Johnson & Johnson Company) over a microcatheter.

Suppose that the USPTO grants you a patent. This is a grant of property rights to the inventors, or their assignee, to exclude others from making, offering for sale or selling the invention in the US or importing the invention to the US . You must enforce the rights afforded to you by your patent by taking legal actions in US Courts without any aid from the USPTO . If you win the patent infringement case, you may be entitled to lost royalties and , in some cases, to punitive damages . Because of the significant effort spent on the discovery of evidence o f infringement, process ing an infringement case may have a price tag of millions of dollars in legal fees . There is m ore discussion o f patent lawsuits in Section 13.1.

6.5. The Process of Patenting

Once you have an invention, decide whether it is patentable . Will it be considered to be new, useful, and non -obvious? Search the public records to learn if there is a device that is similar to yours . In some cases, before a non-provisional patent is approved, the inventor and the USPTO may keep the patent application confidential for a period of time. There is also the matter of finding foreign patents by means of the Internet. Suppose that you find devices on the market that are similar to yours. If the difference between your device and those that you have found is "non-obvious," you can proceed to file a n application to the USPTO for a provisional or non-provisional patent

If you consider that the invention has commercial potential and your small business has $105 available for the filing fee, you can apply electronically or by mail by yourself for a provisional patent application . It consists of the following parts:

- Provisional Application For Patent Cover Sheet
- Application Data Sheet 37 CFR 1.76
- Drawings of your invention
- General description of your invention

Claims and an oath or declaration are NOT required for a provisional application. Later, you will receive a letter from the USPTO that indicates that an application number has been assigned f or your provisional patent application and the filing date . The letter will also advise that the provisional application will NOT be examined by the USPTO for patentability. You would then have up to 12 months to file a non-provisional application. If you fail to do so, the provisional patent application is considered to have been abandoned. Because the provisional patent application is published, its abandonment can be used by the USPTO as a challenge to the patentability of your future patents of device of a similar nature.

One advantage of filing a provisional patent application is that you are immediately entitled to label your device as "patent pending." As soon as the non-provisional patent has been granted, you will have the right to take legal act ion for any violations of your patent right s that had taken place after the filing date of the provisional patent application.

You can file a non -provisional patent without filing a provisional patent. The key advantage of filing a provisional application is that will have the benefit of an earlier filing date.

If you are 65 years of age or older, you can file a petition to have an earlier examination of your application due to your age. If it is granted, the USPTO examination process will be speeded up.

The United States is the only country in the world that awards a patent to who mever is the first to invent the device, whereas other countries award a patent to the inventor who is first to file a patent application for it. Documentation of your invente d technology or device is important if you hope to convince the USPTO that you are indeed the first inventor. In many cases, the device was invented or completed well before the filing date of the provisional patent application.

The legal protection aff orded to a patent that has been approved by the USPTO applies only to the United States market and its territories . The global market position of your medical inventions may warrant your filing of a patent internationally, as well . See Section 17.1 for mor e information on foreign patent filing.

6.6. Key Elements of a Non-provisional Patent Application

The information required for a patent application is pretty straightforward. It contains the following sections:

- The title
- Cross-references to related applications
- Field of subject matter or technology
- Background
- Summary
- Brief description of the drawings
- Detailed description
- Claims
- Abstract
- Figures

The application for a patent involves a number of forms and is submitted to the USPTO, which grants the patent. The sections above, albeit in a slightly different order, together with the name of the inventor and publication classification, will appear in the public record s of the USPTO in about one year from the time of filing.

The background of your invention must be thorough and accurate, because it will be the first item t o be reviewed by the patent examiner . This is where you provide the patent examiner with an assessment on what is currently available in the market . Good research is required to support the accuracy of your descriptions, as well as to report any comparable patents or similar devices of prior arts . The discovery of an omission of information or over -inclusion of materials in your research from the patent write -up may be used by the USPTO as r eason to invalidate your patent, even in years after it has been granted.

If your patent application covers two or more inventions that are independent and distinct, the USPTO will return you application and require that you limit the application to a single invention.

The detailed description of the invention needs to be as specific as possible. If the dosage of the drug, the operational range of the device, the composition of the materials, or some other factor is essential for the use of the machine o r process for which the patent is being sought, it should be spelled out in the description

The "Claims" section is where the inventor claims what his or her device, material, drug, design, or plant does. It is good to make your claims as broad as possible, when it is appropriate.

You also must describe the purpose of the invention. In the case of a medical device, you would indicate the medical problem that you intend to solve and how this differs from what is described in your competitors' patents. If your device has technical characteristics that are similar to those of your competitor, but your application is for a different disease, it is likely that your device will be perceived to have a new use and thus be patentable for that disease.

A clear explanation of your invention is provided by a series of drawings and/or examples of the device's use in the description section. The drawings should include illustrations of the invention, and the experimental data and theoretical analysis that are critical to the invention's application.

Finally, you should describe the special features of the invention in the context of preferred embodiments. USPTO's rules also make it clear that you do not need to have a workable prototype in order for you to file your patent application.

Who should prepare the patent application? In general, someone who is knowledgeable in research writing should be able to prepare the description part of the application. On the other hand, the claims section of the patent, which can contain many legal terms, may be best left to an experienced patent attorney. A patent attorney will help you to write a clear and concise patent document that will not only enable you to get the approval you seek from the USPTO, but also will eliminate any ambiguities in the application that could be detrimental in the enforcement of your patent from future infringement lawsuits.

The attorney's fees for a non-provisional patent application can range from several thousands of dollars to tens of thousands dollars. This is much higher than for the filing of a provisional patent application. As with everything else, you get what you pay for. Make sure that your patent attorney has experience in the scientific and engineering field of invention and that you put in the effort necessary and funds to help your attorney do the job right.

6.7. Special Patenting Considerations

Orphan Drugs   Many diseases occur only in a small population   .
The prospect of limited sales may discourage pharmaceutical companies
from   developing new drugs for certain diseases, because drug
development is an expensive proposition with considerable uncertainty
about whether the drug that is being developed will be able to control or
cure these diseases . Drugs that are developed for diseas   es that affect
small populations are commonly referred to as orphanage drugs   . In
order to encourage their development, a law was enacted that grants   a
patent for the development of orphan drugs that has a   life that is longer
than the conventional 20 years.

Criticism or Rejection of a Patentable Idea   Suppose   that   your
attorney advises you that your invention may not be new, useful, or non -
obvious, and therefore, it would probably be a waste of your time and
money to file a patent   for your invention . Alternatively, your attorney
may point out that your patent would infringe on a number of existing
patents. Don't be discouraged . Instead, view these criticisms as an
incentive for you to improve your patentable idea.

     If you commit to proceed ing, the USPTO wil l generally notify you in
writing of the patent examiner's decision   within one or two years. If your
patent application is rejected, you can either request reconsideration by
pointing out perceived errors in the examiner's decision, or significantly
amend your application and explain why the amended claim is now
patentable and obviates the objections of the examiner.

     If the amended application is rejected by the patent examiner, you
may have little further recourse   . An appeal of the examiner's final
decision is possible, but it is   greatly restricted in the scope of
permissible amendments.

Patent Policies of Your Employer   Suppose you work in a research
company or university, and you invent something in your garage in your
spare time without using any of your employer's materials or equipment.
Can your employer claim ownership of your invention, or can you obtain
a patent for yourself and then build up a company on the order of what
Drs. Bill Hewlett and Dave Packard achieved? The answer depends
strictly on your employer's patent policy concerning employee inventions.

     Read your employer's patent policy carefully before accepting   his
offer of employment, especially if signing an employee agreement is a

prerequisite to your working for the firm . Some companies allow you to invent things in your own garage and to own your patents if they are not related to your work in the company. Other companies stipulate that they legally own everything that you invent at work or elsewhere.

Strong Patent Operation within   Many high -tech and software companies have   their ow n   patent office s. Besides helping their companies to prepare patent application, they spend significant effort in defending patent lawsuits or pursuing   actions against competitors for patent infringement   .   The annual budget   of such patent offices/departments can be as high as hundreds of million dollars.

For many start-ups in the medical device and biotech field, patents are the key property that they have when valuing their company. If you have an invention with a strong patent of broad claims, your company will have a strong competitive edge that may lead to capturing a large percentage of the market and   consequently a large profit from sale s of the device . For th e potential to raise venture investment   that such a patent would afford, many small companies invest heavily in their patent operation and pursue infringement lawsuits aggressively.

Ten Common Mistakes to Avoid   An   excellent analysis   by Michael Neustell   of how to avoid making the   common patenting mistakes appeared i n IEEE -USA Today' s Engin eer (2). Here is a summary of the common mistakes:

- No employee education
- "Can't be patented" attitude
- No intellectual property management program
- Performing patent research too late
- Failure to perform IP audits
- Not taking advantage of "Provisional" applications
- Filing the application at the wrong time
- Patenting the wrong inventions
- Failing to evaluate competitors' patent rights
- Filing unnecessary foreign patent applications

6.8. Value of a Patent

An approved patent is an asset for your company   . Therefore the value should be assigned to "patents owned by the company, " since the assets and liabilities that are reported in the balance sheet are used by potential investors to evaluate the financial viability of your company and the return of their investment in your company.

One way to arrive at a value of a patent is use the sum of the following two costs and one worth estimate:

- The cost of obtaining the patent
- The fees you pay to keep the patent active
- The estimated worth of the patent's probable contribution to the profitability and competitiveness of your company.

Because of the uncertain reliability of the worth estimate, it is difficult to determine how good this valuation is!

Can you estimate the patent value like the market value of a house? For a house, you assess the value based on the selling prices or builder estimates of comparable homes in a similar neighborhood. However, the patent is not a commodity w hose value you know with certainty. In addition, you rarely can find comparable patents that ha ve been sold before. (If you do find one, it means that your innovation is not new.)

Another approach is to assess the company's net worth (which is the total value of its assets subtracted by the total of its liabilities) and then use it to calculate the value of the patent. This will be a challenge if your tangible assets are primarily patents owned by the company and your company does not yet have any earnings.

As you can see, determining the value of a patent is a subjective exercise. Just like the setting of market value of houses, stocks or companies, the final determination of a patent's value w ill be determined only when the investors and the owners of the company agree on the patent 's value. In other words, the persuasive skills of the entrepreneur, based on solid research and an effective presentation, play a key role in arriving at this consensus and consequently the value of the patent.

One final point to consider is that you can earn a fee by licensing your patent to other companies to improve their products . The approach that you would use to set your licensing fee is similar to that used to set the value of the patent itself . The way to prepare a licensing agreement is given in Section 14.4.

The importance of patenting and licensing was clearly demonstrated in a 2007 Associated Press news item concerning the rejection of a valuable Genentech patent by the USPTO. The patent dispute dates to 2003, when MedImmune Inc. challenged the validity of the Genentech patent. According to Genentech spokesman Geoff Teeter, several companies paid Genentech a combined total of $105 million in royalties related to the patent in 2006. Genentech is pursuing appeal   s at the USPTO and in the courts. The appeal process could last two years.

References
1. Landgraff, F.A., Patenting at Coca-Cola, www.yet2.com/app/insight/insight/20010401_landgraff (2001).
2. Neustel, M. S., Patents − 10 Common Mistakes and How to Avoid Making Them,   www.todaysengineer.org/2008/apr/patents.asp (2008)
3. Rodengen, J.L., *The Ship in the Balloon*, Write Stuff Enterprise, Fl, p. 173 (2001).

CHAPTER 7

FDA REGULATIONS

7.1. The Food and Drug Administration

What Does the FDA Regulate? The Food and Drug Administration, or the FDA, was authorized by the Federal Food, Drug and Cosmetic Act in 1938 to regulate products that are covered by the act's name, although its scope has grown through the following years.

In 1968, for instance, the Radiation Control for Health and Safety Act brought some medical devices under the oversight of the federal government. The Medical Device Amendments of 1976 were passed to ensure the safety and effectiveness of all medical devices, including diagnostic products. As a result of these and other legislative charges, the following product categories are regulated by the FDA today, according to the agency's website (www.fda.gov):

- Food
- Drugs
- Medical devices
- Biologics
- Animal feed and drugs
- Cosmetics
- Radiation-emitting products.

In addition to the legislation mentioned above, other Acts of interest to entrepreneurs in the field of biomedical engineering include the Safe Medical Devices Act of 1990, which requires manufacturers to conduct post -market surveillance o f permanently-implanted devices whose failure might cause serious harm or death to a patient, as well as the FDA Mode rnization Act of 1997, which contain s, among other items, measures to speed up the approval process o f medical devices. Product user fees were also implemented.

FDA Research Tools   Federal government regulations are first published in the Federal   Register under Code of Federal Regulations (CFR). Title 21 CFR is reserved for FDA   regulations. The section that deals specifically with medical devices is codified in Title 21 CFR Part 800-1200.

The FDA also has a set of Compliance Policy Guides (CPG)   for each of the product categories listed earlier   . The guides for medical devices are provided in Chapter 3 of the CPG.

The two documents mentioned above are available online from FDA websites. They are the research tools   that are necessary to learn abou t the FDA approval process for your particular invention.

In addition, the website for the FDA's Center for Devices and Radiological Health   (CDRH) contains a   document called "Device Advice." It provides a comprehensive description of the rules, regulations, and processes that are important in seeking approval of your device, as well as in manufacturing and marketing it.

The following   sections contain information about other important issues that you will need to keep in mind or pursue while you engage i n the research and development, manufacturing, and marketing of your device. Since many   medical device companies will be submitting   a Traditional 510(k) Premarket Notification,   Chapter 8 elaborates on this topic.

7.2. The Safety and Effectiveness of Medical Devices

Safety and Effectiveness   Part of FDA's mission is to reasonably assure the safety and effectiveness of devices designed for human use   . Some FDA regulations   that are intended to support th is mission are fairly broad, while others are quite specific.

The Radiation Control for Health and Safety Act, for example, contains a general paragraph that basically says that the FDA should not allow the U.S. public to be exposed to radiation, as radiation is harmful. The Safe Medical Devices Act, on the   other hand, spells out   very specifically who can serve on a medical device advisory panel   . However, the U.S. Congress has given the FDA a fair amount of discretion to write regulations   that are in between these two poles of generality and specificity, based on the latter's interpretation of the law.

How Does the FDA Determine What is Safe and Effective?

One way is by relying on valid scientific evidence. A device manufacturer needs to carry out investigations using laboratory animals, conduct certain investigations involving human subjects, or undertake in vitro studies to demonstrate that the use of a medical device outweigh s any probable risks and impose s no unreasonable risk of illness or injury. When well-controlled investigations are conducted withi n a substantial portion of the target population, clinically significant results from the investigation are taken to mean that the use of the device is effective.

In determining safety and effectiveness, the FDA also considers factors such as:

- The persons for whom the device is intended
- The conditions under which the device is used
- The probable benefit to health, and
- The device's reliability.

Other considerations may include the following:

- Will the device be used in children?
- Will it be used in a hospital?
- Is it a prescription device or will it be sold over the counter?

The answers to these or other similar types of questions will determine the device's classification and how its safety and effectiveness will be evaluated.

7.3. Device Classification

What is a Medical Device? By law, its definition is broad, with one part of the definition considering it as a physical device, and another part considering it on its intended use. Consequently, the FDA may classify it as an instrument, apparatus, implem ent, machine, contrivance , parts, or accessories, or as a medical device intended for use in the diagnosis of disease, treatment of disease, or functional improvement of the body . For example, the Kolotkoff blood pressure cuff to measure blood pressure non-invasively is a medical device, while a weighing scale used by a nurse to determine the obesity of a patient is a consumer product that the FDA may decline to regulate.

Every medical device is classified in one of 16 medical specialties, such as Cardiovascular Devices, Neurological Devices, and Orthopedic Devices. These medical specialties are further divided into subcategories. For example, t he 137 generic types of devices that are found in the Cardiovascular Device medical specialty fall into one of five subcategories: Diagnostic, Monitoring, Prosthetic, Surgical and Therapeutic Device s. Overall, approximately 1,700 different generic types of medical devices fall within these various specialties and subcategories.

The FDA also classifies medical device   s as Class I —General Controls, Class II—Special Controls, and Class III—Pre-Market Approval (PMA). These three classifications are based on risk, with Class I posing the lowest risk to the patient and/or user and Class III posing the greatest risk.

Class I Devices   These devices are subject to the   fewest regulatory controls. Examples of Class I devices include stethoscopes, elastic bandages, examination gloves, and surgical scissors. In keeping with the commitment of the FDA to speed up patient access t   o new medical devices, the agency exempted 122 generic types of Class I devices from 510(k) submission in 1996   . These newly -exempted devices include oxygen masks, pacemaker chargers, dental floss, patient scales, examination lights, and therapeutic massage rs. This FDA action ma de approximately 572 (or 74 percent) of Class I generic types exempt from 510(k) of the Food, Drug and Cosmetic Act, which requires device manufacturers to notify the FDA of their intent to market a medical device.

Class II Devices   These devices require more consideration by the FDA than Class I devices to assure safety and effectiveness   . A 510(k) submission is required for most Class II devices in order for the applicant to establish that the device is substantially equivalent to   a legally marketed device . Electronic stethoscopes, blood pressure cuffs, infusion pumps, steerable catheters, cutaneous electrodes, surgical drapes, and powered wheelchairs are considered   to be Class II devices. With the implementation of the Modernizati on Act, the FDA reclassified 111 generic types of Class II devices as Class I devices.

Class III Devices   These devices are generally those that support human life or prevent impairment of health   . They require the PMA to assure the safety and effectivenes s of devices before they can be used . Class III devices include implants, such as metal knee joints, replacement heart valves, silicone gel   -filled breast implants, and cerebella stimulators.

If your Class III device was available in the market prior to adoption of the Medical Device Amendments in 1976 or substantially equivalent to such a device, you may want to consider using the 510(k) process as a better route to the market, because it is easier and faster than going through the PMA process.

Think of it this way . While the NIH will be interested in funding your research and development of a medical device , even if it is an improvement of some existing device, you may still want to market your device by advertising it as new and totally novel. To do so, you must go through the PMA process . This is laborious and time -consuming. You, as the manufacturer, may face a much greater financial burden to get to market and pay more in user fees and consultant costs.

On the other hand, even if you think that your device may provide a more accurate diagnosis, but you can demonstrate that it is substantially equivalent in terms of safety and effectiveness to other Class I or Class II devices on the market, the 510(k) process is the route to use.

If the FDA finds t hat your device is equivalent to a Class III device, and you believe that the device is more appropriately a Class I or II device, you can petition the FDA to reclassify the device to a lower class. Anyone can file this type of petition, even someone who i s not marketing the device . If the petition is successful, it will no longer be required to go through the PMA process for the Class III device.

According to the 510(k) policy unit within the CDRH's Office of Device Evaluation, 90% of devices are cleared v ia 510(k) with others either going through the more rigorous PMA path or being deemed 510(k)-exempt. Clinical trials are required for about 10% of 510(k)s.

7.4. Investigational Device Exemption (IDE)

When you are developing or modifying a medical device, your small business may need to perform clinical or animal trials to obtain data that demonstrates the safety and effectiveness of the device. An approved IDE permits a device that has not received 510(k) approval or PMA to be tested for human use . Having no such facilities, the small business needs to work out a contractual arrangement with the teaching and research hospital of a university by which they will become a sponsor for the execution of the trials . The sponsor will be responsible for selecting i nvestigators, usually faculty members, for the trials . The investigators will submit a research protocol and an assurance of the humane care and use of laboratory animals for approval by the university's Institutional Review Board for animal test ing and cl inical use. Only with formal approval by this Board can the company and the investigators carry out the animal experimentations and/or clinical trials.

If you are going to use human subjects to develop the data needed by the FDA for approval or to market the device, you must first ask yourself if there is a significant risk to the patient in the trial of this device. If the trial poses only an insignificant risk, the investigator will submit the research protocol and patient consent form s to the Institution al Review Board for human investigations. If the Board grants you an IDE for your device, you can begin . When a device is considered by the IRG to involve risk to the patient, the sponsor of the clinical trial must obtain an IDE from the FDA before beginning any clinical trials of the device.

As an alternative, you may out-source the clinical trials entirely to a contract research or services organization.

An application for an IDE from the FDA contains several things, including a description of prior inv estigations of the device; a description of the methods, facilities and controls used in manufacturing the device; a signed agreement by all investigators to comply with their investigator's obligations; a list of the Institutional Review Board(s) that have been or will be asked to review the investigation; and a plan of investigation. The plan of investigation includes a description of the device, a description of the proposed use of the device, a clinical protocol in order to obtain a reasonable assurance of effectiveness, informed consent material and, if available, information about the device's expected performance . The FDA will act on your exemption request within 30 days.

The law states that you can only ship FDA -approved medical devices within the United States. Upon receipt of an IDE, the shipment of testing devices to institutions for clinical trials becomes legal.

However, the primary rationale for the IDE process is to assure that the rights, safety, and welfare of all research subjects are pr otected. This is an important consideration . It was legislated by the Safe Medical Devices Act of 1990 to avoid the abuse of patients in clinical investigations.

When Barney Clark received an artificial heart in 1982, the artificial heart (known as the J arvis 7) had been implanted only in calves to test its performance . At this experimental stage, there were no data that would indicate how long a patient who had an artificial heart would live and how risky the implant would be to the patient . However, Clark, who understood the risks of artificial heart implantation, the probable future benefit to other humans if the implantation worked, and who wanted to do something altruistic for his fellow men, could be, and was, accepted as a volunteer for the clinical trial because the Jarvis 7 had received an IDE from the FDA.

To assure that a patient fully understands his or her rights, the patient consent form describes his or her role in the clinical trial, the risks posed by the trial, and the countermeasures and protections that the clinical trial's physicians and investigators will take. All statements are in layman's terms. The patient consent form also stipulates that the patient may withdraw from the trial whenever he or she chooses to do so.

7.5. Premarket Approval Applications

If your performance data show that your device is, to a large extent, equivalent to a Class III device without exemption, you must submit a PMA application before you market your device. Usually the Class III device is something for implantation in a human body. This means that you will need to obtain clinical data in order to demonstrate that every part of your device is safe and effective. When you invent a new material, you must first show with appropriate animal implantation that your new material is a good material suitable for implantation in the human body. With this animal study, you can obtain an IDE from the FDA so that you can begin clinical trials. You must carry out a full scientific investigation that will support your PMA application. Although this requires a lot of work, the FDA has a great deal of information available to help you prepare the PMA application.

The FDA takes a minimum of 180 days to reply to a PMA application, which will be reviewed by an advisory panel of medical device experts. The panel may skip a full review if it believes that similar implantable materials have been reviewed and approved by the panel members previously. Finally, the advisory panel will make a recommendation to the FDA to approve or not approve the application. The FDA nearly always accepts the advisory panel's recommendation.

7.6. Post Approval and Post Marketing Requirements

Post-approval Manufacturers of Class I devices with exemption must follow general control procedures for the following:

- Registering your company with the FDA as a device manufacturer,
- Listing the device being marketed with the FDA;
- Implementing FDA-defined Good Manufacturing Practices[1]. This includes documenting how the device is made, ensuring that the labeling of your device is truthful, and ensuring that you have developed adequate instructions for its use.

If no adverse effect from use of your Class I device is reported, no post-marketing requirements may be necessary.

The factory will probably not have an inspection by the FDA for a Class I device, unless someone complains about your device and the FDA feels compelled to follow up on the complaint with an on-site inspection.

In order to receive post-approval market clearance for Class II devices with a 510(k) application, you must not only follow the general control procedure required for Class I devices, but also ensure that your Class II device follows the special labeling requirements and satisfies the mandatory performance standards. Typically, the facility in which you manufacture your Class II device must be inspected every two years. During the first inspection, the FDA inspector will examine performance data to make sure that what you stipulated in your 510(k) application is applicable to the manufactured product.

Post Marketing Requirements Once your Class II device is on the market, post-market safety surveillance also should be implemented. The 510(k) approval may specify that the Class II device can only be sold as a prescription device under the direction of a physician. If not, you can sell your device as an over-the-counter device. Record keeping should include any correspondence with the FDA, clinical study data, shipping records, and a complaint file (if any complaints have been received), and the design record, including modifications.

Once a PMA order has been issued for a Class III device, the FDA will require more extensive controls beyond the general control procedures for Class I and Class II devices. For example, Class III devices will involve frequent and thorough site inspections. In fact, the FDA will need to inspect your factory and running production line before you can market your device, even with a PMA order in place.

---

[1] As set forth in the Quality System regulation promulgated under section 520 of the Food, Drug, and Cosmetic Act.

You may be asked to restrict the sale or distrib ution of your device. You will need to evaluate continuously the safety, effectiveness, and reliability of your Class III device and to report your findings on a periodic basis to the FDA. Warnings and precautions   must   be prominently labeled. Device-tracking and various other precautions and restrictions that are contained in the PMA order must be implemented. In addition, the law requires that manufacturers report to the FDA   any death or serious injury   that the device may have caused and   any malfunction that would be likely to cause death or injury.

If failure of the Class III device would have serious health consequences or if its implantation in the human body is for more than one year, or if the life -sustaining device is outside of the body of the device user, the FDA may ask you to carry out a post market surveillance study. If so, you, the manufacturer, must submit a plan for the study within 30 days of receiving the PMA order from the FDA . The FDA will have 60 days   in which to evaluate the study plan and order that the study be conducted.

7.7. New Drug Development on Premarket Approval Application

"From Fish to Pharmacies, The Story of a Drug's Development" is employed by the FDA to illustrate how a drug developer/sponsor can work with the FDA to bri ng a new drug to market. The FDA also has an interactive chart (Fig. 7.1) to explain the time frame for the development and application process. In this chart, the process of bringing new drugs to market is divided into three segments: preclinical research   , clinical studies and New Drug Application (NDA) review.

Osteoporosis, the wasting away of bone mass, affects as many as two million Americans. The salmon produces a hormone called calcitonin. Taking by osteoporosis patients, salmon calcitonin, which is 30 times more portent than that secreted by the human thyroid gland, inhibits the activity of osteoclasts and enables bone to retain more bone mass. In the first segment o   f preclinical research,   the drug developer/sponsor worked on the synthesis and purifi   cation of calcitonin. With the approval   of an Institutional Review Board, the developer/sponsor carried out animal testing with an injectable form of synthesized calcitonin.

After   obtaining   promising data from animal studies, the developer/sponsor submit ted an Investigational New Drug (IND)

application to the Center for Drug Evaluation and Research (CDER)   .
The developer/sponsor started the second segment o f clinical studies 30
days following submission as the CDER did not find a ny problem with
the IND application in this particular case.

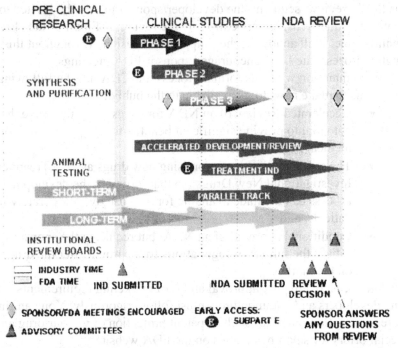

Fig. 7.1. FDA time frame   for the development and application process for a PMA
product.

The following three phases of clinical studies were carried out
during the second segment of research:

Phase 1   A clinical trial, invol   ving twenty to eighty healthy
subjects conducted to investigate some basic actions, dose
ranges and side effects of the drug.

Phase 2   Early controlled clinical studies, involving several
hundred people, to obtain results on the effectiveness of the
drug, short term side effects, and risks associated with the drug.

Phase 3   Expanded controlled and uncontrolled trials, including
several hundred to several thousand pe   rsons, to gather
additional information about the drug's effectiveness and safety

in order to evaluate the drug's overall benefit s-to risk relationship.

With all supporting evidence necessary to meet FDA's requirement for marketing approval available, the developer/sponsor submitted a New Drug Application for review by the CDER's Advisory Committee. In this third review segment, the developer/sponsor m ay be invited to answer any questions that arise in the review . Finally, the FDA commissioner will announce the approval decision. Throughout this lengthy process, the FDA encouraged sponsor/FDA meetings.

In conjunction with this formal process, the FDA has the following provisions to make new drugs available to the public:

- Accelerated Review of an NDA for drugs that have the potential to provide significant benefits for un satisfied medical needs,
- The consideration o f promising new drugs as Treatment Investigational New Drugs so that drugs in the development process can be made available for use by desperately ill patients, and
- Conditional approval of an NDA, but requiring the sponsor to satisfy the full set of regul ations for approval after the drug is on the market.

In addition, there are post approval and post marketing requirements that drug developers and manufacturers must follow rigorously. You can find more information on topics such as patent protection of y our drug and special offers for small businesses on the FDA website.

CHAPTER 8

THE FDA 510(K) SUBMISSION

8.1. Overview

Section 510(k) of the Food, Drug and Cosmetic Act requires device manufacturers to notify the FDA, at least 90 days in advance, of their intent to market a medical device. This is known as a Premarket Notification (PMN) or 510(k) submission. The number of 510(k) submissions that are received may be as high as 3,000 to 4,000 a year. As many as 2,000 to 2,500 new devices enter the market each year. Many are competing products that offer incremental improvements over existing products.

To assist your preparation of the submission, we discuss issues in this chapter that are associated with the following four questions:

- Do you need to file a 510(k) submission?
- What need to be done before the submission?
- What is included in a 510(k) submission?
- What does the FDA do following your submission?

8.2. The 510(k) Submission

When you introduce a Class I or II device to the U.S. market for the first time or propose a different intended use for, or modify a device that you already market, you should consider the submission of a 510(k) notification. Once you submitted this, you may receive within 90 days a letter from the FDA that contains the following:

"We have reviewed your Section 510(k) premarket notification of intent to market the device referenced above and have determined the device is substantially equivalent (for the indications for use stated in the enclosure) to legally marketed predicate devices marketed in interstate commerce prior to May 28, 1976, the enactment date of the Medical Device amendments, or to devices

*that have been reclassified in accordance with the provisions of
the Federal Food, Drug and Cosmetic Act.....*"
This letter is enclosed with your 510(k) summary statement that bears
the 510(k) num ber assigned to the device and   the FDA official seal.
Now, you can proceed to market your device.
     There are four exceptions to this 510(k) process:
1.   If you file a 510(k) and do not hear from the FDA within 90 days,
     you can market your product.
2.   If you deem that your device is substantially equivalent to a Class I
     or Class II device with exemptions as stipulated by Title 21 CFR,
     you are not required to file a 510(k) application   . It is important to
     document that your decision not to file a 510(k) was made in g   ood
     faith and to keep a file of that documentation so that it can be made
     available to the FDA for inspection   . Even with such precaution s,
     you want to avoid accumulating up a huge inventory to meet market
     demand in case an FDA inspector informs you that yo u need to have
     510(k) approval because the intended uses of your device differ
     from the uses of currently marketed devices that you have identified
     as being substantially equivalent.
3.   If you import or distribute an approved device, you need not apply
     for a 510(k). If you re -label a device under your company's brand
     that had received previously 510(k) approval, you may need to apply
     for a Special 510(k), which is described later.
4.   If you are not marketing the device but using it in clinical trials, you
     need an IDE, not a 510(k), before you can proceed with clinical trial.
Two alternative approaches with shorter review time s were introduced
with the enactment of the FDA Modernization Act:
1.   The Special 510(k) Application can be used by medical device
     manufacturers if the proposed device is a modification of a FDA
     granted device and the modifications do not affect the device's
     intended use or alter the fundamental scientific technology   . The
     Office of Device Evaluation 's 30 -day processing time for Special
     510(k) Applications provides an incentive to submit such an
     application.
2.   An Abbreviated 510(k) Application   can   also be used by
     manufacturers who have been able to find FDA -generated guidance
     documents or information   about special controls and consensus
     standards for their devices . The FDA has published a number of
     device-specific guidance documents to communicate   its regulatory

and scientific expectations to industry . Information is also available from the FDA   about the concept of special controls   to assure the safety and effectiveness of Class II devices   and o f the consensus standards applicable to these devices. This second alternative to the Traditional 510(k) Application is easier   for the manufacturer to prepare and for the FDA   to review , thus resulting in a m   ore expeditious evaluation of the 510(k) submission and decision.

If you have a change in the device that could significantly affect the safety or effectiveness of the device , or a major change in the intended use of the device (2), you must submit a 510(k) notification for the new device.

8.3. Preparing for the 510(k) Submission

Suppose that you decide   that your device   qualifies for a 510(k) submission. By this time, you should have the device in a form clos e to the final one that will be marketed . The first thing to do is to file at the FDA web site and pay for the user fee to obtain the User Fee Cover Sheet. If your company is a small business entity, you can submit that information to the FDA to obtain a small business identification number. Inputting this number into the user fee process will   enable the site to reduce your user fee by half. The following items are things to prepare next for the submission.

Identification of Predicate Device(s)   Go to the FDA website to find predicate devices that are substantially equivalent to your device. A device can be deemed substantially equivalent to a predicate device even if it has different technological characteristics, as long as it has the same intended uses, d oes not raise new questions of safety and effectiveness, and is at least as safe and effective as the predicate device   . Get the 510(k) summary statement of the predicate devices from the website so that you can select the one that offers the best likelihood that you will be able to demonstrate the substantial equivalence of your device.

If your device has the functions of two different medical devices, they can be considered to be   the predicate devices for your 510(k) submission.

Using commercial channels, obtain a sample of the predicate device in its original container and   with its instruction manual. Some of these materials will be used in your write-up and enclosed in your submission.

Biocompatibility If your device will come into contact with patients or users, you need to do biocompatibility tests (1). The FDA has issued Blue Book Memorandum #G95-1, entitled "Use of International Standard ISO 10993, 'Biological Evaluation of Medical Devices' —Part 1: Evaluat ion and Testing" for all premarket approval and 510(k) submissions. Device manufacturers in the United States should use this memorandum to determine which kinds of biological effects are of concern for materials used in your device. Such biological effects include closed patch sensitization, skin irritation, cytotoxicity, hemo - compatibility, and reproductive or developmental changes.

Software, Electric Safety and Electromagnetic Compatibility For the 510(k) submission, you will need to know and address th e level of concern that the FDA may have about your software and device (4). If the software device provides diagnostic information that directly affects a decision about a treatment or therapy that could result in serious injury or death , the FDA would be very concerned. If a malfunction of the software device can lead to an erroneous diagnosis or a delay in delivery of appropriate medical care , the FDA will have a moderate concern . If these and many more simila r scenarios do not ap ply to you r device or software, the level of FDA's concern will be minor.

Similar logic appl ies to the subject of electric safety and your device's electromagnetic compatibility.

Sterilization and Shelf Life It is desirable to determine if your device needs to be sterilized or what its shelf life will be, based on the materials used in the device and the frequency of the device's use.

The Performance Testing-Bench, Animal and Clinical The r esults presented here serve as a basis for showing the substantial equivalence of your device . The FDA recommends that the submission include the following information:

- List the specific bench tests conducted
- Describe each test protocol
    o Objective of the test
    o Test articles used in the test
    o Test method and procedures
    o Specific parameters measured
    o Pre-defined acceptance or pass/fail criteria.
- Summarize the results
- Describe your analysis

- Discuss your conclusions

Similar descriptions will be provided in the submission if animal and clinical performance of your device was tested.

8.4. Writing the 510(k) Submission

Guidance for Industry and FDA Staff   (3) and   *Device Advice* (www.fda.gov/cdrh/devadvice) are wri tten by the FDA to help you prepare the submission. The sections in a 510(k) notification are:

Section	Description
0.	TABLE OF CONTENTS
1.	USER FEE COVER SHEET (FORM 3601)
2.	CDRH PREMARKET SUBMISSION COVER SHEET
3.	510(k) COVER LETTER
4.	INDICATIONS FOR USE STATEMENT
5.	510(k) SUMMARY
6.	TRUTHFUL AND ACCURACY STATEMENT
7.	CLASS III SUMMARY & CERTIFICATION
8.	FINANCIAL CERTIFICATION/DISCLOSURE
9.	DECLARATIONS OF CONFORMITY AND SUMMARY REPORTS
10.	EXECUTIVE SUMMARY
11.	DEVICE DESCRIPTION
12.	SUBSTANTIAL EQUIVALENCE DISCUSSION
13.	PROPOSED LABELING
14.	STERILIZATION & SHELF LIFE
15.	BIOCOMPATIBILITY
16.	SOFTWARE
17.	ELECTROMAGNETIC COMPATIBILITY & ELECTRICAL SAFETY
18.	PERFORMANCE TESTING – BENCH
19.	PERFORMANCE TESTING – ANIMAL
20.	PERFORMANCE TESTING – CLINICAL

The table of contents is placed at the beginning of the hard copy   . It identifies which tab to choose for each of the sections of the hard copy of the 510(k) submission. When the section number is combined with the section description to form a file name, e.g. 000_Table of Contents, the above list looks almost identical to the file listing of the CD or DVD that you will send to the FDA.

Sections 1, 2, 3, 6, 8 and 9   in this list   primarily constitute the administrative part of the submissi   on. Since your device is class II, indicate in section 7 that the section is not applicable. Sections 14 to 20 cover the test and materials you   described in the previous section . A total of 30 sections are   permitted. You may use the last 10 sections to include your device's instruction manual, that of the predicate device, its labeling and packaging description, and your publications or scientific papers that are relevant to the submission. In   the remainder of   this section, we will deal with completing Sections 4, 5, 10, 11, 12 and 13.

Section 4 covers indications for use. It should be written like those for the predicate device . Throughout your submission, the indications for use should be identical as any differences in wording may   cause the FDA staff to call for clarification. This could cause a delay.

All sections, except Section 5 (510(k) Summary), are treated as confidential by the FDA . The Summary contains the name of predicate device(s) and its 510(k) number, the description of your device, its intended use, its performance data,   a device comparison table,   its substantial equivalence, and the conclusion.

Once your submission has been approved, the FDA will post your 510(k) Summary on   its website. The regulatory affair s consultant of GMI recommends that you keep Section 5 of the Summary as brief as possible because your competitors may use this document to understand what new things you have provided to the FDA.

The FDA recommends that   you describe the performance specifications of your device in the section on Device Description and include a brief description of the device design requirements . You may begin by explaining the reason for submission , which is similar to the presentation of the medical problem   that you intend   your device to resolve. Then give a narrative description   of the device's overall function. Next, describe the performance specifications of the   device's components. Use diagrams and schematics to fully describe the function of the device and its components . Include a table about the components, part numbers, a description of   their material, whether the component s will be in contact with the patient so that the FDA can understand the biocompatibility of your device.

You may   begin the presentation of the section on   Substantial Equivalence by giving an overview o f the scope and analysis of what you are doing and then the conclusions you formed from your analysis .

Answer the following four questions t   o show that your device is substantially equivalent to the predicate device(s):

- Does the new device have the same statement of intended use?
- Does the new device have the same technological characteristics (e.g., design, materials, etc)?
- Are the descriptive characteristics precise enough to ensure equivalence?
- Does the performance data demonstrate equivalence?

Then, a table is   provided to demonstrate   clearly the functional similarities of the predicate device(s) and yours, as well as their differences. Finally, provide a detailed comparison in the form of a table to summarize the similariti es and differences in indication   s for use, device description, contraindications (conditions   in which one should not use the device), sterilization and uses, technology, labeling, component characteristics and materials . Use these two tables   as the basis to explain further why the differences do not affect the safety and effectiveness of your device.

The section on   Proposed Labeling presents the labels that will be used on the device and its package. In general   , the labels may contain some of the following information:

- Company name, logo, address and website
- Device Name
- Model name
- Key words constructed from indications for use
- Contraindications
- "Use as directed by the physician in accordance with the instruction manual"
- What does the package contain?
- Size information
- Patent pending, if appropriate
- Rx only?

The similarities and differences   between your labels and those of the predicate device need to be discussed.

The FDA encourages the use of electronic copies for Pre   -Market submissions. An electronic copy is an exact duplicate of a paper submission, but   is in the form of a CD or DVD   that must   be accompanied by a hard copy of the documents that bears the signature of an officer of the company. To provide an electronic copy,   it is recommended that the pr eparer of the 510(k) submission has software , such as Adobe Reader 9.1 , that can create PDF files with optical character recognition so that the FDA examiner can use the " *find"* function to locate specific word(s) in the file.

Writing the submission is not the same as writing a research paper. Here are a few pointers for you to consider:

- Proving substantial equivalence must be done with products that are approved under FDA authority.
- The p redicate d evice comparison require s an actual marketed product, whic h has been cleared under FDA 510(k) notification or a preamendments device. Referencing general categories of devices to serve as predicate devices is not acceptable.
- Many clinical devices have been reported in the scientific literature with good results . Because they have not been approved yet by the FDA, they cannot be used as predicate devices to prove substantial equivalence.
- Do not use medical journal articles as proof of product effectiveness and safety . Substantial equivalence is based on intended use (or indication s of use); product claims and technology similar to existing marketed products that are already deemed safe and effective by the FDA.

In this section, we give an overview of submission preparation. Please consult the guidance documents an d 510(k) submissions that are available from FDA websites (3, 4) to prepare your own submission that is specific to your device.

8.5. Outcomes

Suppose you have a 5 10(k) submission that passes the FDA checklist as complete. The FDA has up to 90 days by law to reply to you . Normally they will get back to you sooner. How soon is soon?

In an ideal situation, the FDA will send you a letter saying that your device is sub stantially equivalent to an approved device . There is also likelihood that the FDA will exempt your device from 510(k). If you have a letter or exemption, you can legally proceed to market your device.

However, you might also receive a letter from the FD A that states that they need more information about your device before they can approve it. The letter will describe in some detail what the FDA wants, and will state that you need to expand your application to include this additional information and then resubmit it to the FDA . Your resubmitted submission usually can be processed in less than 90 days, as the FDA has already gone through your application once.

In other s cenarios, the FDA may ask you to provide more clinical data to justify your claim of s ubstantial equivalence . Since collectin g more data will take time, the FDA is very likely to remove your application from their docket. If so, you will need to refile your 501(k) submission after you have the requested data.

The worst scenario is having the FDA find that your device is not substantially equivalent to any Class I or Class II device . If your device is not an implant, and you think that it should not be classified as a Class III device, then you can petition the FDA to create a new generic t ype or category to reclassify your device as Class I or II in accordance with the 513(f) process . After the reclassification, you can then proceed with your 5 10(k) submission.

References

1. Wallin R.F. and P. J. Upman, MD&DI, January (1998).
    www.devicelink.com/mddi/archive/98/01/023.html
2. www.fda.gov/MedicalDevices/DeviceRegulationandGuidance/GuidanceDocuments/
    ucm080235.htm
3. www.fda.gov/MedicalDevices/DeviceRegulationandGuidance/GuidanceDocu ments/
    ucm084365.htm
4. www.fda.gov/MedicalDevices/DeviceRegulationandGuidance/GuidanceDocuments/
    ucm089543.htm

CHAPTER 9

OBTAINING HELP AND SUPPORT

According to the website of the Small Business Administration (SBA), the 23 million small business entities in USA employ almost half of the private work force, produce half of the private sector output, and account for 97% of all U.S. exports (6). Almost 40% of jobs in high technology sectors are in small businesses. Small businesses contribute significantly to the US economy in both innovation and job creation.

In 2008, there were some 6.1 million businesses having employees. About 627,000 of them were new, 596,000 have closed and 43,000 have filed for bankruptcy. It has been suggested that one out of seven new businesses may grow and earn some profit. In recognition of the risks and the importance of small businesses, the government and private sectors provide many forms of support to help small businesses to succeed. In this chapter, we will discuss:

- Support from SBA for small businesses
- Government grants to sponsor the research and development of small businesses
- Community support for small high tech businesses.

9.1. SBA Support for Small Businesses

Small Business Administration   The SBA was created in 1953 as an independent agency of the federal government to aid, counsel, assist and protect the interests of small business concerns, to preserve free competitive enterprise and to maintain and strengthen the overall economy of our nation. As explained in its website, the SBA has four programs to assist your business development. They are:

- **SCORE** (Service Corps of Retired Executives). This is a resource partner of the SBA that is dedicated to entrepreneur education and the formation, growth and success of small businesses nationwide.

- **SBDC** (Small Business Development Center) . This provides management assistance to current and pro spective small business owners.
- **WBC** (Women's Business Centers) . These are a national network of nearly 100 educational centers designed to assist women start and grow small businesses.
- **SBA District Offices** . The SBA operates full service district offices in every state of the nation.

The assistance of SBA and local government is oriented toward the service industry, some retail, and a few manufacturing and construction industries. Even though the needs of ventur es in biomedical engineering may differ from those of the mainstream industries that receiving SBA assistance, support from these four programs and their partners will be useful for the growth of biomedical engineering ventures.

Business Development   Your business development may help you to find a city in which to locate your company, to develop a viable business plan, and to obtain financial assistance   . The local SBA office and government will be happy to help you develop and grow your company.

To help you in your decision to build a factory in a particular locality, the economic development office of the local government, the SBDC, and the Chamber of Commerce can provide information about the labor force available for employment, the names of comparable companies that are situated in that locality, and the availability of local resources such as space, roads and tax incentives . The possibility to collaborate with various laboratories of the university at that locality will be another factor that will he lp you decide where to locate your business.

What should be done to start or grow the business? How do you prepare a strong business plan, resolve business problems, acquire management skills, and find resources to support the business operation? These are the problems that the SBDC and its local partners can help you resolve. A number of attorneys, certified public accountants (CPAs), bankers, and small business people serve in the SBDC to assist its operation and course teaching.

If you want to buy a business, sell a business, or start a business, the SBDC will advise you how to go about doing it. It can tell you the local rules and regulations for your business, wh ich permits you w ill need, how to structure your business . With regard to the last -mentioned subject, the SBDC can help you to set up your business as a sole proprietor, partnership, limited liability company (LLC) or corporation. In the area of sales and marketing, they can advise you on the ways to carry out an initial market analysis and put your marketing plan into action. If you intend to market your service locally, the SBDC will help you identify your competition, regardless of your market, and the demographics of your market – number and sizes of households, median income, etc. It can help you set up your accounts or books and also advise you on the long-range outlook for your market. In order to obtain some information about running a small business, there are a number of training courses or workshops that are offered by the SBDC and its partners. The impact of the SBDC on the Commonwealth of Virginia is mentioned next.

Virginia, which has a population of 7.6 million persons, has 29 local SBDCs. According to the websites of these SBDCs, more than 4,500 business owners and managers received one-on-one counseling in 2006 and more than 9,200 attended a training program offered by a local SBDC. SBDC professionals assist with business planning, marketing, financial analysis, access to capital, business start-up and other specialized services, as requested. Many companies have given an account of the impact that the SBDC has had on their operations and attributed much of their success to their relationship with the SBDC. In 2006, loans of more than $73 million were obtained, total capital of $109 million was formed, 4,170 jobs were created or retained, and sales increases of $99 million were reported for Virginia.

The SBA has a web site spells out in detail how to prepare a business plan. The SBDC firmly believes in the need for a business plan. First, a business plan describes what you do when you start a business. You need to keep working on the business plan and applying it to your business rather than flying the business by the seat of your pants. You will be constantly updating it, at least annually, as suggested by SBDC. Very often, an entrepreneur has a great idea, is technically sharp, and can usually find someone to put money into it. However, when it comes to managing the business and really making it successful, his business skills are not always that great. SBDC views the business plan as something that compensates for many weaknesses. Once you get your business development ideas down on paper and have some experts, like a banker or investor, look at your business plan, they can tell you if you have a good handle on the business and where you will need help with the operation. As described later, SBDC will help you obtain financial assistance from various SBA programs.

SCORE is a sister organization of SBDC. Retired CEOs, company presidents, and businessmen serve as volunteers to staff SCORE. There are more than 10,500 SCORE volunteers in 374 chapters operating in over 800 locations to assist small businesses with business counseling and training. SCORE also operates an active online counseling initiative. You can ask them to review your business plan and introduce you to people who can assist your business development.

Financial Assistance   If you want to establish an office to practice your profession or build a manufacturing facility t   hat can generate income within months, the topics covered in this subsection will help you obtain financing to develop your business.

Loan assistance is a big part of what SBDC 's operation. Generally, SBA is not in the business of making loans, but   it doe s provide loan guarantees. You will want to use commercial bank financing to move your company to the manufacturing and marketing phase or to put you in a position to obtain VC investment in the future. At this time, you don't have much collateral or an ex tensive track record, especially if your enterprise is a   start-up. The bank will likely consider your small business loan application, if you can   secure an SBA guarantee. Just as your parents may   co-sign a loan for you   , the SBA may agree to guarantee part of a bank loan in order to help you   to secure the bank loan. The SBA's loan guarantee mechanism is known as the SBA's 7(a) Standard Loan Program . An SBA pre -qualification loan and a Small Business Investment Company are other avenues   available for small business financing.

How much money can you   obtain from a bank? If you have a business plan to show that you need $1 million to carry out your plan, the SBA will guarantee 75% of the loan for the required funds and you, as an owner , must come up with the r emaining 25% of the money for your development. In essence the maximum loan   will be $750,000 and you will have up to 25 years   for repayment. For smaller amounts, the SBA may guarantee 85% , leaving you to come up with 15%. The loan can be used to pay for   a building, equipment, working capital, and salaries. The fund s you personally put in constitute your   stake in your business development.

At this point, most banks will want you to submit a loan application, including a business plan. Without a plan, most banks won't even discuss a loan. The bank's utmost concern is how you will repay the loan. In the business plan, you must be able to show your sales projections, what anticipated expenses, what will remain after you pay all expenses, how much will be available to repay the bank and also to pay a living wage or salary to yourself. The bankers look at the 4Cs of you and your business development. They look at your character (have you ever been in jail?), your credit (what is your credit record and have you ever been bankrupt?), your capital (how much capital can you put into it?), and your collateral (what collateral can you provide?). If you have a patented invention, completed its R&D, and built a pre-commercialization model, that will be your collateral. With this collateral and a good business plan, the SBA will enthusiastically provide a loan guarantee and the bank will not turn you down for lack of collateral like real estate or stock. What bankers want are a good business plan, a good product, good character, a good credit record, and you to make some investment in the venture. The SBDA will help you to develop the loan strategy, package the business plan and present it to the bank. If you like, they can accompany you to the bank to help explain the proposal.

The SBA pre-qualification program is designed to help small businesses in certain locations of the country and also those owned by minorities or women. In the case of a husband and wife that are starting a business, 51% ownership by the wife will qualify for this particular program. Also, if you're a veteran or have a rural business, you can qualify. The other requirements for loan guarantee are similar to those of 7(a), except that the loan amount limit is about $250,000.

The for-profit Small Business Investment Companies are licensed and regulated by the SBA. They provide management assistance to start-up and early stage businesses. The financial assistance is a combination of debt and equity investment. If you approach these companies, they will work to find investors who can supply investment capital to your company. They will also provide some debt financing. The investors will own part of the company. The rest of the financing will be provided as a bank loan with an SBA loan guaranteed.

9.2. Government Support for Technology Development and Commercialization

Small businesses contribute much more to the US economy and society than can be calculated from the spending and profit that they generate . These businesses are more innovative than l arger companies and more able to respond to changing consumer demand s. Small businesses produce more patents per employee than do large firms and small businesses patents are twice as likely than patents held by larger firms to be among the 1% of patents most cited (i.e. , most significant). These comments were made by Derek Leebaert, an adjunct professor of government at Georgetown University (2).

The development of biotechnology products requires years to accomplish. Some products require large capital investments to carry out the necessary research and development and to commercialize them. As Hector Barreto, SBA Administrator, stated (1), " *But small businesses cannot do it alone. The U.S. government plays a crucial role in creating an environment in which entrepreneurs can flourish . .... Government investment in small businesses benefits not only the businesses themselves but also our national economy and our society at large.*"

Many state governments have programs or agencies that focus on entrepreneurs who have a record of innovation. These federal and state programs are reviewed in this section to provide you with an opportunity to decide whether you would like to a pply for federal and state funding to carry out research, development and commercialization.

Federal Grants In 2001, nearly $1.5 billion in federal funding was awarded to small businesses to develop technology concept s or products. By 2007, the Small Business Innovation Research (SBIR) programs of 11 federal agencies ha d awarded $12 billion t o various small businesses. The SBIR program is a "set-aside program" that the agencies allocate 2.5% of their research funding for domestic small businesses to en gage in R &D that shows potential for commercialization. In 1992, the Congress authorized the establishment of the Small Business Technology Transfer (STTR) program to support small businesses working to commercialize technologies developed in universities or non-profit research institutions.

The National Institutes of Health of the Department of Human Health and Service is one of the federal agencies most likely to fund the R&D of your medical device . NIH regularly offers SBIR Conferences throughout the nation. The technical and administrative staff of NIH man these conferences at one-on-one tables to discuss NIH's interest in SBIR, project planning, proposal development, cost accounting, intellectual property, commercialization, and forming teams with the medical industry and universities. State agencies, universities, and private organizations partner with NIH to offer workshops to help small businesses understand the issues that are important in SBIR programs, make more competitive grant proposals, and develop strong commercialization plans.

In many cases, you can strengthen your research program and enhance your chances of receiving SBIR funding, if you partner with well established investigators or institutions to carry out the R&D. For example, you may subcontract part of the SBIR grant to a certain investigator of a university to carry out clinical trials or basic animal studies of your product because he can provide facilities and expertise that your small business does not have. Conversely, the university faculty may collaborate with you to apply funds received from NIH to examine the impact of your product on certain diseases. A contractual agreement that specifies the rights and responsibilities of each party to the collaborative project is essential to assure the benefit to both your company and the university. This agreement is especially important if you plan to apply for STTR funding.

To learn more about the application process for SBIR funding, please refer to Chapter 10.

Supports from State Governments In recognition of the tremendous potential in permitting the private sector to commercialize the research findings of universities, Virginia established the Center of Innovative Technology in 1984. The State hopes that job opportunities, tax revenues and other economic benefits will be gained by helping universities commercialize their intellectual properties through CIT (3). Many states have similar agencies, which are identified at the www.gnet.com website. We will use CIT to illustrate more specifically what these agencies do.

In order to help universities carry out cutting edge research in all areas of technology, CIT helps create potential applications of university research in business and industry, accelerate the transfer of that knowledge to the marketplace, and promote the growth of entrepreneurial firms and start-ups within the state.

CIT's mission has evolved to the following: to accelerate the development of the next generation of technology and the building of technology companies through its research investment and entrepreneurship programs . CIT's goals are to expand Virginia's technologies into world -class research hubs and to enable Virginia to become a development leader in entrepreneurial technology ventures.

CIT and its partners h old SBIR conferences, TechStart Bootcamps, and Proposal Assistance Awards to help you win SBIR/STTR grants. CIT has been instrumental in helping Virginia companies win R &D dollars for high -risk technologies from the Advanced Technology Program of US Department of Commerce. The Federal and State Technology Partnership (FAST) Program operated by CIT can assist companies to solicit government funding, especially from the federal government. Virginia universities also receive funds from CIT to operate Technology Innovation Centers to facilitate collaboration among researchers in universities and companies.

CIT has nine regional offices in Virginia. Because CIT is committed to the support of companies in Virginia, the regional directors are knowledgeable in all aspects of business development , such as market analysis, intellectual property protection, and the commercialization of products. One of the regional directors ha s a Ph.D. in microbiology and really enjoys the variety of the work for the CIT, start-up companies, and university research laboratories . These regional directors offer one -on-one consulting, technical data and information about your industry, access to expert ise in universities and federal laboratories, and referrals to a statewide network of partners who know your industry.

The CIT office in Charlottesville serves the Central Virginia Region and has close relation with the University of Virginia. There are many start-up activities in Charlottesville that receive support and advice from the CIT. It s staff is focused on advanced materials, advanced manufacturing, biotech, electronics, information technology, and telecom sectors. To monitor trends in those indu stries and funding opportunities for them, steering committees have been set up and staffed with experts for the advanced materials, electronics and biotech areas.

CIT maintains a database of all patents that have been issued in Virginia. This helps Virginia universities market their patents and you as an entrepreneur to find some one in the Virginia system who has something beneficial to contribute to your company and who resides not too distant. CIT also helps with patent licensing. If you need something concerning the patents that are owned by a university, CIT will be of great assistance and the university's patent office will help young start-ups get their businesses off the ground.

9.3. Community Support

Charlottesville Venture Group Many localities have private organizations that promote business and technology development. For example, Charlottesville and Central Virginia have the Charlottesville Venture Group (CVG). This is an organization that is staffed by volunteers and committed to smarter ventures and smarter investments through education (5). They have a quarterly publication, "Capital Talk," that covers various topics, such as what not to say in a business plan. One of CVG's activities is the Business Spotlight, which calls for a business plan competition. This is intended to give you an opportunity to present your plan to an audience of venture capitalists, entrepreneurs, and other interested members of the Charlottesville and surrounding business community. CVG is partnering and collaborating with various organizations in Charlottesville to bring their wealth of expertise in a wide range of business topics to the members and to build entrepreneurial activity essential to business growth.

When the author moved from Charlottesville to San Diego, CONNECT was the organization that had given GMI the most guidance on its development. Many aspects of CONNECT that appear in THE CONNECT STORY and the CONNECT website are described here so that you may appreciate the kind of community support that you can find in your own locality.

CONNECT This is a technology and business accelerator that is dedicated to the rapid and sustained growth of high technology and science companies that have a vested interest in the San Diego region (4). Serving as a proven neutral broker, CONNECT directly addresses the critical business needs of companies, ranging from start-ups to large public corporations, as well as universities and entrepreneurs. CONNECT is supported by more than 2,000 volunteers, many of whom are seasoned entrepreneurs, CEOs of successful companies or attorneys of various specializations. Below are some of the 25 programs that are operated by CONNECT.

- **Access to Capital**
  - **Springboard and Springboard Spotlight**. Mentoring to companies in all stages of development for three to five months by Entrepreneurs in Residence. Quarterly Spotlights profile the graduates for investors.
  - **Venture Roundtable**. Connects venture ca pitalists to early stage venture opportunities in technology, diagnostics and devices, life sciences, therapeutics and clean technology.
  - **Tech Coast Angels**.   A n   etwork of private investors in early-stage Southern California companies.
- **Entrepreneur Education**
  - **Entrepreneurs FrameWorks Workshops**
  - **CEO Strategy Forum**
  - **MIT® Enterprise Forum**
- **Networking and Recognition**   Programs and opportunities specifically designed to bring the community together to create a dialog and to recognize innovation and   identify successful individuals and companies.

So successful is CONNECT that   San Diego is on its way to becom ing the premier region in the country for innovation.

Tech Coast Angels   This is the largest angel network in the United States (7). It has 280+ members who have invested   more than $100 million in over 130 start   -ups in Southern California . The San Diego Chapter has an annual Quick Pitch program   that enables companies to present their business plan s and network with the ve nture community. As a result of the efforts of Tech Coast Angels, the sponsored start -ups have gone on to raise a total of $1 billion in venture funding.

References

1. Barreto, H.V., eJournal USA - Economic Perspectives, 11:1 (2006)
2. Leebaert, D., eJournal US A - Economic Perspectives, 11:3 (2006)
3. www.cit.org
4. www.connect.org
5. www.cville-venture.org
6. www.sba.gov
7. www.techcoastangels.com

CHAPTER 10

SBIR GRANTS FOR PRODUCT DEVELOPMENT

10.1. Vision of Small Business Innovation Research (SBIR) Program

In recognition of the risk that high-tech small businesses have, the Small Business Innovation Development Act of 1982 sets aside 2.5% of the agency's extramural research funding to support the R&D of domestic small business entities . In accordance with this l egislation, NIH awarded $566 million of SBIR grants and contracts and $73 million of STTR (Small Business Technology Transfer) grants to small businesses in 2008 (1). This investment has enabled small businesses to accomplish a great deal in getting new medical products to commercialization, to improve the delivery of healthcare and the health of people, and to contribute to the economy of the nation during the last twenty years.

The mission of NIH is to improve human health through biomedical and behavior research, research training and communications . Your medical device or pharmaceutical produc t development f its into this mission. NIH will be interested in evaluatin g your device for SBIR grant funding consideration.

Since tax dollars are used for funding small businesses , NIH has established an extensive and thorough review process to evaluate the innovation and strengths of SBIR/STTR proposals that are submitted to NIH and to prioritize the funding of these proposals.

Obtaining a VC investment for R&D for pre-commercialization of a device or drug is very challenging. One uncertainty for VC i s that your business model has not been shown yet to be feasible or the medical device or drug to be marketable. SBIR grants give you funds to advance from feasibility and R&D phase of the product to the manufacturing and marketing phase. The SBIR grants p ut you in a much stronger position for getting VC investment to commercialize your products.

10.2. NIH SBIR Funding

NIH has two types of SBIR funding. Almost 90% of the funding goes to support SBIR grants . For SBIR grants, your company decides what R&D you w ish to undertake and what product you want to commercialize. The project depends completely on your own initiative. If y ou feel that the project is important to medicine , you submit a SBIR grant application to NIH for R&D funding of a pre -commercialization device or a drug . The second type of funding is by a n SBIR contract. NIH needs certain R&D done or products to be developed and NIH has no in -house people to do it, NIH will offer to fund small business entities to carry out the specific R&D under a contract. A much smaller number of grants are also awarded in the form of an STTR, which is somewhat similar in form to an SBIR grant, but with more emphasis on technology transfer.

In addition to the requirement that the company must have no more than 5 00 employees, the business must be owned by US citizens or permanent residents who own at least 51% of the enterprise and have control of your research facilities . The 51% ownership requirement prevents the company from being a subsidiary of another company. The aspect concerning control of research facilities also requires you to have a place to carry out the proposed R&D . Thus, you the company can either rent space for the R&D or own space for it so that no one except you can use that facility.

In general, your company activities can be divided into three phases:

- Phase I: Assessing the f easibility of making your product and evaluating its technical merit
- Phase II: Conducting research and developing your product to its pre-production model
- Phase III: Comme rcializing your product.

The government will support the first two phases . Funding for Phase III is expected to come from non -SBIR/STTR sources, meaning that you must raise the capital yourself, borrow it from the bank, or obtain it from venture capitalists.

Suppose that you propose the development of a medical device to achieve a certain sensitivity . A device of such sensitivity is not available in the market . The scope of this project will fit well with a Phase I SBIR grant from NIH for you to undertake R&D to demonstrate its feasibility (i.e., that you can produce you r conceptual model of the device). Of course, you must demonstrate that the project has technical merit, meaning that it will provide important technology or solve some clinical problems. For a Phase I grant, the R&D guideline requires you to have a budget of no more than $100,000 for a period of six months.

The Phase II grant is intended to enable you to continue the R&D initiated in Phase I . In other words, the preliminary results obtain ed during Phase I will be the basis of your Phase II SBIR grant application submission. The guidelines used by NIH for Phase II grants limit the total costs budgeted to $750,000 and the period to two years. When you have sufficient results to demonstrate the feasibility and technical merits of your device, you may consider the submission of a Fast Track Award to obtain both Phase I and II money from NIH . Before you pursue this track, you may wish to ask NIH about others' success in obtaining Fast Track Awards and the percentage of funding set aside for this track.

R&D in genetic engineering or medical development can be expensive sometimes. The R&D may call for the use of expensive reagents or the development a new genetic line of animals . Thus, NIH will allow an exception if you can justif y your large proposed budget. You must c onsult the NIH staff i f you have a budget that exceeds the guidelines of $100,000 for Phase I and $750,000 for Phase II.

The budget contains two types of costs : direct costs and i ndirect costs. Direct costs include the salaries of the PI and researchers who do the R&D covered by the grant, the equipment and supplies required to perform the tasks, attendance at a national meeting, and any R&D work that has been subcontracted. The rental of space, book keeping charges, and salary o f the PI to manage non -R&D supporting activities are indirect costs . Indirect costs are usually calculated as a percentage of the direct costs. However, for the percentage applicable to the operation of your small business, you should consult with NIH . You can elect to set a small percentage of the total costs as profit for your company.

The funds received from SBIR grants differ from a bank loan, as you do not need to repay the government after your compa ny becomes profitable. Consult the government about expenditures that you cannot charge to the grant . For example, NIH thinks that the patent application is a by-product of your R&D and thus you cannot use SBIR grants to pay filing fee s for patent applications. On the other hand, the government normally grants your company the patent ownership of the invention , which gives the company the right to earn royalties.

10.3. NIH SBIR Grant Review Process

NIH and the Department of Defense are the federal governm ent's two main funding agencies for funding basic research in universities and the R&D of small businesses. NIH has a peer review process that ranks the priority of grants for funding . Respectable researchers and university faculties (the peers) serve on study sections to evaluate grant applications and establish funding priorities. The grants manager relies completely on the recommendation of the NIH study sections. Because other agencies have specific mission to fulfill , their managers have considerable leeway in deciding whether to fund your grant.

To assure that you receive an exceptional review, NIH invests time, manpower and money to make the review system work fairly and effectively. I f your grant application receives no funding , you will receive a constructive review and valuable feedback to help you to revise your research plan for another application for funding by NIH.

The research plan that you submit for NIH SBIR grants is reviewed for five aspects:

1. Significance of the research
2. Viability of the proposed approach
3. Innovativeness of your project
4. Training and experience of the investigators
5. Suitability and adequacy of the research facility.

Although the word innovation appears in the official name of the SBIR program, a significantly improved produc t is also acceptable and qualifies your company to receive NIH funding . The first three aspects deal with the technical merit of the proposed research and the last two deal with the ability of the small business to carry out the R&D . The reviewers will look at these five aspects and give you a score, which will decide whether your grant will be funded.

After you submit a SBIR grant to NIH, NIH will assign it to a study section for review. If you wish, you can recommend which study section reviews your gra nt. Overall, the NIH study sections review some 5 ,000 to 6 ,000 new applications each year. Some sections include bioengineering or medical imaging in their section name and biomedical engineers serv e as reviewers for many sections . Each section has 20 to 30 members . They meet three times a year in Washington, D. C. to review and score about 60 to 80 grants during each two-day meeting.

As an example of the reviewers' qualifications, one SBIR grant study section has three members who have a dual degree of PhD/MD, 12 PhD's and 10 MD's . Three of these reviewers come from industry and the rest are employed in universities or research institutes. The executive director of the study section appoints two to three reviewers to serve as the primary reviewers of your grant application. In the review meeting, these primary reviewers will summarize for the review panel what you propose to do and how you carry it out . They will discuss the merit of your proposals and give the panel a feeling of how high they would score your grant proposal. The next action is to triage the proposals into three categories: insufficient merit for funding, sufficient merit for consideration, good proposals requir ing detailed consideration . After further discussion, each member submits a scor e (1 to 5 , with 1 designating best) for the grant proposal. The score is given in the increment of 0.1 . Then the executive director of the study section sums the scores and multiplies the average by 100 to yield a final score.

The greater the score, the lower it is in priorit y for funding . The final score and the reviewers' comments and evaluation are transmitted to you. In a sense, the best score that you can get is 100, implying that you can be absolutely certain that you will obtain the NIH grant. If the score is 200, your research proposal is probably on the borderline for funding. The total fund allocated to each R&D topic decides the last grant that will be funded on that topic . If you receive a score of 300 or more, your proposal is unlikely to receive any funding from NIH.

Whether the principal investigator (PI) under an SBIR grant should have a Ph.D. or an M.D. is an issue that has been raised . NIH's official statement is that this is not necessary. On the other hand, they do require you to demons trate that the PI has sufficient expertise to oversee the research projects scientifically and technically. Describe your education, scientific and engineering training, and research experience in the grant application to show that you are qualif ied to be the principal investigator. T o assess your qualification, t he review panel critically evaluates your research publications in refereed journals.

10.4. SBIR Grant Application Research Plan

The main body of the research plan should contain the following f ive sections:

1. Specific Aims

      2.   Background and Significance
      3.   Preliminary results (not needed for Phase I grant
          applications)
      4.   Research Design and Methods
      5.   Product Development   or Commercialization   Plan (not
          needed for Phase I grant applications).

In the first Section on specific aims, you spell out what you want to do .
Then in the second Section   you describe   the background and
significance of what you want to do   . In this Section y ou also address
why this SBIR grant is important for you to do it and why it is important
for NIH to support your SBIR development . When you have carried out
your Phase I R&D, you describe the preliminary results , supporting the
need for further R&D in the third Section. The fourth Section describes
how you will do it. Finally, for Phase II a grant application, you have
Section 5 to provide an   overview of your plan to commercialize your
product.

      The page requirement for   the three key sections of the Phase I
research plan is 15 pages   and 25 pages for the first four sections of   a
Phase II gr ant. It is recommended that t   he commercialization plan
contain no more than 10 pages . Aside from these page limitations, the
other parts of the research plan include human subjects, vertebrate
animals, literature cited, contractual arrangement, and consultants.

      NIH prefers   that you do not   proceed directly to patient studies
because they want to be assured by animal studies that your invention is
safe before you test it on human   . It is important that you set a few
realistic goals for your Phase I R&D that you can accomplish in six
months and with the $100,000 budget. For example, you may set a goal
of developing a prototype of a blood volume monitor . Larger or more
ambitious aims, such as to   develop a fully functional blood volume
monitor and test it with p atients, cannot be done with in the constraints
on time and budget of a Phase I grant. If you exceed your budget, the
NIH will not supplement your grant to pay for the difference. You can
request for a n o-cost extension of your Phase I grant for another six
months. Similar budget constrain ts apply to the operation of Phase II
grants and no-cost extension can be requested for one more year.

      Suppose that you accomplish the aims of the grant   during Phase I.
Presenting this evidence in the preliminary study section in the Phase II
grant application will help to convince the reviewers that you can carry
out what you propose in that application.

Hopefully, t his section gives you an overall review of what   to consider in submitting an SBIR grant application to the NIH. To prepare a good application, read the   *Advice on NIH SBIR & STTR Grant Applications* by Gregory Milman, National Institute of Allergy and Infectious Diseases (gmilman@niaid.nih.gov). This presentation of 88 slides provides a great deal of   excellent advice that may help you succeed with your NIH SBIR or STTR application (2). In addition, you should obtain a funded SBIR grant application to learn how   to do it successfully. NIAID has an outstanding Phase II grant application available for your examination (3). Equally important is hav ing a seasoned researcher to review your grant application   and utilize his comments to improve your grant application well before its deadline for submission.

10.5. Timelines for SBIR Grant Funding

It normally takes about one year from submission of your grant application to receive the funding from NIH , i f approved, to begin the Phase I research. If you satisfactorily completed the Phase I research and then submitted a Phase II SBIR grant application promptly, it may take slightly less than one year to receive Phase II funding . In essence, you need to be prepared well in advance of that time with whatever funding may be available to pick up the slack   between Phase I and II   of NIH SBIR funding.

Suppose that your company ha s two products for development and that both can be done sequentially, overlapping somewhat in time. You can submit a pr oposal for a   grant for one product, and then submit another for the second product in the following   year. If you are able to receive grant award notices in accordance with the timelines suggested above, you will have continuous funding to develop your two   products for five years. Again, this continuous funding arrangement can be easily disrupted if the funding for one application   is not granted due to a low score.

References

1. www.nih.gov
2. www.niaid.nih.gov/ncn/sbir/advice/advice.pdf
3. www.niaid.nih.gov/NCN/sbir/app/default.htm

CHAPTER 11

WRITING AND PRESENTING YOUR BUSINESS PLAN

11.1. Overview

A business plan is multi-purpose. First, writing it forces the executives to organize their thoughts , plans and dream for the company into a business plan that can serve as a blueprint o r roadmap to build the venture into a successful and profitable business . The plan provides a conceptual picture that answers:

- What do you plan to do?
- Why do you want to do it? and
- How you are going to achieve success?

The plan provides a map that lays out the goals, timelines, and actions for everyone in the company to follow on and the company's financial goals. The plan identifies the employees' responsibilities and describes the benefits provided to patients by the company's product . Thus , it serves in ternally as guidelines for the employees in carrying out their work and mov ing the company ahead in doing goods for patients . The plan motivates potential employees to join the Company, which offers more powerful diagnos es or treatment s for patients. Externally, the business plan can be utilized as a means to stir up the support of existing investors and attract new capital from outside sources, such as venture capitalist firms (VCs).

In this book, we address the development of the company in three phases: Assessing the Venture, Launching the Venture and Building -Up the Enterprise . The product development, actions to be taken, and financials required for each phase differ. As you begin the development of your company in the Assessing Phase, it is important that executives and employees know what needs to be done . Thus, it is appropriate to prepare the business plan as a roadmap for company development . When you launch the company and have many actions to carry out, you need a r oadmap that has been rewritten as an Action Plan. Both the

Roadmap and the Action Plan have the structure of a business plan, but are more in line with that phase of development. As you move into to the Building-up Phase, you will need capital to carry out your   plan to develop manufactu ring, marketing and sales . Thus, you will write a Business Plan that has an emphasis on raising investment capital.

Writing the business plan for your venture, therefore, is an evolving process. For example, as you modify the Roadmap to become the Action Plan, you will need to update the presentation detail of what you already have, add the new action items   that you will undertake during the Launching Phase, and then revise your future projections o   f company developments. Before preparing any of these pla ns, it is important to know what you r company has   and also has achieved. This issue is addressed in the next section   . The subsequent three sections cover guidelines and suggestions for preparation of the Roadmap, Action Plan and Business Plan.

Many compan ies can get   the company off the ground with funds from founders, friends, or family . As capital needs increase, you   are bound to look for funds from VCs   . Aside from the obvious need to access capital to fund the growth of your Company, you may   have an interest in leveraging the VC's knowledge and relationships into a strategic partnership for the development of your company.

Successful venture capital firms are frequently approached by large numbers of companies that need financing. Therefore, it is critica l that your business plan clearly and succinctly defines the market opportunity that you are targeting and   in what way(s)   your company is better positioned than your competitors to capitalize on that opportunity   . In this chapter, we present the process of   writing the business plan and presenting it to your internal team and the investment community.

Your business plans include proprietary information about your company. When you show the plan to potential employees, you can   ask them to sign a non -disclosure and confidential agreement. Signing such an agreement is not the custom for VCs . Thus, it is advisable to do due diligence on potential investors to determine how ethical they are before you send them your business plan with a reminder of confidentiality.

11.2. Company Status before Preparing the Roadmap

Must Have   Once upon a time, while several biomedical engineers were having a friendly discussion o f a hot research topic in a private setting, they came up with an innovative concept f or a medical device that may benefit patients . After several brainstorming sessions, they have:

1. Gained a commitment by several persons to work together in an entrepreneur team to build up a company. One of them has the training, expertise and experience that make him an ideal choice as the one to serv e as the Chief Technology Officer (CTO) and the PI of a Phase I SBIR grant application to demonstrate the feasibility of building the device by state-of-the-art technology.

2. Completed a conceptual description of the innovative device and what it may do for patients.

3. Completed a l iterature survey showing the importance of the medical problem that the innovative device is intended to resolve.

4. Concluded from the number of patients affected by the medical problem, that the potential market is large.

5. Discussed the device and the c ompany with several angel investors. This led to a promise by one investor to invest $100,000 for seed money to get the company going , if a satisfactory business plan for the new start-up is submitted.

6. Interviewed and consulted s everal experts w ho are knowledgeable about the particular medical problem. They are enthusiastic about the development of the new product and its potential to solve the medical problem. The experts agree with the entrepreneur team's belief that the functionality of the product is superior to those of devices marketed by the competitors. These experts are willing to serve as consultants to the Company.

7. Have a vision and company mission statement.

If you are in a comparable sit uation and can point to achievements like these, you can go ahead and prepare the Roadmap.

In the next s egment of this section you will be able to review the vision and mission statements of Microsoft, Medtronic and Global Monitors, Inc . The importance of having Medtronic 's statement is explained later in th e subsection. Use these three examples to write vision and mission statements that are specific to your company and the impact of its device on patients.

In the last s egment, we present ed a medical probl em that GMI's two products could resolve as an example to help you   elaborate on points 2 to 4 listed previously.

The Vision and Mission of Your Company   The vision is the guiding statement of the Company and responds to:

- Why you want to develop that medical device.
- Why you want to market it.
- What benefit your device offers patients.

In e ffect, you use the vision statement to tell the VCs   and anyone else why you're doing what you do.

A very good example is the   Microsoft Corporation's   vision statement (3). The vision of Bill Gates and his partners who founded the company is to put a personal computer on every desk and in every home. They thought that this vision would serve to   meet the needs of   the coming Technolo gy Century by   helping to   improve productivity, efficiency, the search for information, and so on . This vision addresses the problem that they s aw at that time - the lack of operating systems that could be used easily by common people. Following the tremend ous growth of Microsoft, its vision now empower   s people through great software any where at any   time and on any device. Such a   mission statement tells people that, with the products of Microsoft, they can do a lot more than they've done in the past.

The ben efits of the vision, as described by Collins and Lazier (2), are that:

- Vision forms the basis of extraordinary human effort,
- Vision provides a context for strategic and tactical decisions,
- Shared vision creates cohesion, teamwork, and community,
- Vision lays the groundwork for a company to progress beyond dependence on a few key individuals.

The mission statement, the focus of your Company's vision, should address this question: What does your Company want to achi eve? If you want to put a computer on every desk, you would be talking about hardware, software   to manage the operating systems, and various applications for office and home use . Because Microsoft had received a contract from IBM to develop DOS for personal computers,   Bill Gates and his associates decided to concentrate their mission statement on the development and s ale of software to enable Microsoft to become the largest provider of PC operating systems, software and all programming tools required for various applications, such as office operations, hospital information management, etc.

The mission statement of Medtronic (1) is:

- *To contribute to human welfare by application of biomedical engineering in the research, design, manufacture, and sale of instruments or appliances that alleviate pain, restore health, and extend life.*
- *To direct our growth in the areas of biomedical engineering where we display maximum strength and ability; to gather people and facilities that tend to augment these areas; to continuously build on these areas through education and knowledge assimilation; to avoid participation in areas where we cannot make unique and worthy contributions.*
- *To strive without reserve for the greatest possible reliability and quality in our products; to be the unsurpassed standard of comparison and to be recognized as a company of dedication, honesty, integrity, and service.*
- *To make a fair profit on current operations to meet our obligations, sustain our growth, and reach our goals.*
- *To recognize the personal worth of employees by providing an employment framework that allows personal satisfaction in work accomplished, security, advancement opportunity, and means to share in the company's success.*
- *To maintain good citizenship as a company.*

The first statement is really Medtronic's vision. Here is the story told by Earl Bakken on the adoption of this statement by Medtronic and the impact it had on Medtronic as the company reached the age of 25 (1):

> *"Medtronic's financial data in early 1960s revealed the bleak reality* (i.e., near bankruptcy). *The exhilarating growth that followed the development of, first, the external pacemaker and then its implantable successor was hugely expensive for a small, undercapitalized, relative inexperienced company like ours.*
>
> *It didn't take us long, then, to decide what we wanted to concentrate on as a company. We would dedicate ourselves in the development, manufacture and sale of devices that restored people to meaningful lives. We would focus on implantable therapeutic technologies – as opposed to diagnostic or other laboratory products – and build the company around those technologies. Our written mission statement would reflect that decision.*

My role, I decided, was to encourage our engineers in their activity, remind them of the corporate mission, help them see the big picture, and make sure they didn't limit their imaginations or stifle their creative urges.

In 1974, Medtronic celebrate d its 25 th anniversary. For those of us present at or near the company's creation back in 1949, such a milestone scarcely seemed possible.

For a company that has established itself as a leader in the field of biomedical engineering, is the world's largest manufacturer of pacemakers, and will soon gross $100 million annually, Medtronic certainly had a modest beginning some 25 years ago."

The vision and mission of Global Monitors, Inc. is to improve the delivery of hemodialysis through better blood volume ma nagement and to provide devices and methodologies enabling dialysis clinics to deliver safer hemodialysis at lower expense . GMI has two products. **Anti-pooling Vest** is used to alleviate or prevent the development of intradialytic hypotension (ID) for patients undergoing hemodialysis. The **Lee Monitor** is used to diagnose the causes of the development of ID: blood pooling in abdominal organs of patients or low blood volume induced by the hemodialysis process.

The Medical Problem and Products that GMI is Working on   The problem and products cited here are mentioned to assist you in writing your plan, especially in ways gathering quantitative data to support your assertion about the medical function and financial impact of your products. According to the National Kidney and Urological Disease Information Clearing House (6), the 2008 E SRD statistics (adjusted for an annual increase of 5%) are:

- Prevalence: 560,000 US residents were under treatment
- New incidences: 120,000 were new patients taking treatment
- Mortality: 100,000 deaths among all patients who are undergoing treatment or about one out of six die each year
- Cost: $37 billion in public and private funding
- Patients who are regularly receiving dialysis treatment: 390,000
- Dialysis survival rate: 78.7% or one out of five die each year
- Patients doing home hemodialysis: 2,700 or 0.7% of the total hemodialysis population

- Number of kidney transplant performed: 20,000 (or about 5% of patients who are taking dialysis).

As discussed in Section 1.6, the occurrence of ID is the main reason why hemodialysis patients have such a high mortality rate. GMI assumes that its products w ill alleviate and prevent ID and thus lead to an improvement in patient's quality of life by reducing the incidence of ID, thereby lowering the mortality rate. Patients who require dialysis treatment are our customers and their discomfort and high mortality rate are our "medical problem" to resolve.

Many countermeasures to ID have been introduced for patient use during hemodialysis treatment . However, the incidence of ID and the mortality rate remain relatively unchanged (5). An inflatable abdominal band was recently reported to be in use to treat orthostatic hypot ension that occurs in patients post -dialytic or with a number of diseases . GMI has designed some features into the anti -pooling vest for it to be more effective than the band in reducing blood pooling in the abdominal organs. In view of the benefit of the band in alleviating hypotension and the basic research done by the author on blood volume control, it is possible that the vest can more effectively alleviate ID than the methodologies that are currently used to counter the development of ID.

Blood poolin g in the abdominal organs and a reduction in total blood volume are two key reasons that lead to ID (4). The blood volume monitors available in the market do not have the sensitivity necessary to measure blood v olume. Their prediction o f change in blood volume of patients who are undergoing hemodialysis is constructed from an unrealistic model of circulation. As a result, the countermeasures called for by the prediction often do not result in an alleviation of ID. The Lee Monitor has an accuracy that is five to ten times greater than those blood volume monitors currently marketed by our competitors so that the Lee monitor is capable of identifying which of the two causes leads to ID . If blood pooling is the cause, then the use of the anti-pooling vest is required. If low blood volume is the reason, then saline infusion or the use of the vest is appropriate as a countermeasure.

Please note that the reasoning given here merely suggests that the products of GMI may h ave an impact o n hemodialysis patients . More studies need to be undertaken after FDA approval o f the devices so that GMI can show how much better off the patient is by using GMI technology and how great a saving and improvement in the delivery of hemodialysis clinics can gain by using the technology.

11.3. Roadmap for the Assessment Phase

With the scenarios of the Company that were described in the previous section, you can build t he answers to the following two questions into a business plan or roadmap for the company. The roadmap is written to convey the message that <u>the company has a good plan for the following three short-term goals and one-long term goal:</u>

- To recruit qualified executives and employees who will help to move the company forward
- To demon strate the feasibility of manufacturing the medical device
- To prepare the company to attracting funding with which to move the company to the next level of development
- To become a market leader with the sales of effective medical devices.

First Question: What Do You Have Currently? The scenarios described in the previous section are used to answer this question by indicating that your company has the rudiment s of a promising entrepreneur team, a conceptual model of the medical device, and the agreement by an angel investor and several medical experts on the potential of the company.

Many other scenarios can result in similar answer to this question . In one situation, a successful CEO, who had just sold his/her medical device company, was visiting a biomedi cal engineering professor to learn more about the research done in the professor's laboratory . As a post-doc described his/her research project, it dawned on the ex -CEO that this project could evolve into the development of a new medical device. As a resul t, the CEO and the post -doc at that quickly formed a new company and soon would get to the stage of preparing a roadmap for the company.

In a networking party organized by a local entrepreneur chapter and a research university, several invitees had the opportunity to discuss their careers and work. Pretty soon, they discovered a common interest in the use of a new technology to deal with a certain medical problem. After these individuals met for a few more brainstorming sessions, they appointed a CEO and a CTO and established a company with funds from their families or their own savings.

Second Question: What Do You Want to Accomplish in the Coming Six-months or Year? The answer to this question can be explained by a plan that details the execution of th e following four tasks for the scenarios described in the ***Must Have*** segment of Section 11.2:

- Recruit a CEO and establish the organization structure and responsibility chart
- Undertake further study of the market to identify the technology, competition, and barrier to entry
- Submit a Phase I SBIR grant to conduct a feasibility study
- Develop the research plan to carry out the feasibility study.

Research Plan of Feasibility In the third task, what will be written in the research plan is exemplified by the Phase I research plan of CardioResearch Inc. (CRI, the predecessor of GMI) . The grant application propos ed to develop the Lee Monitor to measure the sound velocity of blood with the aid of two unique features: an accuracy of five to ten times greater than the b lood volume monitors being marketed at the time and a monitor design that does not have its ultrasound transducers in contact with the flowing blood. The monitor would accurately assess the transient changes of blood density in a clinical environment[1], with a sampling rate of blood density or sound velocity at no less than five samples per second.

It may be noted that most blood volume monitors currently marketed by GMI's competitors also measure the ultrasound velocity of blood, while their transducers ar e in contact with the blood flowing through the circuit of dialysis machine. Because of the greater sensitivity of the Lee Monitor , one can use it and saline dilution technology to measure the blood volume of patients (4). Because the flowing blood is not in contact with the transducers in the Lee Monitor , there is less chance for contaminat ion of the patient's blood . The proposed data processing arrangement would use 10 to 100 times more data points than that used by the competitors. Therefore, the success of this development depends on showing that the use of more data for cross -correlation would yield a more accurate assessment of sound velocity than possible with a conventional arrangement.

The grant application is accompanied by a 15-page research plan. It details the construction of an ultrasound probe that is not in contact with

---

[1] Because there is a one -to-one relation between sound velocity and density of blood, a sound velocity monitor is also known as a density monitor.

the flowing blood . The probe, a standard signal generator, a general purpose data -processing unit and a PC   are assembled to form   the Lee Monitor for the processing of ultrasound signals into a measurement of sound velocity . To demonstrate the accuracy of the Lee Monitor, its performance is compared to that of the most accurate density monitor [2] when both monitors are connected to an   *ex vivo* blood line for blood density measurement . This performance check is   used to verify the objective of the grant   , which is to show that the Lee Monitor so constructed has the accuracy required for blood volume measurement.

General Guidelines on Writing a Business Plan   A business plan consists of an executive summary, five sections as the main body of the plan, and supporting documents   . At this early stage, it is recommended that the page limit of the executive summary be   one quarter to one half of a page in length and that the main body require no more than 10 pages. Supporting documents are not included in   the page count. In presenting of the process to write the three plans, *the part of the guidelines that apply to the writings of all three plans is italicized.*

The Roadmap for the Assess ment Phase is prepared by combining your answers to the two questions posed previously in this section with the responses to the general guidelines below into one to   convey the message underlined in the first paragraph of this section.

Executive Summary   This summary   highlights these two messages: your technology is the best in resolving the medical problem faced by many patients and your team can build   the company up into the market leader. *Construct an elevator spe ech of 30 seconds from the summary to convey the two messages to potential investors and employees.*

1. The Company   *This section may cover the following topics:*
- *The vision and mission of the Company*
- *The organization of the Company*
- *The entrepreneurial team*
- The background, past experience and capabilities of the CTO, who has the qualification s necessary to get funding for an NIH Phase I SBIR Grant and to get the technology developed
- *Current ownership*

---

[2] Developed for use by the chemical   industry, a Parr density monitor has the accuracy required for blood volume measurement using saline dilution methodology. However, it can not be   used for clinical measurement of blood   volume because of the challenge in sterilizing the Parr density monitor.

- *Investment received and current financial status*
- *The product being developed and the medical problem to be resolved.*
  - *Organizational development*
  - *Product development*
  - *Market development*

Since the developments to be pursued in the last three subjects during the Assessing Phase are covered in the next three sections, any description of them in the Company section would be short as the latter will concentrate primarily on the long-term development of the company. Use the material that you collected for the list of achievements in the previous section for a discussion of the company vision and mission, organization, entrepreneur team, technology, and development plans in the Company section.

2. Technology Development   In general, *this section is used to show that your product has the following four characteristics:*

- *Your technology is really the best available for solving the medical problem*
- *Your technology has sustainable competitive advantages (7)*
- *Your product can achieve a high penetration rate and can gain a large market share with a minimal entry barrier*
- *Your product can generate profits for your Company.*

In the Roadmap, you use the materials that were collected from interviews and literature to support your assertion that your conceptual model can soon be shown to possess the four characteristics above.

Suppose that it is your plan to secure an SBIR Phase I grant to fund your feasibility study, which is to show that you can build the conceptual model into a functional device. You will use one page in this section to describe the research that you would undertake with the Phase I grant.

Conclude this section by outlining the technology that the Company will develop in coming years.

3. The Management and Organization   *This section describes the establishment of a management team under an organization structure that will efficiently handle the business side of product development, employee management, marketing and sales.* Use the materials that you collected in the previous section to write this section and the next. Some organization structures for the company are suggested in Chapter 5.

4. The Manufacturing and Marketing Plan   *This section describes the actions to be taken to have the product manufactured at an affordable cost and to persuade prospective customers to buy your product.* In writing this part of the Roadmap, you describe the research to be undertaken so that the investors will know how you will overcome the hurdles in manufacturing and marketing your products.

5. Financial Projections   *This section presents the financial projections to show that the company is able to use its resources and capital in this phase to undertake the R&D and facility expansion established by the business plan,* i.e. the Roadmap. Do a cash flow analysis to show that you give close attention to financial matters and will not be caught in a situation of having insufficient funds in your bank account because of inadequate planning. Use your knowledge of the market and your product to estimate the market share that you can probably obtain in five years. Next, prepare a projection of income and expenses to show when your company will become profitable.

Supporting Documents   *Enclose at the end of the business plan such documents as the executives' CVs, scientific publications concerning the product, an abstract of the patent, the product's instructional manual, and the FDA letter for the 510(k) notification, if available.*

11.4. Action Plan for the Launching Phase

Action Phase   Once the company has recruited a competent CEO and obtained a satisfactory result from the feasibility study, the CEO and CTO can proceed to convert the Roadmap into an Action Plan. The message of the Action Plan is that you will soon be able to show that your product has a sustainable competitive advantage and will generate sales to create a profit for the company. In writing the plan, you should emphasize the following points:

- The research done in the Assessing Phase and for the Phase I SBIR grant puts the Company in the position of being able to do the work on infrastructure, manufacturing, quality and regulatory control necessary to move the company to the manufacturing and marketing of the medical device.
- The updated market survey and evaluation of the competitive advantages of the medical device further supports the assertion

that the company can become the market leader in the field that
the medical device serves.

- The tasks to be done w ill enable the question of whether a
  prototype of your device can be built at a reasonable cost to be
  answered. This question is known as the cost question that the
  Launching Phase will address.
- The submission of a n SBIR Phase II grant for the R&D of the
  device.
- The sales of medical device w ill increase the value of the
  company and provide a good ROI for the investors.

In addition, you include in the plan how you will prepare the following:

- A prototypic device that can be mass produced and
  demonstrated through a Phase II SBIR grant.
- A detailed cost analysis to manufacture the device
- A demonstration o f its diag nostic or treatment power by
  collaborative research with physicians and biomedical engineers
- A detailed documentation o f the cost effectiveness of the device
  and the potential for insurance reimbursement
- A revenue generating projection o f the sales of your device and
  associated disposable products
- A non-provisional patent application for the device
- A 510(k) submission for Premarket Notification of your Class II
  medical device

The Action Plan covers a period of two to three years with a funding at
the level of $500,000 to $1.5 million to do the tasks listed above . (See
also Table 5.1 for comparison). A good Action Plan can be used to
apply for funding from angel investors and venture capital firms to speed
up the completion of these tasks and to begin the work of the Building -
up Phase sooner.

To rewrite the Roadmap into an Action Plan, you need to
strengthen the parts in the Roadmap that describe what you have
accomplished during the Assess ment Phase. Then, you use Chapters 4
to 10 to lay out a management s trategy that can convince internal
personnel and investors that the management team members are goal
achievers. With improvement in these two parts, you next revise the
part that describes what you plan to do in the future. Limit yourself to a
half page t o one page for the executive summary and 15 pages for the
total Action Plan.

More Elaboration To complete the Action Plan, four more items should be discussed further . The f irst is the submission of a Phase II SBIR grant. This will be dealt with next . Although your class II device may not require clinical trials, it is desirable that you look for others to collaborate with you in clinical studies of your device as a second action item to do in this phase. The clinical studies will determine whether your device w ill benefit the treatment or diagnosis of patients . The r esults should be published in a scientific journal . Thirdly, provide more detailed milestones (including dates) to mark your c ompany's progress during the next five years, especially for the following:

- Completion of the R&D of a prototype
- FDA approval and start of production
- The first sales
- Reaching the breakeven point
- Achieving the full market share of your projection.

Finally, present a description o f the exit strategy and show, by the financial projections , how good a return the investors will receive on their investment and what employees will receive for their work.

Phase II SBIR Grant One action to do in the Launching Phase is the submission of a Phase II SBIR grant . Achievement of its overall objective would show that you have a prototype that is patented, approved by FDA for marketing, shown to have clinical benefits to patients, performed better than your competitors, c an be manufactured at a reasonable cost and f ulfill the requirem ents for insurance reimbursement.

The author would like to share the CRI's experience in obtaining a Phase II SBIR grant from the NIH and subsequently the results after the conclusion of the grant . At the completion of the Phase I grant, it was shown that the use of more ultrasound data for data processing indeed increased the accuracy of sound velocity monitor ing by the Lee Monitor by five or more times that of its competitors. As discussed previously, the gain in accuracy makes Lee Monitor the only one that can assess the blood volume of patients with the saline dilution technology (4). However, because of the use of general purpose systems, the manufacturing cost was estimated as two to three times the listing price of the blood volume monitors marketed by competitors . One specific aim of the Phase II grant was to show that CRI could manufacture the Lee Monitor at a cost as low as one fifth of its competitors' list price .

CRI wrote in its proposal that the devi ce design would include a dual channel A/D converter to sample ultrasound data at 64 MHz, a high speed I/O device to store the digitized data, and a microprocessor to compute the digitized data to determine sound velocity. CRI provided an estimate o f the c ost to manufacture th is. Ways by which the manufacturing cost could be decreased further were also included in the grant application.

Once CRI received the Phase II grant, it connected the evaluation board of the A/D converter to that of the I/O device an d a PC to carry out the testing. It quickly showed that this system did have the necessary accuracy. The cost to purchase these three components now dropped the manufacturing cost of the Lee Monitor to one half of the competitors' price. With this demonstr ation, GMI took over the development and designed a much simpler circuitry that would perform only the specific data processing and outsource d the prototype manufacturing and software development. The estimate that was received from the subcontractor indicated that GMI would be able to reduce its manufacturing cost to about one seventh of the competitor's price. When GMI goes into mass produc tion of the Lee Monitor, the cost of manufacturing may have dropped to one tenth of the competitor's price. CRI also received a Challenge Award from Virginia's C IT for clinical studies of the Lee Monitor . The work done with this State funding showed that the Lee Monitor could be used with the saline dilution technology to measure a patient's blood volume.

11.5. Business Plan for the Building-Up Phase

With the completion of the action items proposed for the Launching Phase, you move to the Building -up Phase, which involves the building of manufacturing capability, testing facilities for quality and regulatory assuran ce and creation of marketing teams to sell your medical device and its disposable product s. The message to be delivered by the Business Plan of this phase is that your management team will move the company forward into the manufacturing and marketing of medical devices that are highly beneficial to patients and generate good ROI for investors.

What you have done in the Assessing and Launching Phase will enable you to write a strong Business Plan and probably get your Company known by the community as a bri ght young company . With the Business Plan, a prototype and publications   that show its medical benefit, you have a better chance   of raising the needed capital to build up your Company   on terms that both you and   the investors will be comfortable with.

In addition to improving the Action Plan and including the building plan for manufacturing and marketing, you   can add more supporting evidence to strengthen   your Executive Summary and Financials . The Business Plan should be limited to 20 pages   , including an   Executive Summary of one or two pages.

Executive Summary   This summary is written with the goal of stimulating the interest of investors to invest in your Company   . You need to make your summary to stand out so that the investors can be convinced that you hav e a promising company and they will get a good return on their investment.

The Company   By including new information obtained in the Launching Phase, this and the next three sections of the Action Plan are revised to become the corresponding section of the Business Plan.

The Technology   In this phase, you may want to   conduct a user satisfaction survey to obtain information   with which to refine your device design. Since it would be necessary to manufacture many devices to carry out the survey, you   will gain some information   about manufacturing costs that will enable you to confirm that you can mass produce your device at an affordable cost.

The Management   In addition to the revision s, describe your plans for hiring supervisors and workers for production, quality control, regulatory affairs, servicing, marketing and sales.

The Manufacturing and Marketing Plan   Use the materials covered in Chapter 15 and 16 to prepare this plan. Include in it the plan to set up a service and quality control unit . Calculate from the research you've done on marketing, pricing and insurance reimbursement, a more realistic projection o f the market share you can gain once your product has been   introduced. Use this projection when you do the financial calculations of the next subsection.

Financials and Exit Strategy

Investor Funding   Stipulate here what funding you will be looking for from investors and how it will be used for infrastructure, equipment acquisition, personnel development, etc.

Assumptions for Financial Analysis   Here is a list of values and factors that you enter into your financial software to do the projections:

- Investment side
  - o Investor funding
  - o Earning before interest, tax, depreciation and amortization (EBITDA) multiple
- Marketing and income
  - o % of penetration for estimating the full market share
  - o Number of years to achieve the full market share
  - o Pricing of the device and consumables
- Expenses in each of the following four major categories:
  - o Cost of goods sold
  - o Expenses for sales, marketing, servicing and regulatory and quality control
  - o R&D expenses, including clinical trials
  - o Administrative expenses, such as salaries, Directors' fees, travel, office supplies, equipment, licensing fee, shipping, storage fees, rents, maintenance and utilities, marketing and advertising

Financial Computations   The computations will be done for a period of five years in the expectation that the exit strategy described next may be implemented at the end of the fourth or fifth year. Here is a list of projections that investors may wish to examine:

- The income statement
- The expense statement showing major expense categories
- Cash flow
- Number of employees
- Use of investor' funds before breakeven date
- Stock price
- Net present value
- Rate of return on investment

A 5-years financial analysis of a monitor company is given in Section 12.5 on Financial Projections.

Sensitivity Analysis   First, the projections can serve as a means for you to check the validity of your business model. In case the projections are bleak, you may need to identify the remedial or contingency action that you should take to correct the deficiencies in the business model and/or assumptions. You should do a sensitivity analysis to examine how a change in the assumptions can affect the financial projections and what impact that change will have on the profitability of the Company and the rate of return on investment. For example, suppose that the

2008 financial crisis (if it ever happens again!) produces a decrease in sales of 20%. The sensitivity analysis with this parameter change incorporated can project how much longer it will be before you reach a breakeven and what the return on investment will be at the end of the fifth year.

<u>Exit Strategy</u>   The investors can receive their investment by:
- Buy-outs by employees
- A merger or acquisition by another firm
- An Initial Public Offering

They certainly would like to know your preference in this matter.

11.6. Presentation of the Business Plan

Quick Pitch   As you progress into the Building -up Phase, you may be invited to participate in a business plan competition . San Diego Tech Coast Angels is an organization that has an annual Quick Pitch Competition in which you can present your venture, expose your company and network with those in the audience and the members of a panel formed by VCs, angel investors, bankers, account ants, lawyers, and executive recruiters (10).

The competition organizers may ask you to submit a brief description of your company and your management team's experience in no more than 200 or 300 words for screening . You can answer questions, such as those below in the write-up:
- What is the market for your product?
- Why will the patient or physician use your device?
- What are your competitive advantages and IP protection?
- How will you make a profit?
- How successful has your team been in managing other ventures?

If the screening committee feels that your venture will be of interest to the panel, then you will be invited to make a two minute oral presentation aided by two to four slides. You may want to expand your presentation to include the following additional points:
- Marketing and sales strategy
- Financial projections and milestones
- Funding request and its use.

With a time limit of two minutes, you w ill not be able to share all of your excitement about developing the venture with prospective investors. Concentrate on topics that can excite and interest the audience in two minutes, so that you will be invited to a more extensive business plan presentation or to submit your business plan for their evaluation.

GMI participate d in the Quick Pitch competition of 2008 . The author was very happy to work with the co aches in drafting the quick pitch and in gaining valuable experience in the pitch presentation. We received several emails the next day from persons who expressed their positive feeling about the presentation. An email from a capital funding company in Huntington Beach, California contained this message:

> *Jen-shih:*
> *I was in attendance at your presentation last night. You did an excellent job.*
> *Once you have purchase orders for your hemodialysis anti-pooling vests, we would be interested in discussing funding with you. Please feel free to e-mail us, or contact me at the number below.*
> *$500k would be no problem for us.*
> *Best regards, (Name withheld for confidentiality)*

The important message here is in *"Once you have purchase orders..."* which echoes Snyder in Chapter 4 *"If you can't put your product in a box and send it out with an invoice and sell it, you haven't got a business."*

The Objective of the Business Plan Presentation   Your objective should be:

- To explain the company's venture as clearly as possible
- To create excitement in the audience about the Company
- To secure a second meeting with the investors.

Following the presentation you may have some time for a Q&A period.

Format for Slide Preparation   You can use 15 to 20 slides to make this 15-minute presentation. Please note that each presentation should be unique with its own flow, although you may use the following template as a start.

In preparing your slides, it is important that you not burden slides with too much information . It is desirable that each slide contain no more than eight lines and fewer than 40 words. More importantly, each slide should contain only one or two key messages . The other points mentioned in the slide should be there primarily to support the key messages. Use graphics to better convey your message. Back-up slides could be pulled out to elaborate on points that might be raised over the Q&A session.

Template of Subjects Covered by the Slides

Slide 1. The mission of the Company. It is also used to introduce the Company's name and the name of the presenter and his or her position in the Company.

Slide 2. Accomplishments and any awards of the key company executives who lead the entrepreneur team. List any patents granted and submitted in this slide.

Slide 3. The device and its unique features.

Slide 4. What you want. You can list two or three needs. One can be funding to raise and the other can be a Vice President of Sales, for example . Further elaboration and justification can be provided later.

Slide 5. The patients who are served by the device . Use this slide to show the number of patients who are likely to benefit from use of the device.

Slide 6. The medical problem that the device addresses. This is also known as the "pain" slide on why patients and physicians really want to use your device for treatment or diagnosis.

Slide 7. Market opportunities. Use a short number of facts or statistics to show the size of the potential market.

Slide 8. Funding that the Company has raised and milestones reached. This slide describes what has been done and with what funding?

Slide 9. Benefits provided to clinics or hospitals by your device . Because of these customers' financial constraint s, you should show that there will be better care along with a reduction of the operation cost by using your device. Use this slide to explain why clinics and hospitals will want to buy your product for use by patients.

Slide 10. Competition and competitive advantage s. Describe the problems in using the device marketed by your competitors.

Slide 11. Feedback from patients and physicians o n the use of your device, if you have this information available.

Slide 12. Go-to-market strategy . Do you want to make direct sales to clinics and hospitals, to serve only as a wholesaler, or to function as an Original Equipment Manufacturer (OEM)?

Slide 13. The company's financial projections. You can list some of the assumptions used. You can use one more slide for this subject.

Slide 14. Milestones to reach. These will include obtaining FDA approval, beginning the promotional campaign, and making sales.

Slide 15. Summarize the strengths unique to your company.

Slide 16. Present three to five points that you want the panel to remember after they have left the room.

Slide 17. Repeat two or three questions that you want the panel to focus on.

Slide 18. Exit strategy for investors. You may let it stay on the screen during the question and answer period.

Summary Remarks   Build a strong company, make good sales, write a solid business plan for you to deliver the message that your technology is the best and your team can build up the company into the market leader. You will succeed.

References

1.   Bakken, E.E. *The Man's Full Life*, Medtronic, Inc., p. 84-93 and p. 150 (1999).
2.   Collins, J.C. and W.C. Lazier, *Beyond Entrepreneurship*, Prentice Hall, p. 53 (1992).
3.   Gates, B., Quotes, en.thinkexist.com/search/searchquotation.asp?search=microsoft+vision&q=
4.   Lee, J.S. Annals of Biomed. Eng. 28:1 (2000).
5.   Lee, J.S., Biomechanics, from Molecules to Man, in "Tributes to Yuan-Cheng Fung on His 90th Birthday" (eds.) S. Chien, P. Chen, G. Schmidt-Schonbein, P. Tong and S. Woo, World Scientific (2010), pp. 219-230.
6.   National Kidney and Urological Disease Information Clearing House, kidney.niddk.nih.gov/kudiseases/pubs/kustats/
7.   Olsen, E., entrepreneurs.about.com/od/beyondstartup/a/whatwarrenwants.htm
8.   www.entrepreneur.com
9.   www.smallbusinessnotes.com
10. www.techcoastangels.com

CHAPTER 12

FINANCING AND ACCOUNTING

12.1. Angel Investors and Venture Capital Firms

Financing a start -up depends largely on the business, its potential and environment, and its financial needs. In today's environment, venture capital is hard to obtain. Angel investors or joint venture deals with well established companies are the best sources . Banks are not likely to provide financing that you want if you have no cash flow with which to service the loan. Because it will take considerable time to get your invention to market, it is important that you establish a second means of activities to create revenue for the company. This can be the marketing of existing products that are similar to yours and consulting services.

The importance of healthcare to peopl e has motivated many engineers, scientists and physician s to found companies in the areas of biotechnology and medical device development for diagnos es and treatments. These companies will be poised to contribute greatly to the world's healthcare in this M edical Device and Biotech Century . A ngel investors and venture capitalists will recover from the present financial crisis to invest in, and promote these entrepreneurial developments.

Angel Investors Many angel investors are successful entrepreneurs who have been benefited from angel investments. The reason why they invest in start-ups is to receive a better return than offered by traditional investments. They are seasoned investors and know fully the risk in start-up investment s. Angel investing is usual ly a sideline activity for these investors. They can provide good management advice that will help you run the company . It is less time consuming to obtain angel investments than to secure financing from venture capital firms . Their due diligence is less i ntense than that of VCs, as described in the next section. Networking, business plan competitions, and web search es are some of the ways you can use to identify angel investors who may be interested in investing in your company.

Some angel investors are known as FFF, families, friends and fools. They may be new to venture investments and may make their decision to invest largely on the basis of their trust in you. Although you may be confident that their investment in your company will grow, remember that a majority of new businesses fail during their first three o r four years. Thus, it is your responsibility to make sure that these investors fully understand th at they assume a risk when they invest in your company. Do not accept money if it comes from sav ings and pension s that the investor depends on for retirement . It is better to have a life - long friendship than to have caused a financial crisis for him in his later years if your company does not succeed.

The f inancial transactions of start -ups involving these individuals and other angel investors are seldom publicized . As a result, information about angel investments tend s to be somewhat anecdotal. The profile of these angel investors , as described below, should be considered only as guideline s when y ou decide whether to attempt to secure angel investments.

- Angels invest about $20 to $30 billion per year in approximately 50,000 to 60,000 companies.
- The average angel investment is about $30,000 to $40,000.
- Investors expect an annual rate of return of 25% to 30% , or to recover their entire investment three or four times in three to five years.
- Angel investors believe that one third of their investments are likely to fail.

To keep informed, angel investors normally require quarterly report s to assure themselves of your company's progress.

However, there are angel investors who want to have greater control of the company and/or to have a seat on the board of directors. This can be equivalent to acquire another partner for your entrepreneur team . Structuring the relation ship between investors and the company right away is essential for the company's progress of the company.

A good source of funding to call attention to is **high net -worth individuals** who are well established in business and periodically invest. Once committed to an attractive deal, the se individuals can move quickly. Typically, these individuals are less sensitive to company valuation than VCs or angel investors . The a mounts that can be raised from this source typically range from $500,000 to $750,000.

A Distraction in an Investment Deal   The first venture of
legendary biotech entrepreneur Snyder was the Cambridge Mailing
Machine Company. It manufactured and sold   machines to use to stuff
envelopes at high speed . He told the   following sto ry to a   class of
Biomedical Engineering Entrepreneurship at the University of Virginia .
The events in the story occurred in 1964:

*A famous lawyer in New York found me and said, "You know,
Sherry, I hear through someone at the golf club about a machine you
have. It's fascinating, and I'd like to invest in it   . How much money do
you need?"*

I said, "Well, I probably need $150,000 to get it out in the market."

He says, "Fine, fine. How much money have you got?"

I said, "Twelve-thousand dollars is all the money I've got."

*He said, "I'll put in $12,000, you put in your $12,000, and we'll
have 50/50 split of the company . Then I'll loan you the balance." He
said, "The only condition is that I'll have a market research study made
and as long as it says the market is a s big as you say it is, we will go on,
and the loan will become a five -year long-term note. But if it doesn't, I
can call the loan and get a hold of the patents and the company."*

*I had confidence enough to know what this figure was, so I said,
"That sounds pretty good to me on the 50/50 split." And off I went.*

*A few months later, the lawyer's market study was done, and
actually it said the market was about twice the size of the market figures
I'd given to him . All of a sudden, I get a call from his lawyer   , and he
said, "Jeez, I'm sorry, Sherry. We're really disappointed by this market
study, and I think we're going to have to call our note."*

*I said, "Wait a second. The market study is twice the number of my
market estimate."*

He said, "I'm sorry," and they called the note.

*Now, this was around October, and I had until December 31 to pay
back all of the money he had put into the company, which was about
$50,000, or else I had to sign the patents of the machine and the
company to him. Talk about being up against the wall!*

*(Through another cliff -hanging experience, Snyder received
an investment of $74,000 in November.)*

*I waited until December 30, when the New York lawyer was
ready for the transfer of the company. I sent a check to him and told
him what he might want to do with it, expletives deleted!"*

According to Snyder, "*God takes care of young, well-meaning entrepreneurs.*" However, the lesson here is you should be cautious about entering into contracts. Pay special attention to the fine print. And, even after you do, remember that the hardest-working and most ingenious entrepreneurs sometimes still need luck in order to succeed.

Also, be prepared to be tested beyond your intellectual capacity, Snyder says, "*Being able to operate in tough times is one characteristic of entrepreneurship. Things don't always go as planned when you're developing a new company. The market isn't exactly the way you see it starting out.*"

Venture Capitalists   In a New York Times article (1), Claire Miller wrote the following. "*Venture capitalists put $7.7 billion into 1,033 deals, a decrease of 7% from the second quarter of 2008.*" She further stated that "*The number of start-ups getting financing for the first time fell 20% to 259 (in the third quarter of 2008). That is the lowest level since the first quarter of 2004. Investors are hesitant to finance new companies because they have so many portfolio companies in the pipeline that are ready to go public or be sold but are stuck because exit markets are all but closed.*" To buck this trend of VC funding, you need to have a product and an entrepreneurial team that are worthy of the investment and put in extra effort in the preparation of your business plan and executive summary.

In your search for VC funding, identify local VCs first. Check their websites to be sure that they will fund companies that are at your company's present stage (early stage, start-up stage, or first or second round of VC funding). Get a person who can link you to the VC. Participation in activities and networking of organizations like CONNECT and Tech Coast Angels not only will help make the connection, but also improve your business plan presentation. Ask your law and accounting firms for the names of persons to contact at the venture capital firms. Email solicitation may have little chance of success. If a venture capital firm invites you to make a presentation, be prepared to present your strongest statement of the market's need for your product, your competitive position, and your team's performance.

Do your due diligence on the venture capital firm and its managers. Before your interview with the firm, learn as much as you can from its website about its portfolio, companies it invests in, and its investment criteria. The firm's owners expect its managers to obtain a healthy return on the money that they have invested in it. Only if your executive summary convinces them that your company will yield a good return on an investment in your company , will they then interview you and begin the process of negotiation, due diligence and funding that is described in the following section and next Chapter . During this lengthy process, talk to the CEO s of companies in which this venture firm has invested to make sure that you will be able to work with the firm and its operating style.

Once a funding arrangement with the venture capital firm has been concluded, it will become involve in many operational aspects of your company. In addition to gaining financial support from the VC, you need to establish relations with it that will enable your company to benefit from its expertise in management, marketing and technology, instead of interfere with, the operation of the company.

The amount of capital that a venture capital firm can supply is large, leading it to become the majority owner of your company . Because the venture funding may be supplied in installments, beware of the possibility that a small initial investment might give the venture firm an opportunity to take over your company and replace your team. Don't get involved in the kind of potentially-disastrous investment deal that Snyder had concluded with a famous New York lawyer to raise funds for his mailing machine company.

Although many venture firms will count on your expe rtise to move the company forward, disagreement s about the company's operation or how it is managed do develop . Conflicts must be resolved by negotiations that provide win -win solutions so that each party gains something and neither really loses.

Hurdle Rate Return of Investment (ROI) is a measure of the performance of the investment. It is defined by the following:

ROI = (Net Gain in Investment)/(Initial Investment)   12.1

  = (Final Invest. Value – Initial Invest. Value)/(Initial Invest. Value)

If th e ROI is provided over an investment period of n years, then the annual rate of return is

Annual Rate of Return = $(1 + ROI)^{(1/n)} - 1$ 12.2

If the projected Annual Rate of Return of an investment project is higher than the hurdle rate set by a venture firm, then the firm will   probably consider the project.

Table 12.1 shows the guidelines that VCs or angel investors use when setting the hurdle rate for ROI. The hurdle rate depends on the company's stage of development.

Table 12.1. Hurdle Rate

Phase I, Feasibility, Assessing or Seed Phase	80%
Phase II, R&D, Launching or Start-up Phase	60%
Phase III, Commercialization, Building-up Phase or 1st and 2nd Rounds.	40 ~ 50%

If the annual rate of return is 60%, the ROI for an investment period of five years is 949%. If an initial investment of $2 million in your start-up was made five years ago, the venture capital firm would be entitled to receive a net gain of $ 19 million, the value of the final investment, less its initial investment. The annual rate of return is much higher than provided by the annual interest rate of house mortgages, which may be in the range of   5% to 7% . A Venture capital firm require   s such an "outrageous" ROI because of the   risk, which it perceives, of losing the funds that it invests in your company   . Because of the confidence   that entrepreneurs have in their venture s, your own risk assessment will be different from those of investors.

To better understand the relation ship between hurd le rate and risk, we consider a case in which a venture capital firm makes a $ 2 million investment in each of three   Companies: A, B and C   . Company A generates the ROI given in Table 5.5, which shows an ROI of 400% or an annual rate of return of   38%. Suppose that Company B had a value of only $4.8 million, which corresponds to an annual rate of return of 19%, while Company C failed completely   . The returns f rom these investments appear in Table 12.2   . When the results of these three companies (A & B & C) are totaled in the fourth row, one sees that the initial investment of $6 million has a final investment value of $14.8 million now. This corresponds to a n ROI of 147% and an annual rate of return of 20%. If company B also fails lik e company C did, the data shown in the fifth row (A & C & C) shows that ROI drops to 67% and the annual rate of return   becomes 11 %. The actual return is even lower when management, processing and legal fees are deducted .

In essence, a venture capital firm must balance losses in a large number of investment deals with big wins in a few to achieve a better ROI than available from traditional investments.

Table 12.2. Return of Investment for an investment period of 5 years.

	Value of Initial Investment	Value of Final Investment	Return of Investment (ROI)	Annual rate of return
Company A	$ 2 M	$10.0 M	400%	38%
Company B	$ 2 M	$4.8 M	140%	19%
Company C	$ 2 M	0	-100%	-100%
Companies A & B & C	$ 6 M	$14.8 M	147%	20%
Companies A & C & C	$ 6 M	$10.0 M	67%	11%

For the entrepreneurs of Company A, their stocks have risen, five years from the time the venture capital firm made the investment, to a value of $10 million. As illustrated in Table s 5.5 and 12.2, the venture capital firm's initial investm ent of $ 2 million yields a net gain of $ 8 million (the difference between the final and initial investment) . The increase in stock value and investment value is made possible by the infusion of capital from the venture firm and the hard work of the entrepreneurs to commercializ e the invention. It is the joint effort of entrepreneurs and investors that makes both winners.

Let us underscore this point further by the words that Tall Oaks Capital, a venture firm in Charlottesville, VA, uses to describe itself . The firm's mission is " *partnering with entrepreneurs and management teams to build extraordinary companies.*" This venture capital firm was *formed in 2000 and is led by four partners that possess over a century of seed and early stage investment and corp orate experiences.* Their website states that *"Working closely with our entrepreneurial team, we provide both the long -term investment support and the strategic guidance that seed and early stage companies need to grow and prosper."*

12.2. Due Diligence of Venture Capital Firms

To deci de whether to invest in a particular company and then execute the investment, venture capital firms undertake due diligence rigorously to ensure that the opportunity for your company to succeed is real, the business propositi on is sound and the legal and financial matters are addressed. The due diligence that venture investors are likely to undertake is described below . This description was adapted from a course note that Tall Oaks Capital (5) distributed to students in a class at the University of Virginia. The process has three phases before reaching the funding stage.

Phase of Getting to Know Your Company   This is the phase during which the venture firm wants to learn more about your company when you are invited to a brief interview. The VC representatives will ask the following questions:

- Who is this company? They will want to know who the officers of the company are, as well as the names of your legal counsel for corporate matt ers, intellectual property, and regulatory affairs; your accounting firm and your bank.
- What does the company do? What products and services does it offer? How does your company make money? What is the size and dynamics of its market? What is the entry barrier?
- Is the company good at what it does ? The VC will want to know what expertise, qualification s, and track record members of the entrepreneurial team possess. VC personnel may get in touch with references that you have provided for your team and company. They will want to know the status of your company's operations. It will be useful to present your business plan for their review.
- What does your company want from the venture firm? In addition to receiving the details of your funding request, the VC would like to know the valuation of your company, the names of any other venture capital firms contacted in this round of financing, the anticipated value of your company, the exit strategy for the investors and its timing, and your target dates for break-even and profitability.
- What are the risks in management, technology, regulatory affairs, manufacturing and marketing?
- Where will your company be in three years, five years and ten years?

Investigation Phase   Once the venture capital firm considers your company as a legitimate investment, it will commit time and resources to conduct an investigation with its internal experts, industrial consultants and university professors. Due diligence is done for the following:

- **Product.** This includes its funct ionality, benefits and advantages, expansion opportunities, proprietary position, regulatory requirements, and manufacturing.
- **Market.** Target population, competitors and competitive position, pricing strategy, direct or indirect sales, distribution, sales force, service and support capability, and alliance s are areas to be fully investigated.
- **Management.** The venture capital firm will review the curriculum vitae of the principals, Directors of the Board and company's advisors . The CV should include th e credentials, publications, grants obtained, positions held, and references.
- **Entrepreneurial Team.** During the due diligence process, the VC will want to learn what communications skills, level s of enthusiasm, perseverance in entrepreneurship, optimism about the company and trustworthiness that team members possess, as well as their   level of commitment . How much has the team invested in the company? Are team members proud of their ownership? Could they become discouraged by set-backs? Can they make calcu lated risk decision? Do they have a sense of humor?
- **Financials.** The VC will do due diligence on the financial condition of your company by examining its past and present budgets, past expenses for general administration and R&D, assumptions and future budget s, and major anticipated expenditures. They will want to know the sources of your funds and the ways you use them and, in particular, what you require to break -even and when can you achieve this. Also, w hat is required to generate a positive cash flow, profitability and an IPO?
- **Exit Strategies.** The venture capital firm will be interested in knowing the opportunity, time and valuation that will enable it to receive from your company their expected ROI for their investment.
- **Risk Assessment .** This will be made in areas of product and technology, corporate management, financial, market and regulatory issues.

Review Phase   This is the final due diligence . The venture capital firm will spend money to hire:

- Corporate legal counsel to review op   erating agreements, contracts, deeds, titles, shareholder agreements, private placement memoranda, employment agreements, etc.
- Intellectual property counsel to review license agreements, filings, record keeping, claims and pending claims,   and intellectual property strategy.
- Technical experts to provide written evaluation s, critiques and a summary of your technology, product, and service.
- CPA to assure the company's operation in accounting and auditing.

Customer references, collaboration references, and pro   fessional and personal references   that you have   provided will be contacted . To enable the venture capital   firm to carry   out its legal, financial, management and technology due diligence, you need to provide a long list of documentations in a timely fashion   . In the case of a large investment, the funding may be provided by a group of venture capital firms, who will share the expense of due diligence.

Sometime during the Review Phase, the VC may send a term sheet for you r signature that sets forth the key te   rms of the proposed investment. (See Section 13.2 for more on term sheets.) Aside from the amount established for the investment and the valuation of your company, the term sheet contains many clauses inserted by the VC for its protection, but which may   reduce the value of your company . It is important to have your attorney examine and review with you each item in the term sheet . How t o negotiate a deal that is   good for the VC and your company is addressed in Chapter 13   . Be aware that the more of your company that you give the VC now, the less you will have for later rounds of financing. Any renegotiation   later may sour the relationship between the entrepreneurs and VC.

Finally, if everyone likes what has taken place during   this due diligence process and   reaches an investment agreement , you will look forward to sign ing the document and getting to the funding stage . This stage will likely begin a year after you receive d the telephone call to arrange your initial interview.

After concluding the process   and obtaining the funding, the entrepreneurs and the VC are now partners in running the company. At this time, you need to be sure that the closing documents and certificates are delivered to the VC soon after the signing . Schedule a first board meeting as soon as possible or at an agreed time. Updates of company progress need to be sent to investors in a timely fashion.

12.3. Account Management

Importance of Cash   Cash is money on hand or in your bank accounts. More businesses fail because o f lack of sufficient cash to pay for their expenses than for a lack of profit. If you run out of cash with which to pay your suppliers and employees, you will damage your reputation and destroy their trust in you . The top priority of finance management is to have sufficient cash for bill paying at all times.

The topics covered in the next two sections are budgeting, which includes a short-term (e.g., one year) financial plan for operation of the company, financial projections, and a long -term (e.g., five years) projection of the company 's revenue, cash position and/or Profit and Loss Statement. Knowing how to manage accounts with no cash flow problems, do budgeting and prepare financial projections is important to assure smooth operation of your company.

Setting up the Account   Once the company is registered, your company can establish a bank account. You may also need to set up a petty cash account for minor transactions or purchases that require the use of cash, to aid the operation of the company.

It is a good idea to spend a few hundred dollars for an accounting program to perform the bookkeeping and financial aspects of the company. Search the internet to learn what other owners say about software programs, such as Intuit's QuickBooks. Have one of the team members do this important work and arrange to have a CPA to assist him or her in the financial work. A system that double check s the use of company fund s by one or two supervisors is essential to prevent the misuse of funds, inappropriate spending or embezzlement.

The software that you obtain should be able to write salary checks for employees and pay the tax due to the government and the invoices of your vendors. At the end of your calendar year, the software will print out the W -2 form, income and expenditure stateme nt, etc . For your company's tax filing, it is done in accordance with its fiscal year.

The financial operation should be transparent to all members of the entrepreneur team. If the team understands fully the company's financial situation, they will make   the necessary adjustments to assure the company's financial health.

Make sure that you manage your accounts well so that the bank will be anxious to loan you money in the future at a favorable interest rate. ***Account Management and Health of Your Company***   The profit and loss statements and the balance sheets can be printed   by the software so that you can analyze the performance of your company after it becomes profitable. By use of the following ratios, you will be able to determine the health of your company and better control your business's financial future (3).

Net Profit Margin = (Net Profit – Debt Interest)/Gross Sales
(The higher the net profit margin, the more profitable the business is.)

Gross Profit Margin = Gross Profit/Gross Sales
(The higher the gross profit margin, the better the business is.)

Return on Sales Ratio = Net Profit/Gross Sales
(The higher the return on sales ratio, the better the business is.)

Current Ratio = Current Assets/Current Liabilities
(Normally, the current ratio should be around 2.0 or greater.)

Debt to Net Worth Ratio = Total Debt/Net Worth
(A ratio of more than   1.0 indicates that there is too much   debt for a company of that net worth.)

Cash Turnover Ratio = Gross Sales/(Current Assets–Current Debt)
(Generally, your cash turnover should be between 4 and 7.)

Average Collection Period = Accounts Receivable×365days/Gross Sales
(This should be no more than 1.5 times the permitted credit period.)

Investment Turnover Ratio = Gross Sales/Long Term Assets
(The higher the ratio, the stronger the business is.)

Return on Investment = Net Profit/Net Worth
(You should strive for at least a 12% return to have a healthy business.)

By comparing these ratios with those for previous years, you will learn whether your company is becoming financially stronger.

12.4. Budgeting

Once you have the company's finance in the coming months under control, you should start a budgeting plan for the company. You enter your company's income and exp enses for the coming year into your financial planning software to determine your company's cash flow. The income might be investments made by the founders or revenues generated monthly by a consulting service, and/or commissions from the sale of other com panies' products. The expenses in the budget should include salaries for personnel, purchase s of equipment and supplies, rental of office and workshop, travel expenses , etc. This budgeting processing is somewhat like the operation of your household. Y ou want to know how much you can spend when you are stead ily employed and have a salary that has been committed for the coming year.

In essence, budgeting requires a high certainty that you will receive the expected income, such as that provided by a contract for the sale of your medical device with payment on a certain date. If the projected income is based on research of the market or patient needs, you prepared a financial projection, as described in the next section, instead of a budget.

One result of the budgeting exercise is that you will know when your company will need another cash transfusion to maintain your company's "cash" situation. Another outcome could be that you will learn that your company may use up all of its cash before it can receive a transfusion. Then, adjustments need to be made to every item of expenditure. Budget cutting or revisions are always painful, but should be transparent to the entrepreneur team and some employees . Their full support o f cost-cutting and their suggestions to establish a new revenue stream should be sought. Overall, the process of budgeting is a means of assuring that the company operation will experience no cash flow problems.

If your company is preparing an SBIR grant application, your software can be used to g enerate the budget for your SBIR grant application. The budget period for a Phase I grant is six months . It is two years for a Phase II grant. Under the current triage system of NIH, you will receive a non-funding decision from NIH in about six months .

If NIH considers your proposal to be exceptional, NIH will advi se you what amount of funding has been approved and when you can request the wire transfer of the funds on a certain date to your bank account for bill and salary paying. The date on which grant funds become available is usually about a year after the date of your submission.

If you decide to seek investment by angel investors or VCs, go to the next section to work out the aspects of the financial projection to include in the financial section of the business plan . The projection s should include the income statement, cash flow statement, balance sheet, and break-even analysis.

It is possible that the process to secure angel investments will be shorter than the process of obtaining funding from the NIH. Once you receive a funding commitment from the NIH and/or angel investors, you need to revise your operation and budgeting in accordance with the funding schedule of the NIH and/or angel investors.

In summary, the most challenging aspect of budgeti ng is to be certain to obtain future funding. Then , you control the expenditures by the budgeting process without experiencing a cash flow problem.

12.5. Financial Projections

Financial projections provide a big picture o f the budgetary operations of your company. For a start -up or new company, it is very helpful to have projections in answering such questions as:

- What is the sale volume of your device and how much revenue does it produce?
- How many employees do you need to hire to manufacture that many devices?
- What angel investments, venture funding and/or SBIR grants are required to sustain the company's operation?
- When will be the company's operation break even?
- What will be the investors' return on investment?

The financial projections form a key part of the business plan to help investors in their decision to invest in your company . In this section, we will use a simple business model for the Excel software to prepare projections o f income, expenses, cash on hand at the end of each fiscal year, value of the Company and the hurdle rate generated by the Company for a 5 -year period. For the sake of simplicity, this model does not take into account such issues as tax, depreciation, bank loan s, difference in timing of receipts from accounts receivable and expenditures, etc . To generate projections that include all of these issues and have fewer errors in writing your own program in Excel, you can purchase financial projection software (4) or hire an accoun tant to do the calculations.

Sales and Revenues Suppose that your XYZ Company has three products: Diagnostic Monitor, Home Monitor and Probes to sell to hospitals for use by patients who are undergoing hemodialysis . To begin the calculations you need to make some assumption about your sale volumes. We will assume that the number of monitor s sold will be relatively few during the introductory phase, increase significantly throughout the growing phase, and reach a plateau (the potential full market share) in the mature phase. The growth in sales during a period of five years is shown in Fig. 12.1, with the sales in the beginning at 3% of the full market number and the sales at the fifth year at 100%.

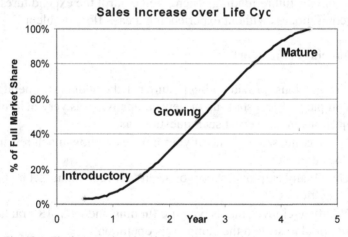

Fig. 12.1. The increase in sales during a 5-year period.

A market survey indicates that the US has some 80,000 dialyzers to serve 400,000 patients. Suppose the XYZ Company decides that the full market number of Diagnostic Monitor s to be sold is 5,000 units . Then by multiplying the full market number by the percentage of the full market share (the y-axis of the growth curve) at each year , you obtain the number of Diagnostic Monitors were sold that year . This data appears in the second row of Table 12.3 . Adding all numbers in that row gives the total number of monitors in use by   the end of the fifth year. It is 12,300 Monitors . The total number of dialyzers being used is 80,000, 15.4% of which would have the Diagnostic Monitor to serve patients. (If the patient population increases at an annual rate of 5%, the 15.4% percentage will decline to 12%.) In view of the monitor's likely benefit to patient's quality of life and   a reduction in clinics' expenditures, this percentage is achievable . This suggests that the full market number of 5,000 monitors is a good   assumption for financial projections.

Similarly, the XYZ Company sets the full market number of Home Monitors sold at 20,000 units . The numbers of Home Monitors sold each year are shown in Table 12.3 . The total number of monitors sold during the five years indicates that 12.3% of all hemodialysis patients would be using   a Home Monitor   for their home dialysis   . This percentage is achievable in   five years in vie w of the two following observations (2). First, 0.8% of dialysis patients in the US were on home dialysis in 200 3, but   about 30% a re suitable candidates for home dialysis. Second, almost 55% of dialysis patients in New Zealand were already on home dialysis in 2008 (2).

The full market sale numbers are   used as the inputs to the Excel program. They can be altered if further market studies are undertaken.

Because of the wear and tear o n the probe, customers who use the monitors need to replace the probe each year t o ensure its functionality with the monitor. The Excel sets the total number of all monitors in use at the end of the first year as the number of probes being sold during that year. The total number of probes sold each year is given in the last row of Table 12.3.

Table 12.3. Projected Numbers of Monitors and Probes sold by XYZ Company.

	Year 1	Year 2	Year 3	Year 4	Year 5
% of full market share	3%	16%	47%	80%	100%
Diagnostic Monitors Sold	150	800	2,350	4,000	5,000
Diagnostic Monitors Accumulated by year end	150	950	3,300	7,300	12,300
Home Monitors Sold	600	3,200	9,400	16,000	20,000
Home Monitors Accumulated	600	3,800	13,2000	29,200	59,200
Probes Sold	750	4,750	16,500	36,500	71,500

The next task is to use the XYZ Company 's market survey to set the prices for the two monitors and the probe . Suppose that competitors are selling monitors at a price of $4,000 each. Although the Diagnostic Monitor may perform better, the Company sets its selling price a t $4,000. Because the Home Monitor is simpler, i ts unit selling price is set at $2,500. In view of the expense to manufacture the probe, its unit selling price is $400 . With the numbers sold and this pricing scheme, the Excel calculates the revenue that appears in the top part of Table 12.4. For the full market numbers used, the revenues of XYZ Company are projected to reach $95 million by end of the fifth year.

The contribution to revenues by product categories is depicted in Fig. 12.2. The lowest curve illustrates the revenue from the sale of Diagnostic Monitors, the middle curve traces the revenue from the sale of Home Monitors, and the highest curve represents revenue attributable to sales of Probes. Although only 12% of dialysis patients are using Home Monitors, their sales make up 53% of total re venues of the Company at Year 5 . The figure also indicates a faster growth rate in revenues from sales of probes as disposable items.

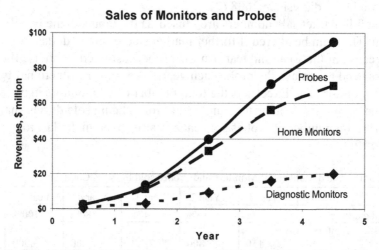

Fig. 12.2. Revenues of XYZ Company generated by the sales listed in Table 12.2.

Expenses As shown in the second segm ent of Table 12.4, seven categories of expenses are considered when determining the XYZ Company's total expenditures . From the knowledge gained in manufacturing prototypes, the material costs for making the Diagnostic

Monitor, Home Monitor, and Probe are estimated at $500, $400 and $150 respectively. The Excel program combines the costs of calibrating and testing the probe, labeling the monitors and packaging, insuring and shipping them and servicing as "manufacturing, packaging and shipping

Table 12.4. Income from sales of three products, Expenses for Administration, R&D and others, EBITDA, Cash Flow, Net Company Value, Return of Investment, Hurdle Rate of XYZ Company. (All are in $ millions)

	Year 1	Year 2	Year 3	Year 4	Year 5
Income					
Sales of Diagnostic Monitors	$0.6	$3.2	$9.4	$16.0	$20.0
Sales of Home Monitors	$1.5	$8.0	$23.5	$40.0	$50.0
Sales of Probes	$0.3	$1.9	$6.6	$14.6	$24.6
Total Revenue	$2.4	$13.1	$39.5	$70.6	$94.6
Expenses					
Administrative Overhead	$0.4	$0.9	$2.2	$3.8	$5.0
Overhead for R&D	$0.4	$0.9	$2.2	$3.8	$5.0
Infrastructure & Rentals	$1.5	$1.3	$4.0	$7.1	$9.5
Materials	$0.4	$2.3	$6.6	$11.6	$15.6
Manufacturing, Packaging, Shipping & Servicing Expenses	$0.2	$1.2	$3.6	$6.4	$8.6
Marketing & Selling Expenses	$1.1	$5.9	$17.8	$31.8	$42.6
Bad Accounts	$0.1	$0.5	$1.4	$2.5	$3.3
Total Expenditures	$4.1	$13.0	$37.8	$66.9	$89.5
EBITDA	-$1.7	$0.1	$1.7	$3.7	$5.1
Beginning Cash: $2.0 M					
Ending Cash	$0.3	$0.4	$2.1	$5.8	$10.9
Net Company Value			$8.6	$18.4	$25.4
Amount Paid to Investors			$4.3	$9.2	$12.7
ROI			115%	360%	535%
Hurdle Rate			29%	46%	45%

expense." It is estimated that this expense represents 55% of material costs. We assume there are two overhead expenses. The overhead incurred by the management team and the board of directors has a fixed expense of $250,000 plus 5% of the total revenue. The same amount is set aside for R&D. A similar arrangement has been made for the expenses incurred for infrastructure and rentals. Because of the need for a large investment in equipment and facilities, we will use a much higher infrastructure expense for Year 1. The marketing and selling expense to conduct the marketing campaign, digital marketing, and workshops has been estimated at 45% of total revenue. Finally, uncollectable accounts receivable are projected at 4% of revenue. These are sales on credit that are not collectable. Total expenditures are shown on the last row of the second part of the table.

EBITDA and Ending Cash   As part of the cash flow analysis, the difference between revenues and expenditures constitutes the net earnings. For the current business model without any bank loans, taxes or equipment depreciation the earnings shown are before interest, taxes, depreciation and amortization (EBITDA). Because of the large expense of infrastructure, administration and R&D, we see negative earning in the first year. With the initial influx of $2 million from the investors, the cash that the XYZ Company has at the end of first year is about $0.3 million. Because of the positive earnings projected for Year 2, the ending cash for that year is slightly larger than for Year 1. The values of EBITDA and ending cash during the five years are listed in the third segment of Table 12.4.

In this table, the smallest ending cash is $0.3 million. In the yearly financial projections, this ending cash serves as the cushion or working capital to prevent a negative cash flow caused by the time lag between expenditures and payments of account receivables. Commercially available financial software can refine the projections to show whether there will be a cash flow problem if data are calculated on a monthly basis.

Company Value, ROI and Hurdle Rate   Suppose that the investors agree to use 5 as the EBITDA multiple to calculate the net company value, which appears in the first row of the fourth segment of Table 12.4. Since the $2 million investment gets the investor 50% of the company, the ROI calculated to the end of Years 3, 4 and 5 are provided in the third row of this last segment of Table 12.4. The hurdle rate is given in the last row. The hurdle rate for Year 4 and 5 are comparable to those established by VCs for companies in the building-up phase (Table 12.1).

Potential Saving for Clinics   The total
amount paid by clinics to the company in Year 5 is $94.6 million. There
are 110,000 patients using the monitors . Thus, the expense incurred by
clinics to acquire the monitors and probes for patients   use is $855 per
patient.

Suppose the annual charge for hemodialysis is $60,000 per patient .
Because more patients   now can u se home care and there is   a lower
frequency of development of intradialytic hypotension, it may be
appropriate to suggest that these improvements produce a 7% reduction
in clinics' operation expense (i.e. , $4,200). Because practioners need to
spend time to administrate the monitor, the labor cost is estimated as 3%
of the annual charge for hemodialysis (i.e.   , $1,800). When the
difference between the reduction in operation expense and the increase
in labor cost is taken as the overall operational saving (i.   e. $2,400 =
$4,200 - $1,800), one sees that   the use of monitors to improve the
delivery of hemodialysis might mean that clinics that spend $855 per
patient to acquire the monitor   will gain an operation saving of $2,400
per patient . This is   a ROI of 181% ba   sed on data in Year 5. (A
verification of these saving projections   by actual record s should be
sought in years earlier than Year 5.)

Limitation of Financial Projections and Sensitivity Analysis
Once you do the projections, ask critics from the entrepreneur team
and outside financial experts to revise the   m. In the current business
model, the overhead is a base expense plus a percentage of total revenue.
Check these overheads against the organization structure of the
Company to see whether the overhead is suf ficient to pay the salary and
fringe benefits of executives and their administrative assistants   who
appear in the organization structure . Similarly, check the estimat es of
the manufacturing, packaging, shipping and servicing expenses against
the number of employees required to do the manufacturing, assembling
and packaging jobs.

Don't overstate your market share   . Overestimation, underperfor-
mance, and financial crisis can always   occur. Having sufficient ending
cash or working capital and   strictly controll ing your expenditures are
essential for your company's safe sailing.

Finally, have fun play ing with the numbers (i.e. , do a sensitivity
analysis on the values used as input) so that you know what impact those
numbers will have on the financial future of the XYZ Company.

References
1. Miller, C. bits.blogs.nytimes.com/2009/01/05/
2. Rubin, R., USA Today,   http://www.usatoday.com/news/health/200908-23-dialysis_N.htm?POE=click-refer (2009).
3. Sitarz, D., Simplified Small Business Accounting, Nova Publishing, IL, (1995).
4. www.planware.org
5. www.talloakscapital.com

CHAPTER 13

NEGOTIATING DEALS

13.1. The Negotiation Process

The Smart Negotiation   As a CEO, you will negotiate with a VC firm for funding, an executive to employ , and another company about joint licensing, a merger or an acquisition. The beginning of a round of negotiations or bargaining is competitive as each side will have different values or goals on funding, employment, licensing right, fees, or price, etc. However, in the end, the negotiation of a good deal that can lead to years of collaboration a nd terms that satisfy both sides can be termed smart negotiation. A good CEO must have the skill to carry out smart negotiation for important actions, such as VC funding, executive employment, and joint venture development.

Be sure to do you r homework and prepare for your negotiations. Think about your opponent and yourself . Work on the answers to these questions:

- What do you want?
- Does each party meet the other's requirement?
- What do you expect to achieve from the negotiation?
- What is the bottom line posi tion of your expectation? What is the least that you will accept and the most that you will concede?

During negotiation, you will learn more about the other side and its position and gain an idea of the likelihood on being able to   come to a realistic outcome. Use the following pointers to help you complete your smart negotiation:

- Negotiate in a "win-win" mode for competing, but collaborative, deals. Don't attempt to out-negotiate the other side.
- Work toward a deal. If   there is   no deal, what are your alternatives?
- Don't get hung up on insignificant issues . Look for trade-offs or alternatives.

- Be creative and flexible, especially if the deal gets "hung-up".
- Bargain with give and take, so that both sides feel that they are getting something extra.
- Be prepared to give concessions. Ask for more, or swap, on issues. You should not win them all. Leave something on the table for the other side.
- Never let yourself be verbally abused by the other side. Use questions to deflect abuse.
- Strive for credibility in your reasoning and compromise.
- Let your strength speak for itself.
- Ask for clarification as a means to justify your position.
- Never use threats. Gently and with great care set a deadline.
- Uncover information that may benefit your negotiation.
- Understand the power of questions and the power of silence in negotiations.
- Take control of the negotiation by having a realistic proposition.
- Maintain good negotiating judgment with balance and moderation, and avoid extreme positions.
- Know when and how to wrap up a complete package deal.

The Hostile Negotiation A few months after your medical device has appeared on the market, you may receive an injunction from your competitor that demands that you stop selling your device because it infringes upon many of its patents. If you fail to do so, your competitor will probably file a lawsuit in the District Court to sue you for damages and a punitive penalty. The receipt of the injunction letter marks the beginning of hostile negotiations and a costly lawsuit. Aside from your competitors, it is also possible that a patent troll may sue you for infringement of its patents. A patent troll is a person, company or a non-practicing entity that owns patents, but has no intention of manufacturing or using the invention, but wants to sue aggressively in the hope that it will receive licensing fees (2).

Here are some of the reasons why you may be sued if you market your invention:

- **To eliminate you as a competitor.** Your competitors don't want you to compete with them as your success may put their non-competitive products out of business. The legal fees for a medium-size infringement suit can be $2 to $5 million. A small start-up may be sued until it can no longer pay an attorney to defend it. Without a good legal defense, you can lose the suit and put your company in jeopardy.

- **To obtain a licensing fee or payment for a settlement.**   In 2001, the Israel Company , Medinol, initiated a lawsuit against Boston Scientific, accusing the   latter of stealing Medinol's stent-manufacturing technology . Boston Scientific settled the lawsuit in 2005 by agreeing to pay $750 million to Medinol (1).
- **To merge with, or acquire, your company.**   In some instances, thi s impl ies that a hostile negotiation will become a friendly negotiation so that both companies can benefit from the merger or acquisition.

Such a legal challenge will immediately cause trouble as you are attempting to raise money for the company . Although your product may be promising, your potential investors may withdraw to the sidelines because of the uncertainty   of outcome of the lawsuit and the   expense that will be incurred to defend it . Your company will be in even greater distress if you do not put   in the effort and money to defend your company. If you do, you may end up doing one of the following:

- **Settle before anyone files a legal suit**   Suppose that your due diligence of   tour adversary 's patent reveals that your product does not infringe upon its patent. However, if there is a possibility of infringement, you   discover that you can design around your opponent's patent so that your new product will no longer infringe upon the patent   . After your patent attorney presents these arguments to your adversary, it may feel that the outcome of its legal action is unlikely to yield a net payment and thus decide to settle for nothing or for a small payment.
- **Settle before trial**   Once a lawsuit has been filed and deemed to have merit by the judge, he or she   will set a trial date. However, a bout 90% of the cases are settled before the date of the trial. Before the trial date, there is a discovery stage in which both plaintiffs and defendants must disclose everything   they know that is   related to the legal case   . The information discovered at this stage may indicate that the opponent's patent is invalid and that there is   no infringement or that there is substantial infringement. Even in the latter case , it is not certain that a jury verdict will favor the infring   ers - or infringees . Consequently, you and your opponent may decide to settle the

case before the trial. Sometimes, the judge and the two parties may request that a mediator be appointed to evaluate the case and guide the two sides in working out a settlement to which they mutually agree before the trial.

- **Settle by trial**   The attorneys will present their cases to a jury for its verdict. The overall legal costs will exceed the two previously mentioned settlements. The verdict will include damages (mostly loss of royalties), compensation for punitive damages, and the fees of attorneys for the winning side. For example, a Netherlands court ruled in favor of Medinol in a summary proceeding for a preliminary injunction that ordered Cordis BV and Cordis NV to stop making, using, importing or selling BC velocity-like stent in the Netherlands (4). Even if you receive a favorable verdict from a US District Court, the losing side can appeal the District Court's ruling to the Appeals Court and finally to the Supreme Court for a final decision.

Historically, U.S. patent owners have been entitled to an injunction upon a finding of patent infringement. Since the ruling in the case of *e-Bay v. MercExchange* by the Supreme Court, several District Courts have refused to grant injunctions to patent trolls (3). These court decisions will have a profound impact on patent licensing as these precedents remove the use of an injunction by a patent troll to stop an infringer from making and selling infringing products. As a result, the strength of a patent troll in licensing negotiations is diminished, the bargaining power of the accused infringer is enhanced, and the "infringing" company can better afford to engage in litigation. In addition, District Courts have granted compulsory licenses to companies found guilty of patent infringement in some cases, making a patent troll more willing to grant a license to an accused infringer.

Dispute Resolution   Arbitration is stipulated as the means to resolve disputes in many employment and user agreements. For this technique, the dispute is referred to a third party to review and to impose a settlement decision that is legally binding. Arbitration is most commonly used for the resolution of commercial disputes. Often the fine print in agreements contain a stipulation that arbitration be used to settle disputes arising from the agreement and deny the use of the courts by employees and consumers as a means to settle disputes. If a dispute is highly technical, an arbitrator who has the appropriate expertise may be appointed. In general, arbitration is faster and cheaper than litigation in court.

Mediation is another technique   used to resolve disp utes. Most judges will recommend that the litigation parties go through the process of non -binding mediation before   proceeding to a jury trial . Many mediators are former judges who know the outcomes of cases that were similar to your case. Mediators use their knowledge and skill to improve the communication between disput ing parties and to help them reach an agreement. They are very experienced in finding a middle ground   to which both parties will be able to agree . The mediators w ill advise all parties that this middle ground will definitely upset them, but is the least objectionable option in view of the high legal expense of proceeding to a trial and risking its   uncertain outcome, with or without   any monetary award.

13.2. The Venture Funding Term Sheet

Overview   If a VC fir m invites you to an interview, you w ill present your business plan to describe what you are offering and what funding you are looking for   . Sometimes during the negotiation s, the VC will let you know that they are interested in financ ing your company and will send you a term sheet   that sets forth the ir key terms and conditions of their investment in your company. This is a non -binding agreement and some terms and conditions are open   to negotiation. If you sign the term sheet   , you are indicating that you will limit your funding negotiation s to this particular VC. The term sheet may stipulate that you pay the legal fee s of the VC firm's legal counsel that were incurred by that firm in its due diligence o f your company if you reach agreement on a funding arrangement.

Before getting to the subject of negotiation, let us examine how the VC operates its business. A VC firm raises fund from institution   al investors, such as pension funds of state   governments or   large companies on the strength of its managers' reputation . Suppose that the investors invest $100 million in this VC firm and set a term of 10 years as the period in which it will   conduct its business . Even though the management fee that a VC firm usually charges is 2 to 2.5% a year, an overall management fee of 2% for 10 years will provide $20 million. If this is set aside, the amount available for investment is reduced to $80 million. If the $80 million are invested evenly over a five-year period, the VC will have $16 million for venture investments for each of the five years. VC firms normally spend the remaining years of the fund's life in managing those investments. A VC firm raises a new fund every three to five years, so that it can continue to actively invest in ventures. The long term health of a VC firm can be determined by how recently it has raised new funds.

Because of the economy in recent years, it is harder to liquidate or maintain the viability of the companies in a VC firm's portfolio. As a result, lower VC funding for new companies creates a buyer's market for VC firms that enables them to be selective when granting an investment deal. Thus, a VC firm will tend to set a lower valuation on the company, so that the same investment can obtain for it a larger ownership fraction of better companies. If you are able to work out funding to sustain the operation of your company, you are in a stronger footing to negotiate a better funding deal.

Company Valuation and the Price of Preferred Stock One of the most challenging aspects of negotiation with a VC firm is to reach an agreement on a valuation of your company. You may use the market potential of your company or its revenue and earnings to justify a valuation. On the other hand, the VC may use the track record or success of your entrepreneur team to arrive at another valuation. Like the process of selling a house, only after the VC and you have agreed to a value, will you proceed to negotiate other conditions in the term sheet.

Angel investors and the company's founders usually receive common shares in exchange for their investments. A VC wants to receive preferred shares, which have priority over common shares in liquidation and the distribution of assets, as well as voting rights that provide greater protection for the VC and full control of the company. The VC's choice of preferred stocks is not negotiable. However, some of the protection sought and the company valuation, which is used to determine the price of preferred stock, may be negotiable.

The VC in Table 5.3 will invest $2 million in the XYZ Company, having reached agreement on a valuation of the latter company of $2.6 million. This valuation yields a price of $2.00 for each share. Thus the VC would receive 1 million shares for their investment. However, because the VC will receive preferred shares, it can stipulate in the term sheet that it will have control of the Board of Directors, even though it is not the majority owner of the XYZ Company as it does not own a majority of the voting (common) shares . After the VC investment, the valuation of the company will become $4.6 million.

Preference in Liquidation   A l iquidation may be   caused by   an acquisition of the XYZ Company by others, a sale of the company, or   a bankruptcy proceeding of the company . The VC has preference in the distribution of cash generated by such a liquidation. This preference can take the form of a return to the VC of an amount that is equal to the amount that it had invested, twice the amount that it had invested or three times its investment, depending on the risk of investing in the XYZ Company. If the preference is 2X and the company XYZ   is sold for $4 million, the VC will receive all of the $4 million, leaving nothing for the other shareholders.

If the selling price of XYZ Company   is $7 million, then the additional $3 million   will be distributed   to the other shareholders, according to their ownership shares. This double dipping, the preference distribution and the subsequent distribution to the other investors, should be negotiated.

Dividends   This is the annual return to shareholders for their investment. For a company in the first or second round of VC funding, the dividends are usually shares, instead of cash   . The dividend to preferred shareholders   may be equal to a predetermine   d and fixed percentage of their investment . Sometimes the term sheet   permits the Board of Directors to vote on the   dividend's percentage of return . This may be lower for common shares . Try to negotiate that any dividends to be paid will be non-cumulative. If the annual return is set at 8%, the total non-cumulative return for an initial investment of $2 million over five years is $800,000. If it w as compounded, the cumulative return would come to $939,000.

Redemption Rights   One condition stipulated by th e VC might be that the XYZ Company   will redeem the preferred shares in three annual installments, beginning on the closing day of the fifth year and at a price equal to the original purchase price (i.e.   , $2 million) plus the accumulated d ividends (i.e. , $800,000). This condition is designed by the VC as an exit strategy when the company is progressing well, but is not yet a candidate for an IPO or acquisition . This redemption right is designed by the VC to correspond to the life span of venture funds.

Board Composition   The term sheet may establish that the holders of preferred shares can choose four Directors to sit on the Board, that the holders of common shares can choose two Directors and that you and the VC will agree on the choice of one independent, additional Director to appoint. Although the holders of preferred shares have fewer shares than do the holders of common shares, the preference enables the former to effect control of the Board and subsequently the company. This control could result in the appointment of a new CEO immediately following the investment is concluded.

Drag-along Rights If the holders of preferred shares decide to liquidate and sell the company, the clause on drag-along rights requires the holders of common shares to agree to the liquidation or sale. Suppose that the preference is 2X (i.e., $4 million) and the dividends due to preferred shareholders are $800,000. If the sale of the XYZ Company generates cash of $4.8 million, the founders and the holders of common shares will get nothing.

Reverse Vesting and Key Employee Matters Before the closing of the investment deal with the VC, the founders have one million common shares. After the closing, the founders must set aside their common shares and then earn them back over the next four years. This stock redistribution process is termed reverse vesting. You may negotiate to immediately obtain a portion of the shares (this is also known as cliff vesting) and/or shorten the vesting period to two or three years. One of the reasons to have this condition in the term sheet is to ensure that the founders stay around and help the company to develop and progress. In addition, a certain portion of stock is specified in the term sheet as a set-aside for an employee stock option plan.

Anti-dilution Provision This protects investors when shares of stock are sold at price per share less than the price paid by the investors. Preferred shares are normally convertible at the option of their holders to common stock on a share-for-share basis. Priced-based anti-dilution adjustments involve increasing the number of shares owned by investors.

Registration Right This is a right given to investors to demand that the company register its shares with the SEC to enable the investors to sell their shares.

Pro-rata Participation Right This right entitles investors to participate in future equity offerings on a pro-rata basis.

For more information on the topics introduced or discussed here, consult a competent attorney or CPA who specialize in venture investment.

13.3. Executive Employment Contracts

Overview   This contract   records   the terms of employment and compensation for the executive , the rights of both the executive and employer, and the company's obligations to the executive . As the CEO, you need to work out an employment agreement that   will motivate the new executive to become a team member without costing the company a fortune. Even if you are the sole founder of the company, you still should have an employment contract for yours   elf to ensure that your hard work and contribution   will be rewarded and that your legal rights are protected.

Your recruitment pamphlet will describe what qualification and knowledge are sought in   the executive being recruited . You can ask a placement firm to help you in the   search for the right candidate. Many entrepreneurs volunteer their time to help the advis   ory work offered by SCORE or organizations , such as CONNECT . These are sources for you to use to find executives to serve in your company.

It is important to do due diligence of the new executive before the interview and signing the employment contract   . Knowing the professionalism and characteristics of the executive and   presenting a legally enforceable employment contract right in the beginning will save many disputes, headaches, and remedial actions . In one case, a company was happy to recruit an executive to work on some patentable inventions. He was granted a significant number of company shares   . Soon afterward, the partners discovered that this executive also worked part time for a competing company on the development of a device of a similar nature . Although this ethical violation   of the executive's employment terms enabled the partners to eventually fire hi   m, hiring him had already put the pa   tentable work done by the company in jeopardy. Because of the lack of a carefully written employment contract, additional effort had to be spent to recover the fired executive's company shares.

The contract for the Chief Executive Officer (CEO)   should include the following provisions:

General Description of the Position, Responsibilities and Term

This spells out the   CEO's position. You need to set out   the duties and responsibilities clearly in the CEO employment contract   . It may state whether you will h ave a seat on the Board of Directors and   how you will report to the Board of Directors and the Chairman of the Board . It may limit the activities that the CEO can engage in, such as consulting work, business activities outside of the company, employment by another company and ownership of an interest in a company that is in competition with your company. The CEO's term of employment is usually set at five to ten years, but is negotiable.

Compensation This includes salary, annual bonus, stock option s, employment benefits, expenses, vacation and other perks and/or a golden parachute.

Trigger Events The contract will define what will happen to you if there is a change in control of the company , as occasioned by a change of ownership, sale of the company, or merger or acquisition of the company. Your position as CEO is an at -will position, meaning your employment can be terminated at anytime for cause, without cause, due to disability or to death, for good reason or without good reason.

Proprietary Information Agreements and Termination Obligations
These agreements deal with the retention and ownership of any intellectual property by the company, the non -compete nature of your future job, the protection of the company's trade secrets, the prohibition of the solicitation of the company's customers and employees, the return of property and documentation, and assistance in litigations when you leave the company.

Arbitration to resolve conflicts, the release of claims, the payment of legal fees and costs and the law governing employment contract will be defined in the contract.

The following issues may require more scrutiny by the executive and his/her attorney:

Stock Options The stock option is a key form of equity compensation that is offered to executives. If it is a restricted stock grant as used in many start-up companies, the executive will be required to pay taxes on the fair market value of the stock on vesting . There may be a problem in paying the tax obligation if the executive does not have the necessary cash or cannot easily sell the shares. This is in contrast to an "ordinary" stock option in which the executive need not pay tax until he has purchased the stock by exercising his options. If the stock option is properly structured under an "incentive stock option" plan, an executive will not have a tax payment to make when his shares are issued, but will pay regular taxes when the stocks are sold.

Definition of Trigger Events and the Compensation   These events not only can lead to the te rmination of employment contract, but also determin e the amount of compensation. A clear definition o f the events is necessary for your protection . The form of compensation may include accelerated vesting of stock option s and/or continued payments of salar y, bonus and paid medical benefits. The amount and timing of these payments may have tax consequences . These issues should be addressed in the employment contract at the outset to avoid additional tax penalties.

Intellectual Property Ownership and Other Restrictive Clauses

As an executive, you may have   an interest in the development of ventures outside of the area   in which the company   competes (or will compete). The right to continue to involve yourself in such ventures and to retain ownership of your inventions should be negotiated. In addition, the restriction on post employment solicitation of customers and employees and non -competition may need to be examined   in order to avoid costly litigation after termination of employment.

13.4. Licensing Agreement

Overview   One objective in   granting a licensing right   for an intellectual property is to facilitate the joint development of a product . Licensing can be the first step   in   forming an alliance   or   the establishment of a joint venture, or the prelude to a   merger or acquisition. You may use the licens ing right as a means of   entering a new   area of   technology.   Most licensing agreements are   created collaboratively, while others are coerced by litigation or the threat of IP infringement.

The company   that grants the licensing right   is known as   the licensor and the one that receives the right as the licensee. A licensing agreement is written with these objectives in mind:

- To define the economic and technical relationship between the licensor and licensee
- To assure the rights and procedures on the use of the licensed IP
- To describe the ways by which the use of the licensed IP will be monitored, regulated and terminated.

Issues in the licensing agreement to be negotiated include:

Licensing Rights   Once you receive a patent from the USPTO, you can exclude any other persons or companies from making, using, selling, or offering to sell in the USA, or importing into this country that for which the patent was granted. The licensing right allows the licensee to carry out these activities without exclusion by the patent owner (i.e., the licensor). If the invention is associated with more than one patent, continuation-in-part or patent application, the licensed patents are referred to as the bundle of these patents. For trade secrets, a licensing right allows the licensee to use the secrets and to access information from the licensor. For copyrights, the right granted by the licensor enables the licensee to copy, reproduce, distribute, publish, create derivative works, display and perform in public that which was copyrighted. Licensed technology, referred to as unpatented technology, includes documents and biological materials, software codes, etc. Its licensing is subject to the rules established for trade secrets and copyrights. The licensee should do due diligence on the validity of licensed patents and technology and ask the licensor for full disclosure. Trademarks for certain products can be licensed for use by means of a licensing agreement.

Licensed Rights and Products   Most products will undergo the following development process: R&D, manufacturing, regulatory evaluations, marketing, distribution and servicing. The licensor can grant this right for all of these processes or to only some of them, as outlined in Fig. 13.1. As an example, the licensor can decide to license only a right to manufacture the device to the licensee. In this licensing or outsourcing arrangement, the licensee will deliver the product to the licensor and the licensee will not have the right to carry out other activities, such as selling or distributing the device.

A licensed product is one that is made by using the licensed patent or technology. It should use a label that identifies the patent numbers or shoes the term, "patent pending." A careful definition of the number of units of the licensed product (e.g., medical device) that are produced or of the way in which the software will be used forms the basis for calculation of compensation to pay the licensor.

Territory   The territory for which the license will be applicable can be negotiated. It may be the USA and its territories or simply one or more specified states.

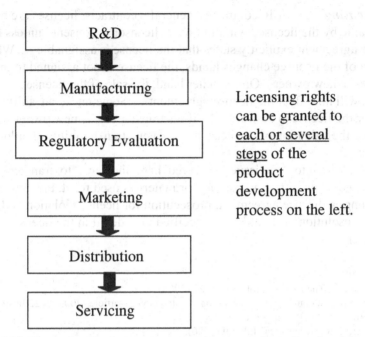

Fig. 13.1. The product development process and its connection to licensing rights.

Field of Use   This defines the type of products and processes that can use the licensed technology or product. A disease may be specified when defining the field of use. For example, if a patented device is licensed for use in neural diseases, the licensee cannot use the device for cardiovascular diseases. Conditions can be spelled out for the use of licensed technology in research and non-commercial uses.

Compensations   If a right is granted to the licensee to sell the licensed products, the compensations are negotiated. This may include the payment of upfront fees for the transfer of the technology and installment payments according to certain developments or attainment of marketing goals. Royalty payments are appropriate. They can be calculated on the basis of the number of units or amount produced or sold. Payments can be based on gross sales, net sales, or net profits. The terms for the calculation of compensation should be clearly defined and the licensor should be given the right to audit and verify the calculation of payments and the figures on which they were based. The manner of payment (by cash, payment in-kind, or product transfer) and its timing need to be spelled out in the licensing agreement.

Sublicensing In contrast to general contracts, licenses are not assignable by the licensee without the licensor's consent, unless the license agreement explicitly states that the license is assignable . When control of the licensee changes hands, the license is not assigned to the licensee's new owner . On the other hand, the sale of the licensee 's shares will not affect the license agreement . Sometimes, an ability to transfer the license is desirable, if its transfer to a new owner will enhance the valuation of the licensee . Then, transferability should be negotiated.

In addition to the issues covered here, the way to transfer and escrow the licensed technology and/or materials used for it, the law governing a license agreement, prosecution for license violation and dispute resolution should be specified in detail in the licens ing agreement.

References
1. Heuser, S, The Boston Globe, Sept. 22 (2005) www.boston.com/business/technology/biotechnology/articles/2005/09/22/boston_sc ientific_medinol_settle_row/
2. Lerer, L., www.law.com, July 20 (2006).
3. Mauro T., www.law.com, May 16 (2006).
4. www.allbusiness.com/technology/6159341.html June 1 (2003).

CHAPTER 14

LEADING PEOPLE AND
MANAGING YOURSELF

14.1. Preparing Yourself and Managing Your Time and Work

The CEO and his/her entrepreneurial team are the heart of a company. Raising fund s for the operation of the company is a full -time job. Leading peop le and managing the team is another full time job . It is important that you divide your limited time between these two jobs , while maintaining a balance between your business and fam ily life. Since your idea o f the entrepreneurial venture will have a limit ed useful life, so will you . To succeed, you will have to constantly change and adapt. Although you may change your business ventures, your family will be with you for many years to come, especially after you have retired from your entrepreneurship.

You need to constantly look for opportunities to create for your company. Finding potential acquirers with financial strength will get your company over and past the Building-up Phase. Examine your company's position to find ways of generating revenue . The bes t position you can put your company in is having sufficient money in the bank to pay your vendors and employees without the need for VC funding.

In Chapter 2, we identif ied a number of traits that an entrepreneur should possess or acquire (Fig. 2.1). Here are a number of rules or bits of practical wisdoms for you to consider for effective, day-to-day operation of the company:

On Interpersonal Relationships

- Be truthful in your dealing s with your team, your customers, your family, and even your competito rs. Above all, however, be truthful to yourself.
- Be honorable and ethical in your business dealings. You will at times be confronted with a deceitful person or company . Learn

194

to recognize deceit and how to deal with it. Avoid direct confrontations.

- Negotiate in a "win -win" mode. Remember that you will often be creating a long-term relationship with "the other side."
- Establish business friends, associates and future contacts by applying the three rules above. In hard times, these contacts will stand by you. Do n't get dropped like a hot potato when the going gets tough.

On Productivity:
- Plan your day and set priorities . Maintain a "to -do" list. Work on high value tasks and get them done on time. Stay on top of your most important responsibilities; the others will just have to wait.
- Define goals and problems clearly. Clarity is everything. When discussing a problem, focus on the future instead of the past. Deal with problems creatively and effectively.
- Always be open to feed-back and listen to negative viewpoints.
- Respond to your co -workers' messages and requests . Clear and timely communication saves time and reduces any anxieties that your co-workers may have. Create notes before making calls and keep them brief.
- Use a system to keep track of names and phone numbers.
- Break up your day in to units, for example units of 75 minutes with a 15 -minute break between. Use the break to return emails and phone calls, hold quick conferences, and get coffee or tea.
- Take one day a week off "just for you and your family".

On Mastering the Internet:
- Learn how best to find useful information online.
- Organize and manage information flows that are somewhat overwhelming.
- Network on the internet to accomplish professional goals.
- Leverage internet tools to accomplish results more quickly.

On the Company's Operation:
- Concentrate on making sales and controlling costs. Learn both and do them well to achieve maximum profit for your business.
- Evaluate expenditure before you make it without exception . Always look for a less costly alter native. Maintain the habit of conserving cash and reducing the costs of everything you do.

- Hire employees after:
  - o Reviewing whether you can afford to hire an employee.
  - o Identifying the type of employee needed.
  - o Defining the work to be done by the employee.
  - o Recruiting and interviewing prospects.
  - o Familiarizing yourself with the legal requirements governing the employment relationship.
  - o Complete all paperwork that is necessary when hiring an employee.

On Self Improvement:

- Read everything and attend every seminar and workshop you can. You will learn new ideas, techniques and methods to save you hours and days of hard work and research. Seminars and workshops are good places for networking.
- Think out of the box, aggressively seek new ideas, question your assumptions, and require accurate information . There are dangers in conformity and complacency.
- Learn the know -how of running a company. 80% of businesses started by experienced business persons succeed. The reason is that they have learned how to purchase, negotia te, raise money, sell and market, manage the finances and lead employees.

14.2. Setting Goals, Incentives and Recognition for the Team

As the leader of your company, you will need to communicate well with your team, develop consensus among team members, delegate jobs and authority to the team, set SMART goals and establish incentives. Make the decision process transparent so that your team w ill not become discouraged with rumors from other sources . As you delegate work to your team, stay on top of the si tuation and have frequent meetings with the team to monitor progress. Give employees the authority to do their jobs, but not treat your delegation as a means to abdicate your responsibilities.

 The SMART goals to be set for the team should have these characteristics (4):

- *Specific* The goals must be in writing and very specific. A specific goal is much easier to underst and and has a greater chance of being accomplished than a general and vaguely-worded goal. You must specify:

- o Who will do it.
- o What you want to have accomplished.
- o Where you want it done.
- o When it should be completed
- o What the support, requirements and constraints for completing the goal are.
- o Why you want to achieve the goal and what the purpose and benefit of accomplishing the goal are.

Avoid non-specific statements, such as "to always work for the good of the company." A team member should only know what is required for his specific assignments.

- *Measurable* Establish a time to reach the goal and specific criteria for measuring progress toward attainment of the goal. To determine whether your marketing goal is measurable and quantifiable, ask questions, such as, "How many devices do I want to sell in the first quarter?" or "By when do I want this goal to be achieved?"

- *Attainable* Specify the action to attain. Your team's attitude, abilities, skills, resources and financial capacity make it possible to reach the goal. If you plan your steps wisely and establish a time frame in which to carry out the steps, you can attain almost any goal that you set. When your goals are attainable, you improve not only your self-image, but also your self confidence.

- *Realistic* There must be a possibility of reaching the goal. To be realistic, a goal must be something that your team is both willing and able to do. A goal can be both high and realistic. A high goal is frequently easier to reach than a low one, because the former will require greater effort - and motivation - than the latter. Do the job as a labor of love.

- *Timely* Timelines must be set within a context. If there is no deadline attached to the goal, there will be no sense of urgency.

To begin developing effective team effort right, adopt the habit of setting business goals daily, weekly, monthly and quarterly, putting them down in writing daily and weekly, and monitoring them daily. Because of Murphy's Law, allow at least 50% more time than you feel is needed for a task. Innovation, R&D and ventures always are more expensive and take longer than expected.

Make sure that every team member knows that time is truly money. Similar to goal setting, a company must have *a SMART incentive plan* to recognize the goal accomplishers of the team. When your company's profit exceeds a certain specific level, then award a measurable number of dollars as an incentive or bonus to reflect the relative contributions to savings and revenue generation made by individuals and teams. Based on the past statements of profit and loss, you can calculate a *specific and measurable* profit level that will be *attainable, realistic and timely* by your team.

Peer recognition is important to the functioning of a team. A good salary and incentive are only two forms of recognition. One of the most effective ways to motivate a team member is by making him feel important as a contributor to his team, his project and his company. The utmost thing that you should do is getting the team to buy into the goals, incentives and recognition.

14.3. Working with the Team

A CEO is empowered to design the organizational structure, assemble the multi-disciplinary team and define the working relationships among the various entities. In doing so, the CEO aims to:
- Ensure that important work gets done efficiently
- Enhance the company's performance
- Aid delegation of job and authority
- Facilitate communication and collaboration
- Encourage team work
- Provide transparency of team management, operation of the company and awarding of incentives.

In the Assessing Phase of your company's development, most of the company work will involve the feasibility and design of the new invention. The Launching Phase involves more work on manufacturing and prototyping. During the Building-up Phase, you expand your capabilities to include production, servicing and marketing. To perform these tasks well and in a short period of time, you need to form a cross-functional team that is staffed with experts in:

- Marketing
- Design engineering
- Manufacturing engineering
- Service support
- Production engineering
- Accounting and inventory.

All asp ects related to the functions above are done concurrently, especially during the Building-up Phase, in order to reach the stage in which revenue and profit will be generated.

If the team is to succeed, the CEO must become proficient in leading, and simultaneously participating in, the engineering team. In getting things done, the team leader needs to pay attention to team discipline, team learning, intra-team relationship s, conflict resolution, and other factors that affect the team's performance.

All m embers need to know the team's objective, although each member will work on those things in which he or she has expertise. The efforts of all are integrated to produce a product for the market that achieves any or all of the following:

- Reduction of product development time
- Reduction of the number of engineering changes
- Effective outsourcing some manufacturing and production work
- Innovation and improvement of a product
- Reduction of manufacturing costs
- Improvement of product quality, reliability and serviceability
- Reduction of the time-to-market.

This engineering team consists of a small number of pe rsons (or all persons people in the small business venture) of complementary expertise and who are committed to work together to achieve the above impacts.

Rolling up your sleeves and willingly do what ever is necessary are essential in being the team leader . Never think of yourself as being too good for a job . In order to encourage team members to learn better and faster, motivate the m to learn new technologies, n ew thinking and new marketing skill . Outsourcing work may be the norm for a small company, if cost effective and appropriate . If you have transparency in decision-making, delegation of jobs and authority, individual accountability, and incentives, you will have a cohesive and enthusiastic team to move the product development toward the marketing phase.

The management of people and project   will be   a challenge as business development grows, activities expand beyond the company, and team members are dispersed. Web-based tools for project management are available to assist you in dealing with the following issues:

- Task and resource management
- Cost management
- Risk management
- Communication
- Knowledge and documentation management.

The ideas covered in this subsec tion were drawn from two chapters of the engineering management book by C. M. Chang (2). These chapters should be consulted for   more ways of "Organizing" and "Managing" your team and company.

14.4. Building the Winning Team

To build a winning team for the company,   your first task is to recruit people with appropriate expertise to work as team members and who can also honor the set of rules set for the team. Here are some working rules that have been extracted from the book by Blair Singer (3); you should consider ad opting for your company and get ting the team to agree to abide by:

- *Be willing to stand behind the purpose, rules and goals of the company.*
- *Be willing to do whatever it takes to support any and all team members.*
- *Have a willingness to stay together.*
- *Support early, often and unconditionally.*
- *Speak supportively and with good purpose.*
- *Complete your responsibilities and assignment.*
- *Make only agreements that you are willing and intend to keep.*
- *If a problem arises, first look to the system for correction and then communicate your solution to the person who can do something about it.*
- *Do not go behind a person's back with a problem.*
- *Agree to work toward an agreement.*
- *Accept personal responsibility. No laying blame, justification or finger pointing.*

- *Do not let personal issues stand in the way of your work.*
- *Make a commitment to win and allow others to win.*
- *Clarify your own communication and verify the response.*

The second task is for you and the team to enforce the rules. Before getting to the point where you show the misfit, troublemaker or non-team player the door, Singer suggests that you just "CALL IT" using the following tips:

- *Pick an appropriate time to make the call, but don't wait too long.*
- *Acknowledge how you are feeling first to the other party*
- *Get permission from him or her to make the call.*
- *Correct the behavior, not the person. Let the rules be the policeman.*
- *State specifically what did not work and offer support.*
- *Make clear what the benefits of correction are for the team and for the individual involved.*
- *Thank the individual for listening and listen to his or her response without interruption.*
- *Acknowledge the individual's proper behavior later when you see him demonstrate it.*

Use the following tips to facilitate the team operation:

- Be concerned about over-management. It may be a waste, is often a hindrance to progress, and , worse yet, a morale killer. Reduce the number of management layers to an absolute minimum.
- Encourage debate on understanding, thoughts and concerns before a decision is made.
- Discourage nay saying , such as "I told you so ," once the decision is made or if something does not go as planned.
- Instill in all team members the importance of doc umentation. Good documentation will not only assure a good understanding of what ha s been done, but also be important in substantiating the validity of a patent, assuring legal protection, and facilitating job continuation and/or reassignment.
- Be prepared with a plan B for critical tasks. No matter how well you plan, problems will always arise. A well thought-out plan B will assure an orderly progress of tasks.

- Require some managers to do technological work to keep themselves up-to-date on technology advancement.

Finally, as a team leader, you need to work on the ability to:

- *Spot and leverage the strengths of others.*
- *Teach others how to succeed.*
- *Use mistakes to strengthen and grow the team.*
- *Use frequency of interaction to build relationship, consistency and, most of all, trust.*
- *Promote a realistic, but brighter, future to the team.*
- *Sell a vision, an attitude, the rules and ideas to the team.*

Technology companies should examine a few exceptions to the teamwork requirements. As stated by Bakken in Reflections on Leadership (1): *"Much success of Medtronic has been due to brilliant mavericks that were difficult for our engineers to work with. Because of the lead of mavericks, Medtronic effected early breakthroughs (in implantable pacemakers). With an enormous amount of imagination and patience, the most effective leaders accommodate the ornery thinkers and give them the attentive ear that their ideas deserve. The challenge to leadership is great, but so, too, are the potential rewards."*

References

1. Bakken, E.E., *Reflections on Leadership*, Medtronic Inc., (2001)
2. Chang, C.M., *Engineering Management, Challenges in the New Millennium*, Pearson/Prentice Hall, NJ, p.44-72 and p.373-428, (2005)
3. Singer, B., *The ABC's of Building a Business Teams that Wins*, Warner Business Books, NY, (2004).
4. www.topachievement.com/smart.html

CHAPTER 15

MANUFACTURING YOUR PRODUCT

15.1. Procurement and Outsourcing

Small medical companies often start as a one - or two-product company. The initial expenditures will include the one-time cost of designing, manufacturing and testing a new product , as described in Fig. 15.1 , before the company can proceed to scale d-up production . The design

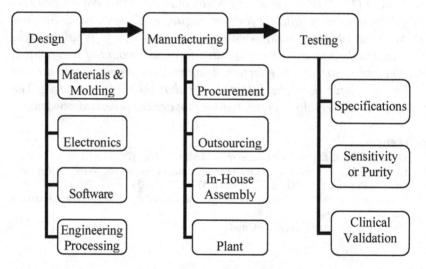

Fig. 15.1. Record keeping, as required by Good Manufacturing Practices of the FDA, for processing blocks that might be involved in t he manufacture of your medical device s or pharmaceutical product s.

step may include the selection of materials, design of electronic circuitries, writing of software, and/or selection of engineering processes. As the company approaches the manufacture of the first few prototypes, it will become involved in procuring components, finding an outsourcing firm, performing in-house assembly, and/or making plan s to expand plant facilities. After test results show that the product matches the specifications, has s ufficient sensitivity or purity and demonstrates effectiveness and safety in clinical usage, the company   will apply for product approval from the FDA. Only then, can the company scale up the production and move to the marketing phase.

Several pointers on how best to procur e the components of your medical inventions or outsource the design, testing and manufacturing of them are described in this section.

There are at present many companies in the USA and the world that have the expertise necessary to carry out this non -recurring engineering for medical device and pharmaceutical companies.

Procurement   Suppose that your new invention is so simple that it consists only of three components . Each component may only require a few modifications to a product that is already available i n the market . You contract several suppliers to remake the modified component s, and then you assemble the components to   prepare your product for marketing. In order to protect your   intellectual property (IP), you can subcontract the manufacturing of the three components to three different suppliers. If your competitors have n o instruction manual that explains how the new invention operates or any   knowledge of how these components will be   put together, your IP right may be somewhat protected for a while.

Even with this advantage, you   should still thorough ly conduct due diligence on   each supplier before you sign a purchase contract that clearly spells out the specifications of the component to be manufactured, the delivery date, the shipping cost, and   the terms of payment. The second due diligence is   conducted to obtain references that reveal how reliable this contractor is in delivering the product as specified. Third due diligence is to assure that the manufacturing practice of the con tractor follows FDA GMPs or ISO Standards that are appropriate for your company's   medical device or pharmaceutical product. The fourth due diligence is intended t   o assure you that the contractor will fully transfer his/her G   ood Manufacturing Practice (GMP) records to your company after he has delivered the goods.

Once you receive the   goods, you should immediately identify the batch and check the products individually or randomly to be sure that the specifications have been met. Call the supplier right away if the delivery product does not meet the specifications. The names of the inspectors who checked the product specification should be   entered in your records. The key message here is that you   must have the record s necessary to demonstrate that diligent and verifiable efforts have been made in the manufacture and assembly of the product.

Outsourcing When your product begins to become more complex, it may be more practical for you to outsource the design, testing and manufacturing to a firm that specializes in your innovation's field and has completed jobs similar to yours.

Use your connection from previous employment to identify such a firm. Your friends working in medical device or pharmaceutical companies may give you name recommendations. There are also a number of websites that you use to identify outsourcers. It is important to be aware that the collaboration between your company and the outsourced firm will be as intense as a partnership (4). Both parties need to do due diligence to assure themselves that they will have a working partnership to manufacture the product properly.

The product development may encounter some unexpected events. Both partners must possess the motivation to work out any problems.

An outsourcing agreement will be somewhat like the licensing agreement that was described in Chapter 13, but will include a description of the development, design and manufacturing work to be done by both partners. On your part, you will need to ensure that the firm to which you outsource the manufacturing is appropriate, capable of doing the work and has the right people to focus on the design and manufacturing work and the facilities in which to carry it out. In addition, it should run a business that follows the FDA good manufacturing practice and be able to sustain the services required for the continuous improvement, development and manufacturing of your devices after the conclusion of the current agreement.

An Illustrative Example You can divide the outsourcing work into several phases as shown in the following case involving the development of a 5 MHz ultrasound processing system. This system will use a newly produced, dual channel, A/D converter and a new algorithm to determine if ultrasound can be used to measure some physical characteristics of biological fluids. Because of the A/D converter's low price, the task will be to examine whether the A/D converter that has a sampling rate of 60 mega samples per second and digitized data at 16 bits can really achieve better accuracy than that offered by a competitor's system, while achieving a reduction in manufacturing cost.

To test the feasibility of this proposition, you prepare a contract for the contracted firm to use the evaluation board of the A/D converter to digitize and store the ultrasound signals and then use a PC to perform the computation.

If sufficient accuracy is demonstrated, you ask the contractor to design a full circuit board in the second phase that will integrate the A/D converter and a microprocessor into a prototype that for your further evaluation of performance. The outcomes of this phase will be a bill of materials (the listing of all chips, resistors and capacitors used in the electronics), the schematics in Gerber files, and the software.

At this stage the assembly of chips onto the circuit board of the prototype will be largely done by hand. It is also essential that you invite a third party to validate chip by chip the bill of materials and schematics provided by the contracted firm. It is much easier to find errors and misrepresentations in documents or products at this stage than later.

The third phase will be to demonstrate that the chips can be assembled in large quantities by machines with the same circuitry performance. In this way, you will more accurately learn the manufacturing cost of the ultrasound system and the assurance of quality products when they are manufactured in large quantity.

This development process is complicated. The first outsourcing of design and manufacturing will be a learning experience. On many occasions, face to face discussion and direct communication are so essential in leading to better solution. Major changes can be made more easily by direct communication. Try to find a firm nearby to work with you in the development of your device.

After gaining more experience and knowledge about outsourcing, you can use the internet to investigate the possibility of outsourcing your manufacturing to firms in other regions of the US or overseas. In fact, it is likely that the firm with whom you have contracted the manufacture of your product already has a subsidiary or partner in China or other countries that is accustomed to mass producing quality products.

If you outsource internationally, the manufacturing facilities that do your work must practice the same GMP as the US custom manufacturer. Because of the large quantities being ordered, a foreign company will set up an assembly line to ensure that it can assemble your product at lower cost and a lower failure rate.

Because of rapid market growth and the emergence of new industry-spanning market segments, medical device manufacturers have begun to seek partners that can provide full service outsourcing, completing all phases of device development from market research to prototype building, equipment design and manufacturing (2).

Advantages of Outsourcing   Here are some of the ways in which your company may benefit from outsourcing (1). Some aspects of international outsourcing are detailed in Chapter 17.

- **Multidisciplinary and Experienced Team**   You are in the position to choose the firm to which you will outsource your work. You can check out what it has accomplished and whether it has the expertise and experience necessary to do your work. In the preceding example, expertise in ultrasound, hardware and software, and more specifically on high frequency signal processing and signal digitization without interference and mis-synchronization, was the key to successful completion of the project. It may be difficult for you to build up an in-house team to do your one-time project. On the other hand, this is the type of job being done regularly by many outsource firms. Consequently, your subcontractor may have already lined up the team to work on other projects after they have completed yours.

- **Expanded Engineering Capability**   Just like having a design and engineering team, the subcontractor may have the necessary engineering facilities to do work that is not practical for you without building an appropriate facility in house for a one-time use.

- **Fewer Errors and a Reduction in Development Time** The expertise and experience of the team should result in fewer errors and enable the development to be completed sooner.

- **Commitment in IP Protection and Confidentiality**   The design and engineering firm knows the importance of protecting your IP rights and keeping your project confidential. Their administration already has a policy in place to assure compliance by the firm and its employees.

- **Better Record Keeping and Compliance with Regulations** Ensure that the firm has done the design and engineering work on medical device or pharmaceutical product of the same field. Specify in the engagement agreement what records must be conveyed when the work has been completed.

Outsourcing Precautions   The success of the partnership depends greatly on the relationship between your company and the outsourced firm. Here is why the relationship is important:

- **Commitments**   Because you are the inventor you are the only person who will know whether the manufactured device can have the functions that you wish. The design and engineering firm will try its best to accomplish what you want. Sometimes a product may not have all the specified functions due to limitations in electronics, chemistry or physics. You will remember that the portable, battery-operated pacemaker mentioned previously could be developed only after the arrival of transistors. The contracted team may recommend changes in the design and engineering of your product, but you are still the one who must make the final decision. You work on the premise of trust in your outsourcer. However, trust yourself even more as you must pay the bill, even if the team does their job according to the contract, but fails to produce a product that meets the specifications.
- **Communications**   It is a good practice to maintain good communications as the project progresses. Schedule periodic meetings of both parties to evaluate the project's status and to make necessary changes and modifications to the design.
- **Expected Costs and Timelines** The   project   budget   and timelines should be set at contract signing. Appropriate resources and manpower should be allocated. You must be prepared for unexpected events in product development, whether the work is done in-house or by outsourcing.
- **Dispute Resolution**   Try to develop a good partnership with the least chance for it to go wrong. However, be realistic so that disputes over work and payments can be resolved.

15.2. Current   Good   Manufacturing   Practice   (cGMP), Accountability and Risk Management

cGMP   GMP is a set of FDA regulations developed to promulgate Good Manufacturing Practices (5). These regulations require that manufacturers of pharmaceutics, medical devices and food products take proactive steps to ensure that the products are safe and effective. The regulations are designed to assure the quality of manufacturing and minimize or eliminate contamination and errors. The regulations also stipulates what is required of manufacturers in matters of record keeping, personnel qualifications, sanitation, cleanliness, equipment verification, process validation, and complaints.

These are open-ended regulations that do allow individual manufacturers to decide how best to implement the controls or to interpret the regulations in a way that is favorable to that company or industry. The "c" preceding GMP stands for "current," meaning that manufacturers must employ the most up-to-date technologies and systems to demonstrate their compliance with the regulations.

The guideline on **Pharmaceutical cGMPs for the 21st Century: A Risk-Based Approach** states "The management is responsible for establishing the quality system structure appropriate for the specific organization. Management has the ultimate responsibility to provide the leadership needed for the successful functioning of a quality system." It is essential that all company personnel practice GMP individually by complying with the appropriate standards established for the particular type or class of employees.

A Quality Assurance Department should be established to set the standards and assure their compliance. This needs to be expanded to include compliance by suppliers and subcontractors. It also may be the best if you arrange to have an external consultant check your compliance. If you are notified by FDA that your facilities will be inspected on a certain date, get your records, facilities, and presentation ready to show to FDA staff when they visit your company.

Accountability The following consent decree may describe the trend toward increased accountability to the quality assurance function of pharmaceutical, medical device and biotechnology companies. In January 2009, the FDA released the news that it had filed a Consent Decree and was awaiting the court's entry of a permanent injunction to bar not only a generic drug manufacturer, but also the CEO, VP of Corporate Quality and a board member from manufacturing and distributing 20 or so drugs until the company and its officers were in compliance with the cGMP. The FDA had ruled the company and its officers guilty of manufacturing and distributing unapproved drugs within the United States.

Because of this consent decree, these officers were held additionally accountable when the company's shareholders sued for security frauds on the grounds that the officers had misled investors about proble ms in the company's manufacturing facilities and had failed to bring the facilities into compliance with federal regulations, including those of the FDA.

A review of the FDA 's records also indicate an increasing number of warning letters being issued to the executives of life science companies for issues related to manufacturing compliance.

The pressure on pharmaceutical, medical device and biotech companies to comply with FDA regulations certainly will have a significant impact on the operation, busines s strategy and resource allocations of your company. As its chief executive, you must devote more effort to assure that your firm's quality oversight and compliance activities have been documented and demonstrated to be effective to both regulatory agencies and your shareholders.

Risk Management Even with the best compliance, unexpected incidents with adverse consequences can still happen. You need to have a response plan to inform internal personnel, FDA and the public of any adverse incident and to decide on a series of actions to identify the cause of the inciden t and the need for recall . As A. R. Lentiani, Jr. advised, you need to be conscientious and avoid the following five mistakes (3):

- Having no response plan or internal notification system
- Putting lawyers in charge
- Shutting out the news media
- Using untrained spokespersons
- Lacking an outside perspective.

To survive such a crisis, Lentiani stated that:

"Bad things can happen to good organizations. The tri ck is to respond immediately and proactively in a direct and honest manner. That sounds easy, but when you are up to your neck in alligators, you might not be thinking clearly. That is why you need to have a plan, test it regularly and follow it.

The othe r important thing to remember after any crisis is to investigate the causes thoroughly and then correct what caused the problem in the first place. The more serious the crisis, the more important it is for you to determine the contributing factors and fix them so a similar event never happens again."

15.3. Lifecycle Management for Maximum Value

The implementation of cGMP is the best way to assure the effectiveness and safety of patients who use your product . You will have to invest manpower to enter data and to analyze the collected data . The added cost will be significantly outweighed by what you can gain if you provide quality service for patients . There are many data management programs on the market that you can adopt for your operation. Several additional benefits are highlighted below. The last three cover the management of the total lifecycle of the product described in Fig. 15.2. ***Better Quality Assurance*** Fig. 15.2 also illustrates the manufacturing lifecycle as one progresses from design to small scale manufacturing, testing and finally large scale manufacturing. The GMP is a reliable

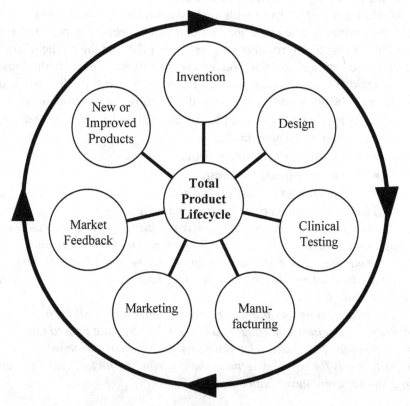

Fig. 15.2 . Data Management during the total lifecycle of the product from invention to new improved product.

means to achieve quality of your product. If one or more processes during the lifecycle were not undertaken in accordance with the GMP, identifying the irregularities will enable the operator to stop and not continue to the next process.

An on-line quality monitoring of the manufacturing process is much better than an off-line testing procedure. First, an off-line testing may rely on random samplings, which may mean that only a small subset of the products will be tested. Secondly, identifying irregularities can only be revealed by an analysis of the final products. Thirdly, standardized and widely accepted GMPs that are implemented in life management serve as a good vehicle by which to assure quality consistency.

More efficient operation   A hypothetical case that can occur frequently in the design of chemical processing facilities, is used below to illustrate why the implementation of lifecycle management can lead to more efficiency in operation. A pharmaceutical company wanted to double its production capacity by building another, identical plant nearby. The projected construction cost was $12 million. Using data in the records that the GMP required the company to maintain, the consultant, who was hired to evaluate the feasibility of plant expansion, was able to identify a few bottlenecks in the processing plant. As a result, resolving those bottleneck locations enabled the company to double its production at a reconstruction cost of about 10% of the projected construction budget.

Similarly, you can model the dynamics of the manufacturing process to determine how to reduce inventories, improve risk management (e.g., financially or by reducing material delivery delays), and to reduce manpower costs. With the globalization of trade, there is a possibility that, for example, a snow storm in China may delay the arrival of your product by, say, two months. Be conservative and play it safe in the modeling analysis.

Improvement in Software Safety   It is easy to revise your software program to enhance the functioning of your medical device. However the FDA increasingly has been finding serious problems with device software because of aging microprocessors and platforms and the addition of new functions and shortcuts in the software. It is also possible that a new evaluation procedure may not be compatible with older microprocessors and platforms for problems identification. Software problems can cause malfunctions in device that could lead to product recall and, in the worst instances, to the death of patients.

With good record keeping for design and software development, you may be in a better position to select the right diagnostic program to verify and validate your software, to prevent defects and failures, to conduct risk analys es, and to   take corrective actions or upgrade your hardware.

Shorter Reaction Time   Suppose that there is a fire in a processing plant. It may be simply human nature that causes the plant manager to postpone reporting the inciden t to top management until some other key problem has been resolved. However, it is the CEO who has the ultimate responsibility for ensuring that the problem is addressed correctly and promptly.   The on -line entry of record   s and timely alert of top management by a record management program can get more people involved in generating a better res   ponse in a shorter time   to correct problems or incidents of an adverse nature.

Facilitation of New Product Improvement   Integrating m   arketing intelligence and patients   '   evaluations in a total lifecycle data management system can result in   further product   improvement and development at a faster pace and with more efficiency.

Moral Enhancement   Suppose your sales rep just landed a big contract. He entered the sales into the record and described how he made the sale . Would you   like to   be alerted by the record   management program instantaneously so that you could call to congratulate the sale rep personally well before the sales rep advises the supervisor who then calls the VP Sales before the message works its way to you?

References

1.   Andrews, R. R., MD&DI's Guide to Outsourcing, S32-S43, June 2006
2.   Andrews, R. R., MD&DI's Guide to Outsourcing, S38S48, August 2006
3.   Lentini, A. R. Risk Management Magazine, June 2009.
4.   Thompson, H. , MD&DI's Guide to Outsourcing, S52S61, June 2006
5.   www.gmp1st.com/gmp.htm

CHAPTER 16

MARKETING AND SALES

Each year, the FDA approves 3 ,000 to 4 ,000 devices under the 510(k) program. Because its approvals are based on showing of substantial equivalence, many of these devices will represent incremental advancements from their com petitors' products. Medtronic stated in its 2007 Annual Report that two -thirds of its revenue came from products introduced in the last two years (6). The problem of competitions may be further compounded by the fact that your company has only limited funds for marketing purposes.

For such a challenging market, evidence -based information, device designs centric to the patients and well -differentiated products are essential to your sale representatives if they are to reach your customers. Then your sales presentation must exhibit sufficient understanding to win the customers and obtain their purchases. We provide some background here to help you become more knowledgeable about your customers, market characteristic s that are important in marketing the medical device or product to the health or pharmaceutical industry , customer relationship management (CRM) and marketing ethics. This should help you prepare your marketing plan . This chapter conclude s with a list of p oints for your use in developing a marketing plan that is suited to your medical device or pharmaceutical product.

16.1. Know Your Customers

Traditionally, customers who have made a decision to acquire your medical device or pharmaceutical product are prescribers, primarily physicians. As our healthcare costs rise from 5% of Gross Domestic Product (GDP) in 1965 to 15% in 2005, the three categories of customers shown in Fig.16.1 are those who have significant influence in the decision to acquire your product. The first category is represented by patients, nurses, clinical engineers, and physicians who use your product. The persons in the second category prescribe or purchase your product. They include physicians and the value analysis teams of

hospitals a nd managed care organizations . The third category   consists
of the payers and policy makers   . These two are grouped together
because, in many occasions,   they are parts of   the government or   an
insurance company . The following   text discusses   these groups of
persons for your consideration in the development of your marketing and
sales plan.

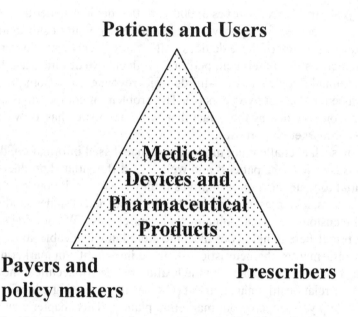

Fig. 16.1. Three categories of persons who are involved in the decision to purchase
your product.

Patients and Users   It is up to   you to convince patients, physicians
and users that your medical product can improve patient experience and
outcomes, maximize compliance and reduce risks . The pharmaceutical
and healthcare market research company Manhattan Research (10)
advises that:

- More than 60% of U.S. adults turn to the Internet for healthcare
  and disease information.
- Physician interest in live video detail   made available by   sale
  representatives is growing   . Currently 45,000 US physicians
  meet with sale s representatives via online video and more than

300,000 more show interest in interacting with sales or other company representatives online.

- The increasing consumer reliance on the Internet for health and pharmaceutical information is transforming digita l direct -to-consumer (DTC) marketing from a "nice to have" tactic to an essential communication channel for companies to use to reach customers.

In view of the great number of devices and products on the market, there is less time for physicians to meet wi th your sales representatives. In essence, your marketing effort must take advantage of an effective means of digital communication to convince physicians to purchase your medical devices and pharmaceutical products without actually meeting your representative.

Equally important will be patient-centered Internet communications and webcasts that serve to educate patients about their own healthcare management, empower them to work on improving their health outcomes and build consumer trust in and loyalty for your company's technology.

Physicians, nurses, clinical engineers, and pharmacists can be users of your medical devices in their work . They want to use devices of high quality and backed by good service. Their opinions are solicited by the hospitals when making the purchasing decision . Good quality and service should not only be your company 's goal, but also an important message that is embedded in your marketing and sales effort.

Prescribers The marketing objective relating to prescribers is to increase the number of times that your product is prescribed. Hospitals and managed care organizations are becoming an important segment in the purchase of medical products as physicians are no longer the only ones who are involved in the purchasing decision. Operating with a low margin, hospitals and managed care organizations are under tremendous pressure to maintain their financial integrity. 25% of hospitals in the US have negative total margins. The future financial prospect s of hospitals are further constrained by (4):

- Weak growth in numbers of patients.
- A l ower reimbursement if health -related expenses from insurance companies and governments.
- A decrease in the collection of fees.

- An increase in costs of operations.
- The impact of the nation's financial crisis.

Hospitals are tackling these problems on many fronts. In the 1990's hospitals were using group purchasing organizations as a means to contain costs. To counter this trend in bargaining power and to facilitate the compliance of government healthcare policies, many medical device companies merged or banded together to form larger organizations . In today's hospitals, the following three cost -containment strategies are particularly worthy of consideration by your marketing and sales team (4):

- *Vendor Access Restriction* Physical access by sales representatives to hospital physicians and staffs can lead to the increased use of the products of those sales representatives. As a means to reduce the influence of the sales representatives, guidelines have been established to limit sales representatives' access to staffs and physicians.
- *Data Driven Supply Chains* The measure of procurement success by the hospitals is changing from the reduction of the cost of acquisition and operation per unit to effective patient outcomes at lowest possible cost. As a result, hospitals are taking a more active role in managing the sampling and trial of medical products . They require that sales representatives have credentials and prohibit the promotion of unapproved products.
- *Value Analysis Teams* With the advance s in information technology, hospitals are more knowledgeable today about their inventories and usage and have more access to the data required to reduce the expense of supplies and operation s. Policies on costs and effectiveness have empowered value analysis teams to make purchasing decision . The teams include physicians, hospital administrators, people employed in materials management and finance, nurses, pharmacists and clinical engineers. Value analysis with evidence -based medicine and government requirements concerning quality improvement of healthcare will continue to play important roles in the process of product evaluation and acquisition.

Payers and Policy Makers Your objective with this category of persons is to establish a funding policy and decision s that are favorable to your product and to create or revise healthcare policies in order to build the demand for your medical devices and pharmaceutical products.

Health insurance is insurance that is provided by a government-sponsored social insurance program or by a private insurance company that has a contract with an individual or his/her employer. The employer or individual pays premiums or taxes to the insurance company or program in exchange for its assistance in protecting the individual from high or unexpected healthcare expenses. The insurance company or program will pay healthcare providers "reasonable and customary" fees for the services provided to the individual. If the providers are in the "Network," they will accept a discounted rate from the insurer. The benefits of an insurance plan and the rules about co-payments and out-of-pocket maximums are specified in the contract. One subject that is important for a medical product company is whether the insurers have established "reasonable and customary" charges for the use of your medical devices or pharmaceutical products.

The largest insurer in the US is **Centers of Medicare and Medicaid Services (CMS)** of the Department of Health and Human Services. This organization operates three Federal healthcare programs: Medicare, Medicaid, and Children's Health Insurance Program. Its mission is to ensure effective, up-to-date healthcare coverage and to promote quality care for its beneficiaries. The CMS 2008 Fiscal Year budget was $458 billion.

To learn more about CMS programs and payments, we will review, as an example, its hemodialysis operation (9). The 2006 Medicare claims data indicated that there were about 4,700 clinics that furnished outpatient maintenance dialysis to an estimated 315,000 Medicare dialysis patients. A total of $8.1 billion has been paid to date by Medicare for expenditures on dialysis and related drugs totaled - or $25,700 per person. The average Medicare payment per dialysis treatment in 2005 was $237. Of this amount, $143 was for partially bundled prospective rate covering dialysis and $94 was for related drugs and laboratory services.

If you are a Medicare patient who is receiving care, you will receive a Medicare Summary Notice like that shown in Exhibit 16.1. The five-digit number in the first column of each line is the code number in the Healthcare Common Procedure Coding System (HCPCS), for that sub-classification, based on the Current Procedure Terminology (CPT) codes. The CPT was developed and maintained by the American

Medical Association (AMA) to provide identifying codes that accurately describe medical, surgical and diagnostic services and procedures that healthcare providers use. The second to the fifth column of the exhibit show the amounts charged by the service provider, what was approved by CMS, how much will be paid by CMS to the provider and the amount that may be charged to your supplemental insurer or yourself. There are deductibles that apply when determining how much you will need to pay for all of medical services and drugs that you receive in a particular year.

Exhibit 16.1. A typical billing notice from CMS for a Medicare patient

CMS			Medicare Summary Notice	
Services Provided	Amount Charged	Medicare Approved	Medicare Paid Provider	You may be billed
Emergency dept visit (99285)	$492.00	$161.79	$70.35	$91.44
Electrocardiogram report (93010)	$46.00	$8.41	$6.73	$1.68
Office/outpatient visit, new (99203)	$188	$92.48	$73.98	$18.50
Office/outpatient visit, Est (99213)	$122.00	$61.15	$48.92	$12.23

If a device is already used in services and has HCPCS codings and yours can serve as a replacement, the provider will be able to compare the profit margin it would have by performing the procedure with your medical device instead of the device it presently uses, and then decide whether to replace the presently-used device with your device for future procedures.

If you have invented a device for use in a new procedure, you should first request that AMA grant you a CPT code for the procedure. Then, you should request CMS to evaluate this new procedure and to establish the amount that Medicare will approve and pay to the provider. The creation of a new code and introduction of a new item for reimbursement is time consuming and expensive.

Then, private insurers may follow by establishing their own reasonable and customary rates for the use of the procedure. Only if approvals for the coding and reimbursement of your device have been obtained will the providers consider purchasing it.

For FDA to approve your device, the effectiveness and safety of your device are of utmost importance. However, the medical need for the device is the first consideration of CMS when setting the reimbursement rate.

In the case of hemodialysis care, the Medicare Modernization Act requires the Secretary of the Department of Health and Human Services to issue a report to Congress that describes in detail the establishment of a fully bundled Prospective Payment System for patients with End Stage Renal Disease by 2011. The System to establish the reimbursement for hemodialysis will account for such factors as the current base rate of $235 per treatment, a facility level adjustment for the wage index, and patient-level adjustments for age, gender, body surface area, low body-mass index, and duration of replacement therapy. The chief Medical Officer of CMS emphasizes that a "quality incentive program" will accompany the new payment structure (11). *"Instead of paying only on the basis of quantity,"* he has said, *"Medicare will also begin rewarding dialysis providers on the basis of quality standards, such as how well they manage patients' side effects."*

Payments for dialysis come from three sources (9):
1. Medicare (the Federal insurance program). CMS sets the reimbursement rate and pays about 80% of that rate to dialysis clinics for 75% of US dialysis patients.
2. Medicaid (insurance available through states for those who have limited incomes and assets). About 10% of all dialysis patients have only Medicaid as insurance.
3. Private insurance, such as an employer group health plan (EGHP). About 10% of dialysis patients have private insurance. Clinics charge EGHP two to ten times the Medicare-allowed rates. What private insurance pays is a closely-held secret, but the reimbursement, on average, would be twice Medicare's rate.

Under many current healthcare plans, providers are paid for each service performed. Thus, providers have a strong financial motivation to perform as many services as possible. The concerns about malpractice may also lead to over-prescribing and over-utilizing healthcare services.

Health Technology Assessments (HTA) now constitute the driving force of changes in the delivery of healthcare (7). Regulatory agencies, government and private sector payers, managed care organization, hospitals and healthcare networks are some of the organizations that undertake HTA s. Regulatory agencies, such as the FDA, want information and/or advice to help it decide whether to permit the commercial use of a particular drug, device or technology . Healthcare payers want to know whether technologies should be included in health benefits plans or disease management programs . They use HTA to address such issues as coverage and reimbursement for use of medical devices and pharmaceutical products. Clinicians and patients want to know whether it is appropriate to use certain technologies for the particular clinical needs of patients . Hospitals, healthcare networks and group purchasing organizations use HTA to decide whether to acquire and manage certain technolog ies. Your company and investors can use HTA to help decide product development, marketing, venture funding, acquisitions and divestiture issues.

In recent years, " **Value Based P urchasing**," also known as " **Pay-for-Performance**," is being implemented by many private insurers and CMS to improve the quality of healthcare and to slow the rate of growth of healthcare costs by linking compensation to providers to their certain performance measures (12). California now has the largest P4P program in the country (2). However, there are not sufficient data to fully determine whether P4P programs , that we re just adopted, do improve healthcare and reduce cost s. For P4P programs, you should give particular attention to the subject of h ow your product will influence the performance measures that are used to quantify the improved care for patients.

At present, President Obama and powerful members of Congress are making plans to remake the US healthcare system. *"What happens during the next 25 weeks* (in Federal regulations) *could affect the* (medical device) *industry for the next 25 years ,"* has stated Steve Ubl, President and CEO of AdvaMed, in 2009 (3). Changes in the methodologies used to assess the effectiveness of medical therapies, 510(k) reform and removal of injury lawsuit protection for PMA - approved devices may be on the way.

In summary, i f your product is an improvement of an existing product, healthcare providers can use the approved fee to pay for the use of your product . For a product that provides a new service, you should incorporate your knowledge of CMS , HTA and P4P into a system to gather evidence -based information for you   and to gain coverage from private and public healthcare payers.

16.2. Market Characteristics of Medical Devices and Pharmaceutical Products

The wide spectrum of customers and inte   rmediaries has disrupted the traditional sales relationship between sales rep   resentatives of medical device companies on one side and patients and physicians on the other side.

Education   Education of users   is still   an important way to   get physicians to know about the product as you introduce it to the market. Courses, workshops and conferences to publicize products are becoming less popular with physicians because of federal regulation   of marketing ethics and the time and cost   to them in being away from their office s. With the   growth in use of the   internet, on -site activities are being replaced by online institutes   , enabling physician to attend lectures, seminars, demonstration of products and procedures and   receive comprehensive training and   follow   educational programs without leaving their offices. Digital marketing is a trend that medical device and pharmaceutical companies can use to   leverage internet technology to improve their relationships and interactions with customers (10).

Patients can exert significant influence on the purchase decision, as evidenced by   the extents we see in   patient-targeted television and magazine advertisements. Of course , the influence of a patient would also depend on whether his or her insurance pays for the purchase or use of your product . Communication of medical product companies with patients on the web and through digital marketing is actively pursued   . They set up websites to help patients understand the causes of their medical problem s, treatment options, the   product's pros and cons, and information about health and disease recovery with use of the product.

Product Lifecycle   The lifecycle of your product has three phases: Introduction, Growth, and Maturity and New Product s (Fig. 16.2) . In the Introduction phase, the product   must "support itself" to   varying degrees with increasing numbers of sale successes and by painstakingly building a reputation for quality and trustworthiness   . Evidence-based information should be avail   able for your customers to assist in their purchase decision . Resources are allocated for you to carry out promotion and training activities, such as on   -line symposia and workshops for education, advertising in magazines and televisions, and training of the sales force.

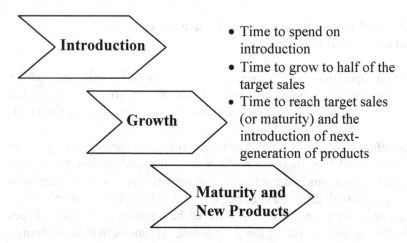

- • Time to spend on introduction
- • Time to grow to half of the target sales
- • Time to reach target sales (or maturity) and the introduction of next-generation of products

Fig. 16.2. The product life cycle. It is described by three times that appear in the right upper corner.

As your sale s increase to a much higher level during the Growth Phase, you should invest further because technology in the field moves quickly, a product life cycle can be short, and even a successful product can be overtaken by your competitor . More real life evidence should be collected during the Introduction and Growth phase that further demonstrates the cost/effectiveness of your product to customers . During the Growth and Matur ity phases, your company can introduce a new and more powerful product to help your company continue its dominant position in the market

Healthcare needs are not driven solely by economy. The demand for medical devices or pharmaceutical products is based on personal health, insurance polic ies and government rules and funding. The key is to sell your customers on the benefits of your product that differentiates it from those of your competitors . Marketing involves communication with your customers . You need to ensure maximum exposure for your new product by making each sale representative not only a spokesperson for your company, but also a specialist in your product 's field . Your websites need to be interest ing to patients and physicians, especially the explanation or description of how your product differs from those of your competitors. Only then will your selling message gain credibility.

Pricing   Your product's price may be based on the cost to manufacture your product, the manufacturing overhead, and your patent position. The economics of your product to hospitals and managed care organizations needs to be considered. If price is one of your advantages, that is great. However, remember that you need service and quality to keep your competitors away and to secure your customer relationships for the future. Evidence of the cost/effectiveness of your product should be considered when setting the price of your product.

Table 16.1. A Comparison of Marketing and Sales Practices, Historical versus 21st Century

Historical	21st Century
Physicians and Hospitals	Multiple Customers
Physician-Focused Teams	Teams with Focus on Patients, Payers, Prescribers and Policymakers
Hard Sale	Well-differentiated Products and Evidence-based Sales
One Size Fits All	Segmentation Based on Functionalities and Geographies
Sales Representatives	Specialists
Prescribers-focused Messaging with Emphasis on Efficacy and Safety	Value-based Messaging Targeted to Payers, Policymakers and Key Opinion Leaders (KOL)
Low Strategic Communication Content	High Strategic Communication Content
Advertisements	Advertisements and Digital Marketing
National	Segmentation, Regional, National and International
Cost and Benefit Pricing	Evidence-Based Pricing, Service and Quality
Silo Approach with Some Collaboration between Marketing and Sales	Collaboration among Management, Engineering, Marketing, Sales and Servicing

The European market has been moving toward greater evidence-based pricing for medical devices and pharmaceutical products. Experts in the US are calling for the use of comparative research of effectiveness to help policy makers determine whether certain therapies and tests are reasonable or necessary. However, there is one unique aspect of US healthcare. It is that the United States has a strong emphasis on patient-doctor relationships. In this aspect, the doctor can recommend a product regardless of its price. CMS prohibits the doctor from considering costs in most coverage decisions as CMS wants to preserve the patient-doctor relationship, while ensuring that patients have reasonable access to new, innovative technologies (8).

Segmentation   Healthcare is segmented. The needs of young patients may differ from those of senior patients. Thus, your marketing strategy needs to be segmented to suit the need of the various populations. Each state may have a different healthcare policy and offer different incentives to users and payers of your product. To optimize your marketing operation, you need to regionalize the allocation of your marketing resources. Similar consideration should be made when you expand your operation internationally.

Key Market Characteristics   To highlight the points made in this section, we summarize the key characteristics of marketing practices in Table 16.1 by contrasting what companies did in the past with what they do in the 21st Century.

16.3. Customer Relationship Management (CRM)

CRM is the management of customer information and its flow for your marketing and sales activities involving current and prospective customers (1). As illustrated in Fig. 16.3, the personnel in management, marketing, sales, servicing and engineering utilize the information from CRM to work collaboratively to assure that all customers are satisfied with your company's products and services (1). The CRM software processes and organizes information about customers and customer interactions for easy access by various company departments. The goal of CRM is to enable the company to gain an understanding of the needs of customers in order to obtain new customers, retain current customers, conduct targeted marketing and generate new products.

Communication is the key to the success of CRM. Every interaction with a customer should be treated as an opportunity to make a new sale, build loyalty and emphasize the benefits of your products. To best manage customer relations, it is imperative that you integrate all your departmental efforts from the perspective of customers. An analysis of customer interaction by CRM can generate business insights, drive customer demand and assure a good ROI.

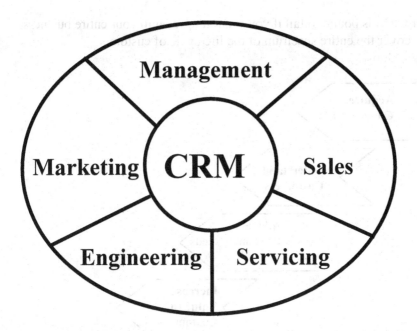

Fig. 16.3. People using CRM and collaboration for success.

The life cycle of a customer relationship involves the five steps depicted in Fig. 16.4. You acquire new customers or patients for your product when it is introduced . You need to promote the benefits of your product to patients and illustrate its cost and effectiveness to customers . Similarly, you will examine whether your product really address the needs of customers. In the meantime, you will work to increase the value of your product to customers . By showing the benefits of using your product and its high use value for patient healthcare, you will have a good chance to retain your current customers and acquire additional new customers.

A CRM initiative is successful only because it:

- Focuses on one specific strategic business issue
- Has clearly defined responsibilities and measurable goals
- Has appropriate organizational structures and team collaboration
- Sets clear customer strategies

Your CRM is bound to fail if you w ant it to revamp your entire business or to cover the entire spectrum of the life cycle of customer relationships.

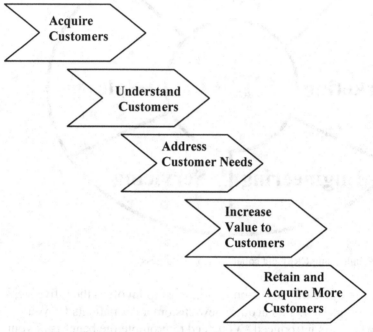

Fig. 16.4. Life cycle of customer relationships

To assure the success of CRM, you need to be diligent with the following assignments to company personnel:

- Management: Assurance of collaboration and goal setting on CRM
- Engineering: Design of cost/effective products and the development of new products
- Servicing: Responsive service for customer retention and intelligence gathering in the field
- Marketing
  - o Messaging, workshops, education programs and digital marketing
  - o Segmentation and targeting
  - o Advertising
  - o Promotional materials

- o   Interaction with Key Opinion Leaders
- o   Gathering patient stories
- o   Public relation
- o   Competitive intelligence
- Sales
  - o   Training programs for sale   representatives   to
    become specialists
  - o   Relationship selling to physicians, hospitals and
    managed care organizations
  - o   Marketing to professionals

16.4. Marketing Ethics and Legal Compliance

Marketing ethically is now a key concern of all medical companies   .
Because of the large retainer payments or gifts   , which they   gave to
surgeons, five major orthopedics companies were fined millions   of
dollars for   the infringement of Federal anti   -trust laws (5). These
companies have been ordered to "clean up their act ." Legal observers
have been   assigned to each company to scrutinize their marketing
activities to ensure strict compliance with the law . The importance of
legal complia nce was further highlighted by a headline news item in
September 2009 that reported that the Feds had fined Pfizer $2.3 billion
and called the drug maker a repeat offender of the illegal promotions of
13 drugs, including Viagra, Zoloft and Lipitor.

Several states have enacted laws to regulate the marketing activities
of medical device and pharmaceutical product companies   . Codes and
guidance on the conduct of these companies   have been released by a
number of trade associations and the   Office of the Inspecto r General,
DHHS. The laws and codes encourage or require the establishment of a
Comprehensive Compliance Program to address concerns   about the
interactions between companies and   healthcare professionals and to
address the public and private sectors' desire to reduce fraud and abuse
(2). A strict limit has been set on gifts, promotional materials items or
activities that a company might give to individual   healthcare
professionals.

There are some exceptions to thi s rule . One is that drugs samples
can be given for free distribution to patients . An other is that financial
support for education forum s can be given   only for those that are

operated by an independent entity. In addition, the compliance program of your marketing and sales plan must be transparent to the public.

16.5. Preparing Your Marketing and Sales Campaign

By this time, you should have some understanding of the complexity of the market for medical devices and pharmaceutical products. While preparing your marketing plan, you should also evaluate whether the marketing of your product is best done by an in-house marketing and sales team or through a well-established distributor. If you elect to do it within, there are three things to consider doing as you move your young company forward by your marketing and sales efforts:

- Have a patient satisfaction survey done and collect evidence on the cost, effectiveness, benefits and safety of your product. Use health models to project the economic benefits from the use of your product. The survey, evidence and models are organized for review and evaluation by prescribers, payers and policy makers.
- Recruit a VP of Sales and Marketing who is well-qualified, experienced, and knowledgeable of the healthcare that you intend your product to serve. If you intend to sell by a distributor, make sure that its sale manager is qualified as if he/she is, in effect, your VP of Sales and Marketing.
- Hire qualified sale representatives and set goals and incentives for them to work with. Train and equip your representatives with the knowledge and presentation required of a specialist.

Once you have built up a customer base, consider the following list for implementation in your expanding marketing and sales campaign (4):

- Acquire CRM software for information processing, set up the process to collect customer information, and provide resources and incentives to assure collaboration among management, engineering, marketing, sales and services.
- Make information on your product available to key opinion leaders (KOL) so that they can inform the medical community of the cost/effectiveness of your product.
- Set up your website with information on causes of diseases, treatment options, your product's technology, and stories of patients.

- Establish education programs, web training and web courses for physicians so they may learn about your product and get in touch with them through relational contact.

If you elect to use a distributor to market and sell your product, go over the prospect list with the distributor and discuss with him/her how prospects on the list should be contacted and who will do it.

Once you reach the mature stage and begin to achieve a satisfactory level of sales, you need to commit to the long term and continual upgrading of your products using input from customers and bringing your marketing and sales campaign to a new high. The following commitments and actions are suggested for your consideration (4):

- On commitment and customer knowledge:
    - o Allocate resources in gathering hospital intelligence on purchasing and product needs
    - o Align hospital purchases with product development, marketing, sales and servicing
    - o Implement a lifecycle approach in the commercialization process
    - o Build collaboration among production, marketing and sales personnel to integrate the knowledge of hospital needs, trends, processes, and economics into the development, marketing and sales effort.
- On action development:
    - o Effectively integrate hospital needs into your company's R&D
    - o Gear the evidence generation processes toward all customers with special consideration to hospitals
    - o Incorporate the product portfolio and positioning strategies with hospital economics and adaptation risks
    - o Incorporate hospital needs and product requirements into marketing materials and the training of sale representatives
    - o Develop and deliver education materials and servicing support to hospital customers
    - o Match product positioning, pricing, and contracting strategies with hospital economics and adoption risk

o   Put into place an account planning process to evaluate and develop a marketing plan for hospital consumers and physicians

o   Train sales representatives and management staff in the tools, tactics, knowle   dge and ethics applicable to hospital's material management and purchasing processes

o   Have sales representatives actively engage hospital customers in product launches and on   -going sales activities.

Concluding Remarks   The spiraling increase in healthcare expenditures in the 21st Century and the availability of so many medical devices and pharmaceutical products for diagnos is and treatment have put pressure on everyone   engaged in sales of these products. You can become the leader in the market for your specialty product if you have a quality and cost-effective product that stand s out from the competition and your marketing campaign can   communicate the benefits of your product to customers.

References
1.   Arnold, J., *Future Pharmaceuticals*, Q3, (2006).
2.   Buckley M. D., and B. J. Flynn, New California Law Required Comprehensive Compliance Programs for Pharmaceutical and Medical Device Companies, www.nutter.com
3.   Filmore, D., S., Levin, *IN VIVO*, Article #2009800091, May (2009).
4.   Hodson, T., S. Inman, *MD&DI*, 30-35 (2009).
5.   Kidwell H., www.medicaldevice-network.com/features/feature40463 Aug. (2008).
6.   Medtronic 2007 Annual Report.
7.   National Library of Medicin   e, Health Technology Assessment 101, www.nlm.nih.gov/nichsr/hta101/ta10104.html March (2008)
8.   Novelli, T., *Med. Device Tech.*, May/June Issue (2009)
9.   Peckham, B., *KidneyTimes.com*, June (2007)
10. Ressi, M. A., www.manhattanresearch.com/presentationresearch
11. Rubin, R., USA Today,   http://www.usatoday.com/news/health/2009-08-23-dialysis_N.htm?POE=click-refer (2009).
12. Wikipedia, en.wiklpedia.org/wiki/Pay_for_performance_(healthcare)

CHAPTER 17

GLOBALIZING YOUR BUSINESS

Globalization during the last thirty years, the result of freer travel and trade, has changed the economy of the world in many ways. It is expected that globalization will speed up further in the next two decades. If your product sells well in the US, you should explore the possibility of selling it globally. To manufacture your product at a lower cost, you may also consider outsourcing it internationally.

The first section of this chapter is intended to provide the operational basics of globalizing the marketing of your product. After seeing the complexity of doing so, a company likes yours would probably choose to engage a trustworthy and established distributor to market your product in a foreign country.

The high healthcare costs and the large number of people who are uninsured certainly pose a big problem for our country. The healthcare expenditures of the Big Four of the European Union are about half of US expenditures (as a % of GDP). The World Health Organization (WHO) ranked these countries high on the quality of healthcare. Do you know anything about the healthcare systems of the United Kingdom, Germany, France and Italy? In view of the fact that China is already the world's manufacturing center, can the US maintain its leadership position in the medical device industry? The BRIC (Brazil, Russia, India and China) are the biggest and fastest growing countries in the Third World. With more purchasing power for this 42% of world population, BRIC are poised to become a large market for medical devices. As a citizen of the medical device community, you should look at globalizing the sales of your product beyond the limits assumed in marketing your own device and outsource its manufacture.

For this reason, the rest of this chapter is devoted to topics, such as the healthcare systems of the UK, Germany, France, Italy, China and Taiwan, the prevalence of diseases throughout the world, the work ethics of the Chinese and Taiwanese, the industrialization of China and Taiwan, the success stories of international alliances, operations in

Canada and Mexico, and the growing market for home medical equipment (HME). They are presented for you not only to find ways of globalizing your business, but also to improve and expand your operation as you adapt to global changes.

17.1. International Operations

Global Market on Medical Devices   According to the International Trade Administration (ITA) of the US, the global market for medical devices had a value of $210 billion in 2008. It is projected to increase to $270 billion by 2012 (20). The market shares of the Big Five of the European Union and the other countries are listed in Table 17.1. The normalization of the market (or revenues) by the population of each country yields the market productivity (revenues or market per capita) of each country shown in the fifth column of the table. As one can see US companies lead the world in the revenues of medical devices and also in market productivity. The US share of the world market has remained at roughly 45~49% in recent years.

Table 17.1. Global population and market share of medical devices

Country	2009 Population (millions)	2008 Global Market* ($billions)	% of Global Market	Market Productivity ($ per capita)
USA	307	$103	48.9%	$335
The Big Five of the European Union	306	$50	23.6%	$163
Japan	127	$35	16.7%	$277
Canada	34	$5	2.2%	$134
Brazil	191	$4	2.1%	$23
China	1,329	$4	2.1%	$3
Australia	22	$2	1.0%	$95
Taiwan	23	$2	1.0%	$87
Mexico	111	$2	.9%	$18
South Korea	48	$2	.9%	$38
India	1,145	$2	.8%	$1
Total of above	**3,643	$210	100%	$58

* Sources: ITA.   ** Total world population: 6,707 millions.

The ITA points out that US, Japan, Germany, France, Italy and UK make up 75% of the medical device market with only 15% of the world's population while China, India, Indonesia, Brazil and Pakistan have about half of the world's population , but consume only about 5% of medical devices globally (20).

In regard to the market productivity of medical device, Taiwan's productivity per capita is $87, not far from the $163 of the Big Five of the European Union and the $134 of Canada.

The total value of US medical device exports in 200 7 was $32 billion with almost 46% of the devices going to the European Union. About 22% went to Japan and other Asian countries . The industry f or medical devices is one of the few USA industries that export more than they import.

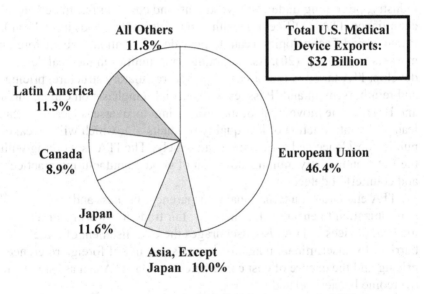

Fig. 17.1. Destination of US medical device exports in 2007.

The Chinese market for medical devices is forecast ed to reach a value of $23 billion in 2011 (1, 3). Currently, it is the second largest medical device market in Asia . China has the potential to be come the largest single -country import market for US medical device exporters . The production and development of high -tech medical equipment in

China continues to be largely small-scale. Fierce competition describes the market in China for medical devices and supplies.

In April, 2008, C. A. Padilla, Under Secretary of Commerce for International Trade, led 15 US companies on a healthcare trade mission to Beiji ng. *"China is a fast -growing market for the U.S. healthcare industry, known for its world-class goods and services. U.S. industry has the potential to raise the standard of medical care in China,* " said Padilla. *"China's pending healthcare reforms will affe ct many American companies doing business in that market—or seeking to do so. A clearer understanding of China's policy environment will enable the U.S. healthcare industry to more easily compete in China, raising the quality and efficiency of medical treatment there."*

Government Support In global trade, I TA is the key US government agency engaged in strengthening the competitiveness of US industry, promoting trade and investment, and ensuring fair trade and compliance. ITA's Office of Health and C onsumers Goods has a Health Products and Technologies Team to provide information about foreign markets to industry (20). As marketing opportunities in medical device develop, ITA target s four areas —quality, reg ulatory structure, pricing and reimbursement and IP issues with special emphasis on China, India and Brazil. The move ment of manufacturing to overseas locations can lead to the introduction of low quality products , which will weaken public confidence and a ffect trade adversely. The ITA is working with the FDA on industry training, adoption of good manufacturing practices and counterfeit detection.

ITA encourages international transparency, fairness and harmonization to ensure that there is fair trade in world markets for medical devices . ITA also discourages the establishment of trade barriers by discrimination against imports, the use of foreign reference pricing and the excuse of cost containment . The ITA can assist you to overcome barriers related to:

- Excessive tariff and custom regulations (reporting it to www.export.gov/tcc, TCC: Trade Competitive Center)
- Discriminatory rules of origin
- Burdensome standards
- Lack of IP right protection (filing a complaint with www.stopfakes.gov, STOP: Strategy Targeting Organized Piracy)

- Non-transparent government procurement.

As described previously, SBA is very supportive for globalization. Its affiliates conduct courses on global ent   erprise, export ing and importing to help your staff learn more about globalization.

Many European governments are taking   a more active role to support entrepreneurial developments . For example, if you   decide to develop a high-tech company in France and are looking for VC funding, the French government w ill guarantee 75% of the VC investment . The governments of many Asian countries are investing in the development of their medical device and biotech industr y. Government investment s made by China and Taiwan are detailed in Section 17.6.

Foreign Patents and Counterfeit Prevention   The legal protection afforded to a patent that has been approved by the USPTO applies only to market s in the United States and its territories   . The global market position of your med   ical inventions may   justify filing your patent internationally as well.

Most countries   are members of The Patent Cooperation Treaty (PCT). A US applicant can now file one "international" application in English to the USPTO . This is not a substitute for pa tent applications to other countries. What you gain with the PCT filing is an   additional 18 months in which to file your patent application to the patent office   s of other countries.

For a European patent , you first apply for approval from   the European Patent Office. When it is approved, you can then pay one large lump sum to have all countries in the European Union grant you the patent right. If you prefer, you can pay the patent filing fees for a limited number of large European countries to protect your i ntellectual property right in those countries . If you want to include the Asian market, you will need to apply for patents in Japan, China, Taiwan, Singapore, etc   . This multinational process is further complicated by   those non-English speaking countries li ke Japan or China , which   only process patents applications that are written in their language.

Counterfeit copies of your products are usually not done under the good manufacturing practice prescribed by FDA and of low quality. The counterfeiter may even duplicate your labels with the result that users may send the imitation products to your company for repair or refund . Other than government effort, y ou should consider adopting additional protection for your device by making it difficult to copy.

Regulatory Affairs and Reimbursements To market your device
to the European Union, obtaining a classification from the European
Medicine Agency is the first step (12). That agency's four
classifications, I, IIa, IIb and III, are not much different from those of the
FDA. The classifications are governed by 14 rules and 24 articles of the
Medical Devices Directive (93/42/EEC). For other products, the Active
Implantable Medical Directive (90/385/EED) and In vitro Diagnost ic
Directive (98/97/EC) may apply.

Once it has been approved by European Medicine Agency, the
medical device agencies of some EU nations review the device classi -
fication again and set the reimbursement. You will need to obtain a CE
(Comformité Européenne) marking to confirm that the product meets all
health and safety requirement of their directives . A "notified body" that
is qualified by the EU nations must be involved in the conformity
assessment process if you wish to sell your product in the EU.

With a mandate to promote cost-effective technologies and to work
on eliminating harmful or ineffective technologies, the Health
Technology Assessment Agencies of EU nations work together to
facilitate the exchange of information and harmonization. On the othe r
hand, the EU Treaty respects the national right of each member to
operate its own healthcare system. EU member nations have independent control o f their pricing and payment method s. Although almost all
of the countries have implemented evidence -based medicine, each
country's pricing, market access and enforcement arrangements differ.

To do it correctly, you and your distributor in the EU may have to
work with a notified body to collect all appropriate documentation and
to ensure that you fulfill all regulatory requirements for submi ssion to
the appropriate agencies for classification approval, CE marking and
device reimbursement.

The regulatory agency of Japan is the Pharmaceutical and Medical
Safety Bureau, Ministry of Health and Welfare . Taiwan's regul atory
agency is the Taiwan Food and Drug Administration . For China, you
may need to submit your device approval application, if the device is
class I or II, to the Pharmaceutical and Medical Safety Bureau of the
Provincial Government . The application for C lass III needs to be
submitted to the National Pharmaceutical and Medical Safety Bureau .
Although China's rules and regulations for medical devices bear
considerable similarities to those for the US and EU, data on clinical

trials of Class II medical devic es, which may not be required by the US FDA, must be included in Chinese submissions.

Complications may arise when you market to countries in Latin America that may not have full fledged regulatory systems.

Issues on Distribution and Marketing   There are   many options available to you to distribute and market your product in a foreign country. You may set up a subsidiary and hire employees to   sell the product. Paying   commissions to   sales representatives or permitting someone to set up a franchise are other   ways of generating sales. You could also engage a distributor, set up a joint venture or license a foreign company to sell the product.

In this process, you will sign a distribution and marketing agreement with some foreign distributor   for it to sell and distribute the product . Certain aspects of the agreement are similar to   those in the   licensing agreement that was   examined in Section 13.4. Below are   additional points to consider:

- On performance and commitment of the distribution entity
  - o Do d ue diligence of the foreign distributor 's business plan regarding distribution. Also, do a   credit check, contact all references, and review past performance.
  - o Determine the extent of the distributor's commitment to the required facilities and staff . What is the m arketing obligation regarding efforts and expenditures?
  - o What will be the t raining frequency and who will pay the training expenses?
  - o What will be the arrangements about   keeping, monitoring and auditing sales record   s, customer information, and competition?
- On sales exclusivity and performance
  - o Consider the exclusivity on a full line of products or a partial list.
  - o Negotiate the n umber of , and investment in, demos, shows and visits.
  - o Who does (and approves) the marketing planning?
  - o Consider p ricing discount s, volumes   goals, payment schedules and incentives.
  - o What l imitations should there be on   the distributor to prevent it from offer "competing" products

- On renewal and termination
    - o What should be the length of the initial term?
    - o Should the contract automatically renew or expire without a confirmation of renewal?
    - o Consider the following grounds for termination: breach of contract, cessation of business, bankruptcy, or deficiency in performance.
    - o What about notices, resolutions, and a transition to non-renewal or termination?
- On financial arrangements
    - o You will need a pricing and payments schedule.
    - o Who pays custom duties, value added tax (VAT), sales and other product taxes?
    - o Who controls the price schedule, timing, and resale?
    - o What about the cost of insurance cost and broker fees?
- On management issues
    - o You will need to make arrangements for shipping, warehousing, responsibility for product in transit, FOB or FCA.
    - o What about the application for import and export licenses?
    - o What about necessary product servicing, customer support and warranty management?
    - o You will need to limit liabilities and establish caps in both amount and period.
- On ownership of rights and properties
    - o Making, manufacturing, copying, modifying and marketing the products
    - o Enhancements, documentations, and their translation
    - o Records and documentations on property ownership
    - o Require timely transfer of properties, documentation and translation materials at termination or non-renewal.
    - o Ownership, use and registration of trademarks
- On dispute resolutions
    - o What are the governing laws and under which jurisdiction will your efforts be?
    - o What will be the role for mediation, binding or non-binding arbitration?

17.2. Healthcare in the UK, Germany, France and Italy

Each country in the European Union operates its own national he alth system. For example, healthcare in UK , which has a population of 61 million, is provided primarily by its National Health Services with an annual budget of about $160 billion (6). Almost all treatments and drugs that NHS offers are free of charge . England does have private insurance that is paid by employers and individuals to supplement their healthcare at a cost of around 10% to 20% of total healthcare expenditures. 92% of in -patients have stated that they are satisfied with their treatment and 87% have said that they are satisfied with their general practioners.

In 2004, the NHS began a major pay -for-performance initiative that is known as Quality and Outcomes Framework . General practi tioners receive a 20% funding increase from the previous level to invest in staff and technology in order to increase the use of electronic health records and the electronic prescription service . The data showed that the pay -for-performance improves the healthcare quality for 10 chronic diseases.

Germany has an insurance-based healthcare system for all of its residents (4). 90% of residents are enrolled in public, non -profit health insurance plans. They have a free choice of heal th insurance and health providers: PPO, HMO and primary care . There is one standard list of benefits for all insured persons.

The healthcare system s of France and Italy were ranked 1 st and 2nd by World Health Organization in 2001 because of their universal coverage, responsive healthcare providers, patients and provider freedoms and the health and longevity of the population . The French law protects a patient's choice of practitioner and guarantees the physician's control o f medical decision -making (5). The French government grants the private insurers the right to run its healthcare funds. The French system makes it more difficult for insurers to deny coverage for preexisting conditions or to those who are not in good health. At $3,500 per capita, the French healthcare system is one of the costliest in Europe, but still far below the cost of $6,100 per person in the US.

The Italian healthcare system is a decentralized version of the UK's NHS. Despite the WHO's high ranking of the Italian system, only about 20% of Italians are satisfied with the quality of their care (13).

17.3. The Healthcare Systems of Taiwan and China

In 1995, Taiwan formed the National Health Insurance (NHI) to provide universal coverage to its citizens (7). The working population pays half and their employers pay the other half to a government-run insurer. Other persons pay a flat rate. In this system, every citizen has equal access to healthcare—free choice of doctors with no waiting times. The system encourages a great deal of competition among healthcare providers. NHI offers a comprehensive benefit package that covers preventive medical services, prescription drugs, dental services, Chinese medicine and home nurse visits. Each person has a Smart Card. Its use enables the physician to see the patient's computerized medical history and prescription record. Then, a prescription is provided and the medical bill calculated for automatic payment. As a result, the cost to administer the healthcare system is 2%, the lowest in the world. Taiwan spends a little over 6% of GDP, and less than $900 per person, for health coverage.

The improved healthcare has led to an improvement in the life expectancy, infant mortality rate and maternal mortality rate in Taiwan to bring it to the level of Western countries. Patient satisfaction is in the range of 70%. However, a number of issues concerning the quality of healthcare require solution are being discussed (18). First the government is not taking in enough money to cover the services that it provides. With so many patients wanting to see a doctor right away, the doctor limits the visit to two to five minutes per patient and works long hours. The large hospitals become larger as patients flog to large medical centers, which are perceived to have the best doctors, the best equipment, and the best facilities. Some hospitals are run like businesses with an emphasis on revenue and incentives for doctors that are based on revenues generated. Although the Taiwan system limits the availability of new medical devices or pharmaceutical products for patients, many hospitals are equipped with the best state-of-the-art medical equipment. (Patients are allowed to pay for additional services that are not covered by the national insurance.) The reimbursements rates are considered by some to be the lowest in the world. In Taiwan, hospitals also operate their own pharmacies for out-patients services. As a result, the profit margin, rather than the optimal treatment for the patient, may influence the type of drug that is prescribed.

By the end of 2008, the migration of workers to China's urban areas had caused its urban population to reach 46% of the 1.3 billion Chinese. The income of urban residents is five times of rural residents. Urban health insurance was initiated in 1999 to provide broad coverage for urban residents. The insurance cost is shared by employers and individuals, with each worker paying 2% of his or her wages and employers paying 6%. In rural areas, On the other hand, even with farmers paying a small fee and public funds paying the balance, only 25% of China's rural population is covered by rural health insurance. As a result, all rural primary health services are provided on a fee-for-service basis.

On the provider side, major hospitals in China are operated by the Department of Health at the national and provincial level. They are well equipped and have qualified doctors. Public hospitals have a high degree of autonomy and are expected to generate revenue sufficient to cover 70% to 90% of their expenses. China has only a few private hospitals for its residents. (Some are built for the treatment of foreign workers and their families living in China.) Many county hospitals are being constructed to serve the people in the countryside. Even with the Central Government of China attempting to allocate more resources to county hospitals, the lack of qualified healthcare providers throughout the nation makes it a challenge for the county hospitals to provide a full service to patients.

17.4. World Prevalence of Diseases

In this section, we examine the prevalence of end-stage renal disease (ESRD), chronic obstructive pulmonary disease (COPD) and other diseases in the world. In Table 17.2., we show for four countries, USA, Japan, Taiwan and China, the number of ESRD patients taking or requiring dialysis and the annual cost of hemodialysis treatments per patient. For comparison purposes, the country's GDP per capita appears in the Table's fifth column. One conclusion that can be drawn for these four countries is that HD treatment costs are higher than the GDP per capita. However, the out-of-pocket payments of citizens in the US, Japan and Taiwan are small.

China's low labor cost is responsible for a significantly lower cost of delivery of HD treatments. On the other hand, the number of potential patients and the low GDP per capita present an enormous challenge for

China in its delivery of HD care to its patients. This affordability problem is further exacerbated for rural residents of China because of their lack of health insurance and their low income, which is one fifth of that of urban residents (as reflected in their GDP per capita of $1,167).

Table 17.2. The prevalence of hemodialysis and its cost of treatment.

Country	Prevalence* (per million)	Dialysis Patients	Annual Cost for HD treatments	GDP per capita
USA	1,300	400,000	$72,000	$46,716
Japan	2,000	280,000	$50,000	$38,559
Taiwan	3,040	70,000	$20,000	$17,040
China	2,000	2,600,000	$6,400	$3,315

* The prevalence in Japan is used to estimate the number of patients in China who require hemodialysis treatments. Current number of patients receiving treatment regularly may be in the range of 100,000 to 150,000.

For the year 2001, It has been estimated that the total number of dialysis patients throughout the world was 1.1 million in the year 2001 (14). A prevalence rate of 28 per million was used to estimate the patient population in China in that year. Recent health data from China shows that its prevalence rate may be comparable to that of Japan and Taiwan. If this is combined with an annual 5% increase in dialysis population for other countries, the number of patients who required dialysis in 2008 can be estimated to be as high as 3.5 million.

The US allocates 1.4% of its healthcare expenditures to provide hemodialysis for 0.13% of its population. When a universal health plan was introduced, Taiwan's rate of prevalence of hemodialysis rose to become the highest in the world. As a result, 11% of the Taiwan government's health expenditures in 2008 were for hemodialysis treatments for 0.3% of its population (26). If all patients in China were to receive dialysis treatment, then the total expenditures would be $17 billion. If China's healthcare expenditures are calculated at 3% of its GDP, the hemodialysis cost for 0.2% of its population with ESRD would be 14% of China's total health expenditures.

Disproportional expenditures as that on ESRD are bound to show up for the treatments of chronic pulmonary obstructive disease (COPD) because too many Asians are heavy smokers. For example, there are more than 320 million smokers in China (67% of its adult males and 4% of its adult females). In 2000, the total cost of COPD and other smoking-related diseases in China amounted to more than $5 billion and

COPD was the second leading cause of mortality in China, trailing only cerebrovascular disease (19).

These COPD patients are bound to become short of breath and require assistance in breathing. The sheer number of COPD patients indicates that the impact o f COPD on healthcare may be even more severe than the SARS epidemic. During the SARS epidemic, many hospitals ran out of ventilators to provide ventilatory support to SARS patients. Although it may be absurd to assume that each smoker will eventually acquire a ventilator, the price tag for 320 million ventilators at today's lowest price of $4,000/ventilator comes to $128 billion or 3% of China's 2008 GDP.

The healthcare problems of patients with diabetes, AIDS and many other diseases are equally daunting. We need to extend the "**One World One Dream**" vision of the 2008 Olympics to citizens of the world , companies of medical devices and pharmaceutical products and governments to encourage working together to achieve the dream of resolving the many health problems that endanger mankind.

17.5. Work Forces of Taiwan and China

West to East   As stated in the National Intelligence Council report on Global Trend 2025, the transfer of global wealth and economic power now underway – from West to East – is without precedent in modern history. What contributes to this shift of the locus of manufacturing and some service industries to Asia? Some obvious factors are:

- Lower labor costs
- Hard working ethics of Asians
- Ingenuity of Asian people
- Government policies
- Generous support from US and Americans.

These five factors are discussed below and the next section covering the fourth item further.

About the Chinese and Taiwanese   To globalize your business, your first step will be to recognize the culture, language and working habits of others so that you can inspire an international workforce to get things done right and to generate profit for your operation.

Chinese have a culture that reaches back more than 5,000 years. The Chinese were so proud of their country that they call ed it their country

中国 (Middle Kingdom) – the country at the center of the world . Ever since the Anglo -Chinese Opium Treaty was signed in 1907, China and its people have been exploited by foreigners and invaded by foreign countries. Together with the internal turmoil caused by warlords and government officials, the Chinese people suffered terrible hardship and extreme poverty during a period of more than 170 years. As a result, the most populous country in the world in 1978 was ranked only 11th with a GDP of $147 billion or 131st with a GDP per capita of $154.

By 2008, China had jumped to 3rd rank in the world with a GDP of $4,401 billion, an increase by a factor of 30 in 30 years. This accomplishment is attributed primarily to the socialist market economy of Mr. Deng Xiaoping and the sweat equity of the people of China . The economic and political policy of the government and the mass of Chinese people drove the nation ahead and created one of the fastest growing economies in the world, and raised significantly the standard of living of the Chinese people.

Many Chinese immigrated to Taiwan in the 17 th Century. Some moved from mainland China to the island around 1949 when the Communists took over mainland China . Taiwanese, with the help of the US government and Americans, made g reat strides in moving their economy forward during the last fifty years.

The people of China and Taiwan are hard working, ingenious, industrious, and peace loving. The author will provide several examples to illustrate these characteristics , which will h elp you to establish working relation ships that can benefit you and the Chinese and Taiwanese who work for you.

The author heard th e following story about the development of a new tennis racket. The chief of an American company that sells sporting goods h ad a new design that promised to increase the power of the tennis racket. He talked to his racket supplier about his design when he was in Taiwan to negotiate a manufacturing contract for the coming year. On the following day he received a prototype of his racket to test. This rapid delivery illustrates the Chinese work ethic and the willingness of Chinese to go the extra mile to satisfy a customer's desire.

Mr. Wang Yung-Ching A highly successful international entrepreneur, Wang, like man y of his fellow countrymen, was a man of strong traditional Chinese work ethic . He labored six days a week and sixteen hours a day . On some 3 00 days each year, he h eld luncheon meetings with his staff who were stationed in Taiwan, China and USA.

At age 16, he started his first entrepreneurial venture , a store that sold rice. Later, he opened a rice -milling factory within 150 feet of another milling factory that was owned by a Japanese merchant. (At that time, Taiwan was under Japanese occupation.) The Jap anese factory operated every day until 6:00 PM, but Wang's factory worked until 10:30 PM at night . Based on each of his customer's ordering history, Wang foresaw when his each customer would need to replenish his rice stocks, and automatically shipped the customer's usual order quantity to him, along with a bill that was payable on the customer's payday . His hard work and this novel customer service enabled Wang not only to overcome many instances of preferential treatments granted by the Japanese merchant, but also to achieve sales far greater than those of his competitor in a short time. This innovative approach to customer service at minimal cost serves as the guiding principle of the management systems that all of his companies employ.

In 1954, the US G overnment set up a program to provide financial aid to private entrepreneurs in Taiwan . Seizing the opportunity, Wang landed a PVC plastic powder production project backed by a US loan . This first entry into the petrochemical business is now known as the Formosa Plastics Group, the largest company in the world in PVC production and processing, with annual revenues of more than $30 billion. This feat earned him the title of "King of Plastics." Employing 94,000 employees, his multi -national petrochemical and electronic enterprises ha ve factories in many cities in Taiwan, China and the United States.

In addition to his business endeavors, Wang established Chang Gung University in 1987 . The School's motto is "Diligence, Perseverance, Frugality and Trustworthine ss". One of its educational objectives is to develop professionals who have solid academic knowledge and practical expertise in order to improve the health of the citizens of Taiwan and to promote the vitality of Taiwanese industries . Because of his philanthropy, this university has the lowest tuition of all private universities in Taiwan . The 5% of the students, who are bright, possess great potential, but are poor, receive full scholarships to pursue their education in medicine, engineering and business m anagement. Many of them are disadvantaged aborigines of Taiwan who go on to become nurses, engineers, managers and doctors. Wang and his brother also established the Chang Gung Memorial Hospital . Its mission is to provide the people of Taiwan with low cost and high quality healthcare.

Wang died in October, 2008 at the age of 92, leaving wealth that was valued by "Forbes" in 2008 at an estimated $6.8 billion. He donated billions of dollars to the foundation that runs the University and the Hospital as a means for Wang and his family to repay society. About five months before his death, he donated $15 million to a disaster relief fund for the regions that were devastated by the 2008 Sichuan Earthquake in China. He is remembered as a healthcare promoter and a "God of Management" who helped vitalize Taiwan's economy and healthcare.

Wang and many Taiwan entrepreneurs owe their success to the assistance that they received from Americans and the US government. Not only was that assistance repaid in the form of job creation in the US, but also by their philanthropic aid to worthwhile causes.

Chinese Americans Many Chinese immigrated to the United States or came for work of a temporary nature. *"The first Chinese was hired in 1865 at approximately $28 per month to do the very dangerous work of blasting and laying ties over the treacherous terrain of the high Sierra,"* said Congressman John T. Doolittle of California in 1999 on the commemoration of a monument to honor the efforts of Chinese in laying the transcontinental railroad. *"By the summer of 1968, 4,000 workers, two thirds of which were Chinese, had built the transcontinental railroad over the Sierras and into the interior plains. On May 10, 1969, the two railroads were to meet at Promontory, Utah in front of a cheering crowd and a band. A Chinese and Irish crew was chosen to lay the final ten miles of track, and it was completed in only twelve hours. Without the effort of the Chinese workers in the building of America's railroads, our development and progress as nation would have been delayed by years."*

In more recent times, many Chinese who possess both wealth and an advanced education have come. Some brought their life savings of a few hundred dollars and others came with a scholarship received from an American university. Some of them become successful entrepreneurs in the US and others returned to China or Taiwan to build their entrepreneurial careers. Here is an example of one such person who became a successful US entrepreneur.

The author's friend, Dr. Naishu Wang, received a medical degree from Chongqing University of Medical Sciences in Chongqing in 1970. She came to the US on a student exchange program for graduate study and received her Ph.D. from Ohio University in 1991. After working as a post -doc at UCSD on research for about two years, she decided to work in industry. When the company she worked for was sold in 1966, she decided to form her own company, Alfa Scientific Designs, Inc (ASD) so that she could do more research and development to s erve patients. She used the equity in he r house and her credit cards to come up $140,000 in funding for ASD. One of her twin daughters served as accountant and the other worked on marketing . They rented 400 square feet of office space in San Diego and bega n operations . Using her previous connection with the *in vitro* diagnostic (IVD) device industry, ASD started to generate revenue within a year by serving as distributor for a number of device manufacturers . Instead of soliciting SBIR or venture capital fund ing, she used her time to generate revenue for the company, but also carried out research and development of IVD devices, which was dear to her heart . Now her company has 12 patents and 300 employees to develop, manufacture and market the most advanced IVD devices for the diagnosis of drug abuse, infectious disease, pregnancy, fertility, cardiac disease and cancer . Her success in building ASD is a reflection of her hard work, her ingenuity, her desire to excel, and her ability to build on what she had , traits that are shared by many Chinese Americans.

Although she often worked sixteen hours a day, she said that the hard work was enjoyable because she knew that getting it done would benefit patients. She started the company as a means to earn a living, but ended with a company that serves people's need s. As a physician and entrepreneur, she sa ys that biomedical engineering entrepreneurship is a career choice that people can become interested and excited in . Some fad areas that many engineers and scientists pursued in the recent past and are pursuing now may fade in time . If you are interested in what you are doing in a discipline that benefits people, only then can hard work become enjoyable . She assure s us that, with ingenuity, hard work and luck, you will succeed.

17.6. Industrialization of Taiwan and China

Taiwan's Development of Industry In 1973, the Industrial Technology and Research Institute (ITRI) was established with the following mission:

- To guide traditional industry in upgrading technology

- To assist the development of newly established industry
- To develop industrial technology professionals
- To promote the global competitiveness of enterprises.

About 60% of ITRI's 6,000 employees have either a Ph.D. or M.S. degree. It has six focus labor atories, one of which is the Biomedical Engineering Laboratory. In 1976, ITRI acquired CMOS technology by a licensing agreement with RCA. Since the transfer of this technology by ITRI to Taiwan, the newly established semi -conductor industry has become Taiwan's most celebrated industry. In 1990, ITRI united 47 domestic manufacturers to form the Notebook Computer Alliance. This Alliance has helped make Taiwan the world's largest notebook computer producer.

Aside from its effect on technology, ITRI's impact on Taiwan's workforce has been enormous. As of 2006, 140,000 of ITRI's 160,000 past employees (or alumni) were working in industry and 60 were CEOs of companies in Taiwan.

The National Science Council of the Taiwan government launched a major biotechnology initiative in 2002. By 2005, annual sales of Taiwan's biotechnology sector reached $4.9 billion and an annual growth rate of 10.4%. Expenditures on biotech R&D by the Taiwan government totaled $485 million in 2005. In 2008, the Challenge 2008 National Development Plan called for an investment of $76 billion to improve living standards and the business and investment climate in Taiwan. It sought to transform Taiwan into a "Green Silicone Island" with the objective of making Taiwan a producer of at least 15 of the best products or technologies in the world.

According to the Global Competitiveness Report 2006/2007 published by the World Economic Forum, Taiwan rank ed 9th of the 125 countries included in the study. In Asia, Taiwan ranks 2 [nd], behind only Japan.

Taiwan's Education Taiwan is not only constructing many more universities for the education of their citizens, but also expanding university research. The Academic Ranking of World Universities ranks seven universities in Taiwan among the top 100 Asian u niversities. This number is comparable to the listing of 31 universities of Japan, which has a population of about five times that of Taiwan.

In 1980, Chuan Yuan Christian University established an undergraduate department of biomedical engineering. The a uthor participated in the first workshop set up in 1982   to help the Taiwan government prepare a long-range plan for the development of medical devices and a biotech industry under the leadership of Dr. Han   Wei. Overall, Taiwan has established undergraduate and graduate programs in biomedical engineering in   approximately 10 national and private universities.

IP Protection in Taiwan   Another issue of interest to the readers of this book is the protection of intellectual property in Taiwan   . The United States had referred Taiwan as a "safe haven for pirates" and was particularly concerned with these three issues:

- The establishment of an Intellectual Property Court,
- The protection of intellectual property right on university campuses,
- The specificity of Taiwan Copyright Law.

By 2008, the Court was in operation, the Taiwan Ministry of Education had adopted positive measures to assure IP protection, and progress ha d been made in the establishment of a specific copyright law.   The United States Trade Representative (USTR) pointed out that the enforcement of intellectual property right s under the rule of law   during the last eight years had now made Taiwan a land of innovation and R&D . As a result, the USTR announced in early 2009 that Taiwan had been removed from its "general watch list" of violations of intellectual property rights.

Taiwan's Medical Device Industry   The medical device sector in Taiwan has an annual production value   of $2 billion (adjusted to the year 2008). Several comments by Andrew Wee, Research   Analyst at Frost & Sullivan, on "Taiwan's Leap to Medical Device Manufacturing" are reproduced below (23):

- *Taiwan's location in Asia and its established trade links with Japan, Korea and South East Asia have al   lowed it to gain a foothold in manufacturing medical devices for the region. Due to the relatively young age of the industry, most of the manufacturing revolves around safety syringes, medical disposables, blood glucose monitors, electronic and infra   -red thermometers, and home use medical appliances.*
- *With no lack of talents and funding, Taiwan's medical device industry has around 397 medical device companies, employing more than 14,000 people in Taiwan.*

- *The majority of medical devices exported from Taiwan are focused on powered mobility aids and 5 out of the top 10 medical device exporters are in this business. It is estimated that Taiwanese manufacturers supply up to 70% of the global market for powered mobility aids.*
- *Several Taiwan companies have in rece nt years established themselves as leading medical device companies. Several of these companies have established an international team with marketing offices and distributors spread worldwide. New start-up companies are also banking on more innovation and a higher degree of research, allowing them to come up with high quality devices which will allow them to compete on equal grounds with global companies.*
- *Medical device companies in Taiwan have conducted more manufacturing activities than research and devel opment over the past few years. However with the increasing competition and costs of production, these companies are now expanding research facilities and investing in them.*

China Development China's jump into the position of the World's third most produc tive country is unprecedented in the history of globalization. What the country has accomplished in the last 30 years is illustrated by the following list of accomplishments:

- The no.1 foreign country in ownership of US treasury bonds.
- The second largest e ngine for world economic growth, after the United States.
- The world's manufacturing center . It mak es 40% of the world's air-conditioners, 50% of television sets and refrigerators, 60% of garments and 80% of toys. It is projected that China will rank number 1 in exports for the year 2009.
- The first choice f or investment by large multi -national corporations, as reported by the United Nations Conference on Trade and Development.
- The only country to have raised hundreds of millions people out of poverty.
- Has 18 institutions of higher education that made the list of the top 100 institutions in Asia.

- The builder of **Three Gorges Dam**, the <u>largest hydroelectric power station</u> in the world and the largest electricity-generating plant of any kind.
- The second largest importer of oil in the world.
- The largest steel producer in the world.
- Has 300 million cell phone users and 87 million Internet users. About 780 million Chinese email messages pass through the Internet each week.

The Chinese have accomplished the foregoing and much more by hard work, ingenuity and a high savings rate. The government is committed to the establishment of a harmonious society (和谐社会) for its people and the world.

Economic Stimuli of China   Even though the 2008 world financial crisis caused about 20 million of Chinese to lose their jobs, the government has already established the following two bold initiatives with their government reserve:

- A \$585 billion two-year economic stimulus package to boost growth and domestic demand. It has four major components, including large-scale government spending for infrastructures, industrial restructuring and rejuvenation, in addition to scientific research and a social safety net.
- An investment of \$72 billion in 2008 to cover the construction of infrastructure projects in water, gas and electricity, as well as in agricultural technology, education and medical services and subsidies for rural residents,

These initiatives and the Western Development Plan that was started in 2002 will generate many more jobs for Chinese citizens, increase domestic consumption, and increase imports from abroad. As David Dollar of the World Bank noted on an East Asia and Pacific blog: *"The global economic crisis is an opportunity for China to reorient its growth model away from so much dependence on exports and industry, and more toward dependence on domestic needs. This includes private consumption, but also includes public spending on social services and on enhancing the quality of life through environmental clean-up and public transportation. The stimulus package is certainly a start in this direction."*

17.7. Alliance of American, Taiwanese and Chinese Companies

Taiwan as a PC-manufacturing Powerhouse The ingenuity of
Taiwan's entrepreneurs in semi -conductor industry is illustrated by the
following excerpts from Intel's Paul S. Otellini's story of Stan Shih, the
engineer who turned Taiwan into a PC-manufacturing powerhouse (15).

*"Thirty years ago, computer manufacturing was an arcane
business inv olving a handful of companies building a small number
of large and expensive machines a year, mostly using components
made in -house. Stan Shih, a mild -mannered Taiwanese electrical
engineer working on gadgets such as desktop calculators, saw a
better way. Among the first to recognize the potential of
microprocessors (those tiny computer chips that today are the brains
of billions of products from cars to cell phones), Shih saw how
marrying cheap chips with efficient manufacturing could spread
computing power to the masses. It was the right idea —so right that
Shih ended up creating a globally recognized brand of personal
computers (Acer), kindling a booming high -tech industry in Taiwan
(where many of the components in the world's electronic devices are
now made), and inspiring a generation of Taiwanese entrepreneurs.*

*At Acer, Shih took a radically different approach to PC making.
By focusing on supply -chain optimization and cultivating a vibrant
ecosystem of tightly clustered component suppliers, Acer was abl e to
introduce new technology faster and at lower prices than
competitors. As early as 1986, for example, then -little-known Acer
released the world's second PC based on Intel's 386 microprocessor,
just one month after industry giant Compaq.*

*Thanks in no s mall part to Shih's pioneering example, the
integrated-supply-chain model is now the hallmark of PC contract
manufacturing worldwide. In other words, he's a big reason why your
PC costs $1,000, not $10,000. Under his stewardship, Acer grew into
a top-five PC brand. But Shih's innovations didn't stop there. Rather
than competing head -on with low -cost Chinese manufacturers, he
gradually moved Acer up the value chain to focus more on design
and innovation. Acer — which once did contract manufacturing for
the l ikes of IBM, Dell and Compaq — is now itself the customer to
mainland contract manufacturers that have emulated Acer's earlier
business model. Instead of merely manufacturing cheap capacitors,
radios and the like, Taiwan's PC industry grew far more ambitio us*

under Shih's mentorship. With ever more countries entering the global information economy, his legacy of innovation-driven business will continue to power economic growth and inspire the next generation of Asian entrepreneurs."

Certainly it is great to see the CEO of Intel, the largest CPU maker in the world, g ive such high praise to Shih . It certainly appears to be justified by the recent big sales in PC, iPhone and consumer electronics that have come from the Shih business model of allying American, Taiwanese and Chinese companies to produce highly attractive devices at extremely low prices.

Shih's Smiling Curve W   hich companies   in this alliance receive the benefit for such marketing   successes can be answered by Shih's smiling curve that appears in Fig. 17.2 (9). Its x -axis indicates the stage of product development a nd starts with the research and development stage and continues to the technology invention and patenting   stage. Having the technology, one the n proceeds to the manufacturing   stage. The combination of low fabrication cost, high product performance, and skillful marketing leads to big sales under a given brand. The final stage

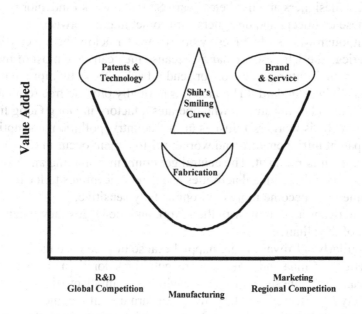

Fig. 17.2 Shih's Smiling Curve that traces the value that is added to a product as it progresses from the R&D stage to manufacturing and then to marketing and servicing (9).

is termed the branding and servicing   stage. The y -axis of the Shih's graph indicates the value added to the product at each stage. The value added to the product during the initial and final stage s of the process is high. The value added by its fabrication is low because of the low labor cost in China.

With no problems in communication between the Chinese and their American counterparts, the Taiwanese engineers and designers build the assembly lines, train the workers, ensure the quality of the products, and deliver the products to America in a timely fashion   . Taiwan's commitment to building its business in China is indicated by the fact that there are 1.5 million Taiwan merchants and their families who work and live in China.

Impact of the Alliance on America, China and Taiwan   According to the reasoning of Atlantic Monthly's James Fallow given to explain why America should welcome China's rise   – for now (10), we first examine whether all parties in the allia nce are satisfied with what they receive from it. How the   alliance functions can be viewed in the following manner. Chinese workers earn $2,000 a year to help American engineers, designers and marketers earn $2,000 a week (and more). The Taiwanese engineers and designers earn something in between.

Although wages of Chinese worke rs are far below the poverty line of America, the Chinese are happy because they can save most of the money for their future endeavors or send it back   home to improve their families' living standard. (The factories normally provide free room and board. A friend of the author who operates a factory in Dong Gong lives and eats with his workers.) Just as in any country, pollution, corruption, greed, patent infringement s and worker mistreatment occur in China . In some cases, it is rampant. The central government is making an effort to crack down on these illegal activities and offers incentives to local governments to become more environmentally-sensitive.

Americans are happy with the ir work and the wages they receive as a result of the alliance.

Similarly, Taiwanese are happy because they can use their knowledge of China and America   to get things done in the way that American and Chinese will endorse while the intellectual property of each party is protected and the Taiwanese earn decent incomes.

The next que stion raised by Fallow can be expressed as "How well does this alliance work? " Let's use Apple Computer to illustrate th e answer. Through the alliance of Apple with companies in Taiwan and

China, Apple had the   inventory necessary to meet the following sal es
that were generated in the third quarter of 2008:

- 2.6 millions MAC computers, up   by about 18% over the
  previous quarter and with a unit price reduction of $300.
- 5.2 million iPhones, up from 3.8 million in previous quarter.
- 1 million iPhone 3GS   units in the first three days of the
  product's introduction. The old iPhone, which was first offered
  at $399, now had a price tag of $99.
- 10.2 million iPods in that quarter.

As a result of these sales, Apple announced a 15% jump in profit   . This
made headlines in the business sections of newspapers in July, 2009. An
accompanying note stated that industry PC shipments had fallen by 3%
to 5% from those of the previous three months. Such news about Apple
profit certainly delighted Apple's shareholders - for now.

More on the Pursue of Alliance   The camera phones and
notebook computers are also lik   ed by the   Chinese. Products are
developed to meet the massive demand of that market . This can be done
without infringing the patents of American and Taiwanese companies   ,
while the alliance generates more profits. The revenues of Taiwan's 25
key tech companies were expected to   hit $122 billion in 2005 (24),
providing one indication of the success of the alliance.

Taiwan's success is also China's success. It is estimated that 40% to
80% of China's export s of information and communications hardware
are made in Taiwanese-owned factories in China.

Such an alliance has been pursued by Taiwanese and Japanese
businesses. Taiwanese companies c an expand their technology horizon
and receive capital investment   by their cooperative ties to Japanese
companies for use in   their development of Chinese business. Japanese
companies, on their part, u se the management know-how and the China-
based Taiwanese companies to develop their business in China.

In a different direction, some Japanese firms have established such
operations in China from which to re -export back to Japan, while other
multinationals have established manufacturing facilities in China to
access the local market.

Due Diligence of Alliance   An alliance is just like a partnership . Its
success depends on finding the right partners for the venture . Your
motive for an alliance in China or any foreign country is to have a good
return on your investment. However, the motives of Chinese partners

are very complicated because they are shaped by three factors . They are the demands of government and government officials, the needs of the partner corporation, and the personal agenda of the partner exec   utives (22). Unlike American partners , it is difficult to assess and verify the credibility of potential Chinese partners.

The success of the alliance mentioned previously could be due to the Taiwanese partner w   ho is trustworthy and has the experience of navigating through the China system to find the right Chinese partner.

Simply said, making an investment in China is the hottest business pursuit, but also the most challenging business task in the world. The book by W. Wang (22) is recommended for reading before you select partners and negotiate for the formation of a partnership or alliance.

17.8. Canada's Medical Device Industry and Manufacturing in Mexico

Canada is a global leader in digital radiography,   in vitro diagnostics, cardiovascular devices, dental implants and materials and   HME (11). It has some 1,000 firms, mostly small and medium enterprises, employing 26,000 people. Canadian's manufacturing costs of medical device are the lowest of the G 8 countries. It is the second OECD countr y in tax relief per R&D dollar spent . Canada ranks #2 among the G 8 for patent protection. Most importantly,   it is   easy for your engine   ers and executives to travel to Canada. This makes it one of the best locations in which to establish a joint venture. Its location leads to the following discussion of "landed costs".

Landed costs are the total cost of purchasing the product and getting it to your warehouse. Let us use the example given by Blankenship (2) to illustrate the landed costs for an order of marble tiles that are   shipped from China to the USA. They are:

- Invoiced price $4,725
- Transportation and duties $4,989
- Domestic delivery $2,035
- USDA exam $500
- X-ray exam $400
- On-site storage container $1,300
- Total $13,849

Although the invoiced price is much lower than the price you can obtain from your local American suppliers, the addition of the other charges makes this order unprofitable. The long list of charges and the possibility of having a fuel surcharge and other additional charges for change in order, etc., require that you be extremely cautious and know the landed cost of your import before signing the purchase order.

Mexico's low landed costs are very attractive in comparison to those of other developing countries (8). Manufacturing in Mexico is especially suitable for US companies that have products that require short delivery times and have a high engineered content. The proximity of Mexico to your US Company makes it easier to meet just-in-time orders. Over the years, the manufacturing capability of Mexico has been significantly enhanced. The establishment of the Border Industrialization Program, which is known as the Maquiladora Program, makes Mexico a preferred outsourcing location for many American companies. Your intellectual property is somewhat protected in Mexico, because Mexicans are more interested in earning wages than the prospect of copying your device for sales to the USA.

Mexico does have some disadvantages. First, its level of corruption is more than Canada or European countries. Second, its employment laws impose severe penalties on companies for laying off employees.

In summary, inexpensive labor, possible duty-free importation into Mexico, favorable US tariffs, lower freight costs and shorter turnaround times are the competitive advantages offered by Maquiladora. However, it is advisable that you seek professional help and advice well before deciding to set up a manufacturing facility in Mexico.

17.9. HME Markets and the Need for an Alliance

What are home medical equipment (HME)?   The following 15 categories provide some examples:

- Glucose Monitoring Systems for Diabetes
- Insulin Delivery Systems for Diabetes
- Breathing Apparatus for COPD
- Home Dialysis Machines for ESRD
- In Vitro Diagnostic Devices
- Drug Delivery Devices
- Infusion Pumps

- Drug Metered Inhalers
- Hearing Aid Devices
- Sleep Apnea Monitors
- Positive Airway Pressure Respirators for Sleep Apnea
- Nebulizers
- Oxygen Concentrators
- Home Monitoring Devices
- Neural Stimulators
- Home Defibrillators
- Home Suction Devices
- Rehabilitation Equipment
- Wheelchairs and Home Care Beds
- Telemetry Devices

Growth of HME   The home medical device market is expected to experience significantly high growth during the coming decades because of the following factors:

- An i ncrease in the aging population (According to the US Census Bureau, the percentage of people who are 65 and older will increase from 12.4% in 2000 to 20.7% by 2050.)
- The ever rising total of expenditures for healthcare
- The limitation of existing healthcare facilities
- The effort to contain hospital operation costs
- A preference for home care over hospital care
- The cost advantage of home care relative to hospital care
- A desire for the continuation of treatment and recovery at home
- The improvement of a patient's quality of life with home care
- The need for better, simpler and safer home treatment devices.

According to the report entitled "The Future of the Home Healthcare Equipment Market to 2015," the global HME market had a value of $48 billion in 2006 and was forecast to grow at 8.9% annually to $86 billion in 2015 (1, 25). The United States and Canada form the largest geographic market for HME with 34% of the global market . The European Union accounts for 29% of the market.

Disease-Specific Needs in HME   The Center for Disease Control indicated that 23.6 million Americans had diabetes in 2007, with nearly a third of them undiagnosed (26). Another 57 million have pre -diabetes, and are likely to have the disease if they do not alter their living habits .

Among various diseases managed or treated by HME, diabetes accounts for the largest share (i.e., 46% in 2006,) of the global HME market.

About 4% of middle -aged American adults have obstructive sleep apnea. The number of patients with COPD and ESRD in the world is alarmingly high. The Report on the HME market uses an 8.9% annual growth rate in its projections for this industry.

In view of the foregoing status of various diseases and the purchasing power of the third world block BRIC, the growth in world HME market may be considerably higher in coming years.

With so many patients wan ting to use HME, the price must be affordable.

For a device to qualify as a good HME, it must be simple to use. As in the case of the home hemodializer, one must have a simple monitoring system to assure the safe removal of a large amount of fluid from t he patient's body during hemodialysis. In addition, the home is a convenient setting for longer and more frequen t hemodialysis treatments. University of Washington Professor Emeritus Christopher Blagg says that about 30% of US dialysis patients are candidates for home treatmen t (17), although only 0.8% now receive it (21). In comparison, about 55% of dialysis patients in New Zealand are dialyzed at home, as are 30% in Australia and 20% in Canada.

The ventilator problem of COPD patients was pointed out by a subcontractor of GMI during the hardware design of the Lee Monitor. In the previous 10 years, he had worked in a San Diego factory of a large ventilator company in the US. He said that the advancement in the manufacturing of DC motor s would enable him to manufacture a ventilator at a cost of $50 to $100 . He was looking for a venture sponsor to build a factory in China to develop, manufacture and market low cost ventilators. If what he envisioned were to be done, the world would be one step closer to providing a better quality of life for millions of patients who have COPD.

Alliance to Meet HME Needs   The success of the alliance of companies in the US, Taiwan and China described in Section 17.6 demonstrates their ability to produce at a high level and low price a camera phone and PC to open up a massive , new consumer market for their products. During the last thirty years, Hong Kong has invested $273 billion as direct foreign investment in China. This is nearly as much as the total of investment in China by all other countries (16). The alliances of companies in Singapore and South Korea with Chinese

companies make them benef iciaries of globalization. (These countries ,
Singapore, South Korea, Taiwan and Hong Kong , are the four Asian
Tigers.) Brazil, Russia, India and China (the Big Four or BRIC) have not
only attracted the most investor attention , but also significantly
increased their purchasing power.

Concluding Remarks The successes of the world's HME industry and
the diminishment of poverty worldwide provide the incentive for world
entrepreneurs to use the alliance business model to manufacture
affordable HME for better home care of all patients in the world.

References

1. Biggs, J., www.massmedic.com/docs/jbiggs05.ppt (2005).
2. Blankenship, D., www.smartchinaourcing.com/shipping/landed -cost-hidden-costs-of-customs-and-shipping
3. China: Accessing the Medical Device Market. *Espicom Business Intelligence* , July (2007).
4. Dietz, U., *Federal Ministry of Health*, Germany, May (2008).
5. Dutton, P. V. *Boston Globe*, Aug. 11, (2007).
6. en.wikipedia.org/wiki/Healthcare_in_England
7. en.wikipedia.org/wiki/Healthcare_in_Taiwan
8. en.wikipedia.org/wiki/Manufacturing_in_Mexico
9. en.wikipedia.org/wiki/smiling_curve
10. Fallows, J., Atlantic Monthly, July/Aug. (2007).
11. investincanada.gc.ca/eng/industry -sectors/life_science/medical-devices.aspx
12. Lloyd, S., C. Mayott III, D. Schenberger, P. De Fazion and J. Burke, *MD&DI*, Aug. (2008).
13. Maio, V. and L. Manzoli, *P&T Journal*, 27:301 (2002).
14. Moeller, S., S. Gioberge, and G. Brown, *Nephrol Dial Transplant* 17:2071 (2002).
15. Ostellini, P. S., *Time Asia*, www.time.com/time/asia/2006/heros/bl_shih.html (2006)
16. Ramzy, A., The China Connection,*Time*, June 7 (2007).
17. Rubin, R., USA Today, http://www.usatoday.com/news/health/200908-23-dialysis_N.htm?POE=click-refer (2009).
18. Shapiro, D. Am *Chamber Commerce in Taipei, Cover Story,*39: 3 (2009).
19. Sin, D. D., and W. C. Tan, *Am. J. Resp. & Critical Care Med.*, 176:732 (2007).
20. Suneja V. and R. Paddock, *MDMA Webinar*, Dec. 16 (2008).
21. US Renal Data System. *USRDS 2003 Annual Report*, NIDDK, (2003).
22. Wang, W. The China Executive, 2W Publishing LTD (2006).
23. Wee, A., *Frost & Sullivan Market Insight,* Jan. 23, (2006).
24. Why Taiwan Matters, *BusinessWeek*, May 16 (2005).
25. www.bccresearch.com/report/HLC054A.html
26. www.diabetes.org
27. www.nhi.gov.tw, e-Health Ins, vol. 95, Nov. (2008)

CHAPTER 18

INVESTING IN THE FUTURE

The knowledge of community leaders, prominent academicians, authors, government officials, entrepreneurs and philanthropists on the subject of **Biomedical Engineering, Healthcare and Entrepreneurship** that the author has collected from news articles, magazine publications and books in recent years form the core of this Chapter. The author is especially grateful to Drs. Peter Katona, Michael Khoo, John Linehan and Robert Nerem who expended additional effort to write the excerpts and share their vision with the readers on investing in the future. At the end of each section, the author makes a brief conclusion to integrate the information presented by those who contributed to that section. Special thanks are due to Dr. Shu Chien who wrote an exciting and passionate Chapter 19 on Biomedical Engineering Entrepreneurism.

18.1. Investing in Your Company and Yourself

On Running a Medical Device Company, Bill Hawkins, Chairman and CEO, Medtronic (Courtesy of *MD&DI*, 3).

1. Core Values: Discipline, Respect, Duty.   These are deceivingly simple concepts that seem to recommend themselves to everybody, but are practiced consistently by few. Having been taught these values at an early age, they have played a role throughout my career in medical technology. From my first sales position to leading a great company like Medtronic—I've never found a replacement for core values like perseverance and loyalty.

2. Thinking Differently.   Like other high-tech industries, the medical device field requires that we think differently: boldly, creatively, and unconventionally. Challenging norms and assumptions is requisite in order to push the innovation envelope as aggressively as possible. Push hard—and then some. Don't ever stop. When we get too comfortable, we lose our edge and fail our customers.

3. The Patient, The Patient, The Patient.   I strive to stay focused on the patients we serve —no matter how challenging or difficult running the business may seem. There's no better   way to maintain the passion required for success than to believe in what you can do for your customer. In medical technology, it's simple; it's the patient. The moment I feel the balance shift away from the patients, who are the ultimate beneficiaries of o   ur products and services, is the moment passion wanes, productivity decreases, and business begins to suffer.

4. Innovation.   There's a belief in some business circles that in challenging economic times, the best companies double   -down on marketing in order to win share from competitors. This may be true, but I believe it's even more important to double   -down on innovation —the science, research, and development behind the new products and technologies that change how healthcare is practiced across the world   . Innovation is our lifeblood—and nothing can replace its importance.

5. Technology = Value. Technology for technology's sake is never our goal. A cool gadget may dazzle the eye, but developing truly useful technology to help physicians solve a practical   problem provides value and drives market-leading performance.

6. Strive to Discover the Entrepreneur in You.   Companies frequently lose their compass and the passion of the entrepreneurial spirit. In our industry, it's critical to stay on the edge of   technology. I always think about the future and what medical device advancements might do. What's more, I retain the best engineers and physicians on staff who will share their own visions with me on a regular basis.

7. Family Matters.   My greatest sen se of pride in my career has been doing what I do each day with my family in mind. The work I do enables many people, including both my father and father   -in-law, to enjoy full lives.

8. Have a Mission. Medtronic's mission is nearly 50 years old and has served us well through both good and difficult times. Every company should have a mission to guide its purpose and serve as a reminder of

why it exists and who it serves. We all should have individual mission statements as well, to ground and guide us through thick and thin.

9. Live a Little.   Working to alleviate the chronic disease burden around the world is serious business. That said, take some time to live a little and remind yourself of the kind of life you want the patients who use your therapies to have. This reminds you that you're not just saving lives—in many cases you're enabling better quality, livability, and happiness for those lives.

10. Give a Little . . . Or a Lot.   I can think of few better ways to measure one's success than by giving back and giving back often. Those who do will know the powerful and invigorating sense of purpose and satisfaction that comes from helping others and be humbled by the gratitude expressed in return.

On Customer First, Earl E. Bakken, co-Founder, Medtronic Inc., in Reflections on Leadership, 2001.

For our representatives in the field, of course, "customer first" is more than a strategy or slogan. "Customer first" is the first commandment, the basic law by which they conduct their professional lives. They see or talk with the Medtronic customer every day of the week. They often go to extraordinary lengths to make sure that the customer is satisfied. Our representatives have been known to drive hundreds of miles in the middle of the night to deliver a pacemaker to a physician. They have gone so far as to arrange for the delivery of a competitor's device to a doctor who needed it when one of their own was unavailable. Our field representatives, I am very proud to say, have demonstrated time and again that they will meet the customers' needs regardless of the cost or the effort.

The same might be said of our engineers, our various support staffs, our receptionists, and other company representatives. In the design and manufacture of our products, in our marketing and advertising, in every one of our employees' diverse activities, the prevailing commandment is, or should be, "customer first." Some years ago our employees wore a button that stated the sentiment effusively. The button read: "I Love the Customer!"

On Guiding Vision,   Robert   Jarvik M.D. (the developer of the first
permanent total artificial heart) on W. Kolff.
In 1971, after my first two years at medical school, Dr. Willem Kolff,
who died Feb. 11 at 97, hired me to work on the artificial-heart project at
the University of Utah. On my first day, he instructed me to create a new
heart design that would keep an animal alive longer than any earlier
models had.

Previous designs had failed, he explained, because they did not fit
anatomically. And that was all he said. He told me what to do , but not
how to do it. That was Dr. Kolff's forte   —finding enthusiastic people,
laying out his visions and then leaving them to their own devices.
Dr. Kolff, who was one of the founders of the American Society for
Artificial Internal Organs, encouraged scores of people to turn their
attention to creating mechanical hearts, electronic devices that restore
hearing and vision, artificial arms and more. He believed that
bioengineering could one day provide a substitute for almost every organ
in the body.

What could not be replaced, however, was Dr. Kolff himself, who
possessed energy, Old World charm and a grand, guiding vision. I count
myself among the many inventors, engineers and doctors who worked
with him and will never forget his indomitable spirit.

On Innovati ve Company , J ames C. Collins and W   illiam C. Lazier,
authors of "*Beyond Entrepreneurship*".
To be an enduring, great company, we believe it must have the ability to
innovate continually —to have a constant flow of new ideas, some of
which are fully implemented. We say some are implemented (rather than
all) because a great company will always have more good ideas than it
can fund. Most companies start with a creative founder. The challenge,
however, is to become an innovative company, rather than a company
dependent on an innovative founder. We've identified six basic elements
of what it takes to be an innovative company:

1. Receptivity to ideas from everywhere   Highly innovative
companies don't necessarily generate   more ideas than their less
innovative counterparts (good ideas are in plentiful supply for all
companies). But highly innovative companies are often more receptive
to ideas—and not only to their own ideas, but to ideas from everywhere.
Furthermore, they d o something about the ideas. Not that an innovative

company executes every single idea, but it is much more likely to act quickly on a partly-baked idea than to spend countless hours deliberating about all the reasons why it can't work.

2. "Being" the customer   One of the best ways to make and keep your company innovative is to have people invent solutions to their own problems or needs. In other words, be your own customer and satisfy yourself. If that is not possible —if you are in a business where you cannot be your own customer —then figure out a way to experience the world as a customer experiences it . The idea here is simple. If someone in your company creates an innovation to solve her own problem or meet her own desire, there are probably other peopl e in the world who would benefit from her invention.

3. Experimentation and mistakes   Sadly, the nature of innovation is that it is fraught with the unknown . The best way to find out if something is a good idea is to experiment, to give it a try. This, of course leads to mistakes – ideas that aren't good —but they are part of the process . Innovation requires experimentation and mistakes. You can't have one without the other two, period.

4. People being creative   All people have the capaci ty to be creative. There is no such thing as an inherently uncreative person; creativity is a capability that resides inside each and every one of us. There is no special breed of person somehow ordained from God with the gift of creativity. Nor is it true that most of us were born deprived of that blessing.

The first step in having people at all levels be innovative is to believe in their inherent creative capability . After all, how can you possible expect people to innovate if you don't fundamentally bel ieve that they can?

5. Autonomy and decentralization   This need for freedom and autonomy is well recognized by companies that remain innovative. Herman Miller allows its designers to work away from central facilities, in whatever environment they find conducive to work. Merck & Company, one of the most innovative pharmaceutical firms, hires the best scientists it can find, lets *them* select targets for basic research (not marketing or corporate), and stays out of their way.

This applies at all levels of hu man endeavor, from a five -person basketball team to entire societies. Indeed, freedom of action -room to experiment—is the primary factor behind the relative strength of Western economies compared to their centralized, eastern -bloc counterparts. In their book, *How the West Grew Rich,* Nathan Rosenberg and L. E. Birdzell, show that the underlying source of the West's economic advancement is the large number of innovations that come about via autonomous experimentation. This experimentation, in turn, comes about because people *can* act, because there are few restrictions holding them back from giving something a try. Just imagine what the United States economy would be like if every new business had to get formal government approval from a ministry of central bus iness control. (Actually, we don't need to imagine; just look at the Soviet economy.)

6. Rewards   We don't mean to suggest that people being creative are motivated solely by money, or power, or prestige. In fact, they're often motivated by the desire fo r interesting work, the challenge of a tough problem, the joy of contribution, or the satisfaction of doing something new. Nonetheless, innovation should be explicitly rewarded. All people, no matter how pure their motivations, are influenced by the reward systems of their organizations. Rewards matter. And if you want to remain innovative, you've got to reward innovation.

On Engineering Management, C. M. Chang, Ph.D . Professor of Industrial Engineering, University of Buffalo, State University of New York (1).
Engineers with excellent managerial skills and superior business acumen are needed to lead corporate America in the new century . As the economy grows increasingly global, technologies advance at a faster pace, and the marketplace becomes more dynamic; countless industrial companies will need technically trained engineers to turn technological innovations into profitability.

The need for engineering management training is obvious from another point of view. The National Science Foundation estimated in 2000 that about 46 percent of American engineers and scientists were actively working in managerial and administrative capacities. This managerial percentage remained more or less constant across the age groups from under 35 to over 55 years old. As the trend continues, almost one out of every two engineers or scientists will be engaged in managing people, projects, teams, technology and other resources to add value to their companies.

Conclusion   It is your vis ion, core values, education and family that enable you and your company to better yourself and the company and make innovations and improvements for the benefit of patients as shown in Fig. 18.1.

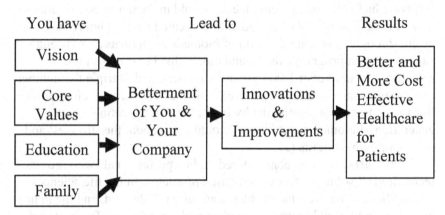

Fig. 18.1. Some key factors for you and your company in making innovations and improvements that benefit patients.

18.2. Contributing to the Profession, the Society and the Nation

On BME Education, Michael Khoo, Ph.D., Professor and D.C. and H.E. Baum Chair, Biomedical Engineering   Department, University of Southern California.
Biomedical engineers who have become successful entrepreneurs are also fountains of knowledge that can be tapped to relay to subsequent generations their experience of how they managed to convert engineering ideas into devices, products or methodologies that can be applied in the clinical arena. The mechanisms of technology transfer, the complicated web of medical product regulation, and the economics of medical device development – these issues that need to b e confronted head-on by biomedical entrepreneurs are generally not commonplace in the biomedical engineering curriculum. Successful biomedical entrepreneurs can play a critical role as mentors and role models in the

education of up -and-coming biomedical engineers, who plan to pursue careers in industry.

On Biomedical Engineering as a Natural Home of Entrepreneurship,
Peter G. Katona, Sc.D., President, The Whitaker Foundation.
Mr. U. A. Whitaker was a successful engineer, entrepreneur, and businessman whos e testament created a foundation in 1976 for "charitable, scientific, literary, and educational" purposes. Since Mr. Whitaker had believed that engineering could make major contributions to medicine, The Whitaker Foundation dedicated itself to improving health through enhancing the field of biomedical engineering. Through a variety of grant programs, the Foundation helped to establish the research careers of over 1,000 faculty members, and to triple the number of biomedical engineering departments, now numb ering well over 80. Such investment was motivated by the belief that educating a new generation of biomedical engineers would bring about the strongest and most long-term benefits (5).

Engineers are often cons idered to be professionals who provide technological solutions to well specified problems. In the life sciences and medicine, however, the problems are often ill defined, and the major task is asking the right questions before seeking answers. The hallmark of a well -educated biomedical engineer is that he or she can participate substantively in identifying important problems, in addition to contributing to technological solutions. This is achieved by drawing upon a rigorous integrated training in both the l ife sciences and engineering.

Identifying problems is especially important for entrepreneurs. Such individuals make their contributions by an in -depth understanding of needs and coming up with solutions that are effective, novel, and hopefully – profitable. They do not design devices that had been specified by others: they design devices, materials and processes that solve real biomedical problems that they recognize and formulate.

Before its planned closing in 2006, The Whitaker Foundation conducted a survey of the recipients of its biomedical engineering research grants. Almost half of the 614 responders had at least one patent, and more than a third created new products, resulting in over 100 new companies (5). This interest in entrepreneurship is especially noteworthy since the research grants had been designed for faculty members early in their careers, rather than to practicing engineers.

Biomedical engineering is a profession that requires knowledge in diverse areas, welcomes risk, poses major challenges, and offers substantive rewards. Thus, it is a natural home for entrepreneurship. Mr. Whitaker would be pleased.

On Demand for Healthcare, Dane A. Miller, Ph.D., President and CEO, Biomet, Inc. (in the Whitaker Foundation 2005 Annual Report).
There are three basic techniques for dealing with the increased demand for healthcare in the next quarter century. One option would be to reduce compensation provided to those delivering the healthcare. The second choice would be to deliver fewer units of healthcare through rationing. The third possibility would be to create advances in technology so that more efficient and higher quality healthcare can be delivered at a lower cost. It is this third technique that offers the greatest challenge and opportunity for the field of biomedical engineering. Approach No.1 will simply not work because eventually the healthcare system will drive away suppliers and providers. Approach No. 2 involves a number of socially unacceptable decisions. Therefore society's focus should be on No. 3.

On Responsibilities, Barack Obama, the 44 [th] President of the United States of America, the 2008 Inaugural Address.
For as much as government can do and must do, it is ultimately the faith and determination of the American people upon which this nation relies. It is the kindness to take in a stranger when the levees break, the selflessness of workers who would rather cut their hours than see a friend lose their job which sees us through our dark est hours. It is the firefighter's courage to storm a stairway filled with smoke, but also a parent's willingness to nurture a child, that finally decides our fate.
Our challenges may be new. The instruments with which we meet them may be new. But those values upon which our success depends – hard work and honesty, courage and fair play, tolerance and curiosity, loyalty and patriotism – these things are old. These things are true. They have been the quiet force of progress throughout our history. What is demanded then is a return to these truths. **What is required of us now is a new era of responsibility – a recognition, on the part of every American, that we have duties to ourselves, our nation, and the world,** duties that we do not grudgingly accept but ra ther seize gladly,

firm in the knowledge that there is nothing so satisfying to the spirit, so defining of our character, than giving our all to a difficult task.

On Partnerships, Harold Varmus, M.D., Director of National Institutes of Health (1993   -1999),   Foreword, 1998 NIH Symposium on Bioengineering: Building the Future of Biology and Medicine.

Bioengineering advances the nation's health by applying engineering principles and techniques to biological problems. The rewards most obvious to the public are n   ovel devices and drugs, but bioengineering also offers further insight into biological processes, new methods for using data from genetics, and increased ability to visualize the brain and other organs. History tells us that most of the revolutionary changes that have occurred in biology and medicine have depended on new methods that are themselves often the result of fundamental discoveries in many different fields. Thus biological problems are too complex to be solved by biologists alone; we need partners   in many disciplines, including physics, mathematics, chemistry, computer sciences, and engineering.

On US Healthcare, Karen Davis, President of the Commonwealth Fund, New York (2).

High healthcare expenditures and the growing number of people without health insurance set the United States apart from all other industrialized countries. The United States spends twice   per capita what other major industrialized countries spend on healthcare, but is the only one that fails to provide near -universal health insurance coverage. We also fail to achieve health outcomes as good, or value for health spending as high, as what is achieved in other countries.

The United States has been slow to learn from countries that   have systematically adopted policies that curtail spending and   enhance value. Chief among these are mechanisms for assessing   the comparative cost - effectiveness of drugs, devices, diagnostic tests, and treatment procedures; implementation of information   technology, including electronic repositories of patient medical   information, across sites of care; easy access to primary care, including organized systems of off -hours care; a strong role for government in negotiating payment for care; and payment systems that re ward preventive care, management of chronic conditions, care coordination, and health outcomes rather than volume of services.

On Biological Revolution   , Robert Nerem, Ph.D., Parker H. Petit
Professor and Director of Institute for Bioengineering and Biosc   ience,
Georgia Tech.

This 21st century is being called the "Biotech Century." It is called
this because the biological revolution, which arguably started at the
beginning of the 20th century, has advanced so significantly that it
provides the foundation   for the new technologies of this 21st century.
Advances in biology are continuing to advance, this at an ever
accelerating pace, and in addition the world of technology has become
global in nature. These developments have several implications.

First, the medical device/implant industry already is being impacted
through the convergence of biology with the traditional electro   -
mechanical technologies developed in the second half of the last
century. As important as these have been for healthcare, the emerging
combination products, i.e., the combination of a biologic and a device or
a drug and a device, offer new possibilities for treating patients   . Also
emerging are regenerative medicine and the use of stem cells of various
types in the replacement, regenerati   on, and/or repair of tissues and
organs. This will provide the opportunity to develop new therapies, ones
that are cell -based and will provide for the treatment of diseases and
conditions where there currently are none available.

Second, this biological revolution has and is impacting not only the
medical arena, but all of biology   . This means biomedical engineering
must evolve into a much broader biology-based engineering, which more
appropriately should be called bioengineering. This is because one might
predict that 15-20 years from now the application and impact of biology-
based information will be just as much outside of the field of medicine
as within it . This new field of bioengineering already is beginning to
address major problems of society   , such a s energy through biofuels,
food through agricultural biotech, and the environment   . Yet there
undoubtedly will be more areas to come.

Third, the global nature of our society demands that a biology   -
based engineering not only address problems of the develope d countries,
but also of the developing countries. In Africa and parts of Asia there is
a need for healthcare technologies that not only can treat the diseases
prevalent there, but also are cost effective and easily delivered . In these
developing countries food is a major issue, and there are increasingly
environmental issues.

Thus, the application of a biology   -based engineering, i.e. bioengineering, is continuing to broaden and diversify   . With this the need for new biology-based technologies and products will also continue to broaden, and this demands a continuing emergence and broadening of the field. Although it is always difficult to predict the future, it is clear that the future is bright . For all the changes that have occurred in the last 30 years,   these driven by the biological revolution and the investments made by The Whitaker Foundation, there will be even more profound changes in the future, i.e. over the next 30 years   . Thus, the future for this field of a biologically -based engineering is excee dingly bright, but one that more than likely will be much different than what any of us can today envision.

On Public Policy and Innovations   , Duane Roth, Chief Executive Officer, in the 2008 Annual Report of CONNECT, San Diego, California.
To prepare for the next 25 years in an increasingly competitive global innovation economy, CONNECT has the following key objectives that are fundamental to our future competitiveness:
- Research institutions are the engines of discovery and we should unite to recruit and   retain the most talented researchers anywhere and offer support for increased federal funding of basic research;
- Intellectual property is our primary asset and we should be diligent about protecting our discoveries around the world;
- The global economy re   quires ever increasing partnerships to remain competitive and as a region we should reach out nationally and internationally and share our contacts;
- Communication between academic leaders and the private sector will be even more essential to the innovation   economy and we should develop ways to continue to improve;
- Risk capital is the fuel of innovation and we must develop new and sustainable models to fund innovation; and
- Recruitment of talented entrepreneurial leaders and creative scientists and engineers is essential and we need to develop tools to ensure we remain competitive.

If one evaluates these objectives, it becomes apparent that public policy in Washington D. C. and Sacramento holds many of the keys to our future success. Federal support of resea rch is the lifeblood of the new idea generation. Intellectual property laws, trade policy and regulation are set largely by Washington policy makers and these policies will determine much of our global competitiveness. Workforce and education arc both federal- and state-governed. As a region, we must become more engaged with our legislators and CONNECT is committed to improving communication with our Washing   ton and Sacramento legislators.

Conclusion   The challenges and opportunities in healthcare and disease prevention are infinite. To deliver better healthcare at lower cost and to be more effective in prevention, the constituents identified in the outer ring of Fig. 18.2 need to work together responsibly, educate themselves, show flexibility, take initiat ives and make innovations and improvements.

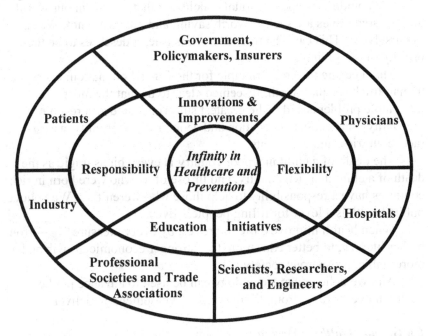

Fig. 18.2. Healthcare and disease prevention are infinite for the improvement of people's health when their constituents (the outer rin   g) work together through education, responsibility, flexibility, initiatives, improvements and innovation.

18.3. Doing Something for the World

On Global Health , Bill Gates , in response to the Tech Museum honoring him with the James C. Morgan Global Humanitarian Award, 2006 (6).
For a long time, I continued to see my largest contribution to the community in terms of creating a successful business. I just didn't have the time and energy to do more.

And then one day, Melinda and I read an article about the millions of children who were dying every year in poor countries from diseases that we had long ago eliminated in this country. One disease I had never even heard of—rotavirus—was killing literally half a million kids each year. I thought: "That's got to b e a typo. If a single disease was killing that many kids, we would have heard about it—it'd be front-page news." But it wasn't.

We couldn't escape the brutal conclusion that —in our world today—some lives are seen as worth saving and others are not. We sai d to ourselves: "This can't be true. But if it is true, it deserves to be the priority of our giving."

That became the core principle for the Gates Foundation: every human life has equal worth. It seemed clear to us that the most intractable problems and the greatest suffering came as a result of inequality—in access to education and economic opportunity, across race, countries, and continents.

The death of a child in a poor country is every bit as tragic as the death of a child in a rich country, and th ose of us who were born in rich countries have a responsibility to help those who weren't . We believe public health is a lever for lifting people's lives.

When health improves, life improves, by every measure —from higher literacy, to better education, to stronger economic growth and a more stable, prosperous society.

And we believe that technology can be used to advance public health in every way—from discovery, to development, to delivery.

On Global Health by Design, John Linehan, Ph.D., Professor of Biomedical Engineering and Medicine, Northwestern University
Bill Gates is correct. Technology can be used to advance public health – if it is affordable!

Global Health by Design is a great way to involve students. They readily respond to the challenge of designing devices to address un - or under-met clinical needs in resource -limited settings. The key to success will be to minimize cost by using *existing* technology in ways that meet the needs of the end user and any limitations imposed by their environment.

Northwestern University provides an example. Four years ago, NU established a medical   -device innovation program, Global Health Technologies (GHT), in collaboration with the University of Cape Town (UCT) in South Africa . Four devices developed with ess ential student participation within the GHT program are either in, or will soon be in, the clinical testing phase of device development.

These device -design projects were initiated in collaboration with the UCT faculty, and in close coordination with healthcare professionals and medical administrators of the Western Cape, and African businesses in the medical and non -medical technology sectors . The geographical reach has gradually broadened to include participants   in other South African provinces and other countries in southern Africa.

The GHT program focuses on device design and innovation, taking a need -based and user -centered approach to solving problems that are specific to under-resourced and medically over-burdened regions of sub- Saharan Africa. T he program is under the purview of both the Biomedical Engineering Department and the NU Center for Innovation in Global Healthcare Technologies (www.cight.northwestern.edu).

Student participation has included undergraduates, MS   students and PhD students from both Northwestern University and the University of Cape Town.

On The Smile Train , Charles B. Wang, CEO and Chairman, Computer Associates and co-Founder and Chairman, The Smile Train (7). Wang said today (March 14, 2009) that The Smile Train, an international children's charity and medical organization, is off to a great start following an international symposium where $20 million was donated to fund a ser ies of joint Sino/U.S. strategic initiatives to help eradicate cleft lips and palates.

"The Smile Train has brought together the finest doctors, nurses, surgeons and scientists from China, the United States and around the world," said Bush (41 [st] President of USA). "Although they may speak different languages and come from very different backgrounds, there are some things they all have in common: the belief that every child counts, and that every child deserves a smile."

"Our initial commitment of $20   million is just the beginning of what it will cost to help the millions of children with clefts in China who cry themselves to sleep every night," said Wang, Founding Member of The Smile Train . "Just imagine what it must be like to live your entire life wi thout being able to smile   . That's why we need so many more people to get on board The Smile Train and help us help these children."

Unlike other organizations that rely on American surgeons to perform surgery in foreign countries, The Smile Train believes that local self-sufficiency is the only realistic, cost   -effective answer to the problem. Through free education, training and equipment, local medical professionals and teams can be empowered to provide the help needed by the local children.

"I can thi nk of nothing more special and worthwhile than helping disadvantaged children who have no place else to turn," said Wang   . "And there's no organization that I know of that has the potential to change the lives of as many children as The Smile Train."

It ca n take as little as 45 minutes for cleft lip surgery and up to three hours for cleft palate surgery. "Smile Train surgery is the closest thing to a modern -day miracle that I have ever witnessed," said Wang   . "It's like giving a child a second chance in life."

In 1999, its first year of operation, The Smile Train funded programs and partnerships at a level of $10 million to $15 million . Since Wang's private contributions have covered all administrative costs of The Smile Train, 100 percent of all additional donations will go to program areas of training, treatment and research.

The Smile Train is a non -profit organization launched in 1999. Its goal is to eradicate the global problem of cleft lips and palates   . The Smile Train's comprehensive approach to the p roblem of clefts involves free training for doctors, free surgery for children and research to find a cure. It is supported by thousands of individuals and private foundations and does not receive any governmental funding.

(In the ten years since the foun ding of The Smile Train by Wang and Brian Mullaney, The Smile Train has provided surgery to 500,000 children. Smile Pinki in Fig. 18.3 is one of these children. With a cost as little as $250 and a rate of 100,000+ surgeries a year now, 500,000 desperate children not only have just a new smile, but also a new life.)

Conclusion   Global health is a problem for all of us to work on in this 21 [st] Century. The three elements —affordable technology, local effort and running philanthropy lik   e a business as depicted in Fig. 18.3—are bound to deliver not only smiles to many children like Pinki but also better healthcare for the third world.

Fig. 18.3. A joint effort to solving global health problems of the third world (courtesy of The Smile Train with Pinki's picture, 7).

References:

1.   Chang, C. M.,   *Engineering Management, Challenges in the New Millennium*   , Pearson Prentice Hall, N. J. (2005).

2. Davis, K., *N. Engl. J. Med.*, 359: 1751-1755 (2008).
3. Hawkins, B., *MD&DI*, p.32 June (2009).
4. Jarvik, R., Time, p.18, March 2 (2009).
5. Katona, P. G., Biomedical Engineering and The Whitaker Foundation: A Thirty-Year Partnership. *Annals Biomed. Eng.* 34: 904-916 (2006).
6. www.microsoft.com.nsatc.net/presspass/exec/billg/speeches/2006/11-15TechMuseum.mspx
7. www.smiletrain.org
8. Bakken, E., *Reflection on Leadership*, Medtronic, MN (2001).
9. Collins, J. C. and W. C. Lazier, *Beyond Entrepreneurship*, Prentice Hall, N. J. (1992).

CHAPTER 19

HOW TO SUCCEED IN BIOMEDICAL ENGINEERING ENTREPRENEURISM WITH REALLY TRYING[1]

Shu Chien, M.D., Ph.D.
Professor of Bioengineering and Medicine, UCSD
Director, Whitaker Institute for Biomedical Engineering, UCSD
President, Biomedical Engineering Society (2006-2008)

Dr. Jen -shih Lee has written an excellent book for undergraduate and graduate students, as well as working biomedical engineers, who want to learn the basic knowledge required for the development of biomedical engineering entrepreneurs hip. In the Chapter on *Investing in Biomedical Engineering*, he has presented the results of his interviews with many successful biomedical engineering entrepreneurs and visionary educators in the field in three Sections . The superb visions, insightful anal ysis, and valuable advices by the interviewees make this an extremely valuable Chapter. It is a privilege for me to be asked by Dr. Lee to write an excerpt . I have made an attempt to summarize these marvelous paragraphs without referring specifically to th e Sections, because there are some interplays between them. Because many of the important thoughts were expressed by several interviewees and for the sake of continuity in reading, I have not made specific references to them in this excerpt. In a few places I have added my own thoughts.

19.1. The Biomedical Engineer as a Person

Core Values The biomedical engineers, including those who become biomedical engineering entrepreneurs, must possess and/or develop

---

[1] The title of this Chapter is a take-off from a comedy movie made in 1967 entitled ⸢How to Succeed in Business without Really Trying?⸥, starring David Morse, Maureen Arthur, and Rudee Vallee.

certain personality traits, many of which ar e common for scientists and engineers, as well as other citizens of the Society . The biomedical engineer must have the core values of integrity, honesty, dedication to truth, fairness, passion, generosity, discipline, perseverance, courage, sense of responsibility, respect, and loyalty. A very important element to be successful in entrepreneurism, as well as biomedical engineering in general, is innovation.

Balance in Life Biomedical engineering entrepreneurship is serious business that takes a lot of t ime, energy and concentration . It is important, however, to balance the many priorities in life . This includes personal health (physical and mental) and family life. Therefore, time management is very important . A healthy mind and body and a happy family c an have major contributions to success in biomedical engineering entrepreneurship, just as in other professions. Work, health, and family are interdependent. The key is how to manage time to enjoy all these elements.

19.2. Development of a Biomedical Engineering Entrepreneur

In order to develop into a successful biomedical engineering entrepreneur, it is important to have an excellent background and education, which should integrate natural sciences, life sciences and engineering. The training should fos ter the ability to identify important problems and the approaches to solve them, as well as the development of a vision for the future . One needs to learn how to convert ideas into products (the work "product" will be used to include devices, technologies, biologics, drugs, etc.) that can be used in clinical medicine. By knowing what is the existing state -of-the-art in terms of opportunities and challenges, the entrepreneur will be able to integrate these into his/her thought process to develop innovative ideas and pursue them. In order to be innovative, one needs to think differently, boldly, creatively, and unconventionally.

Besides the formal training in schools, the influences of outstanding mentors or role models have often been cited as an important e lement in career successes . Such mentors provide the role models for being innovative, visionary, dedicated, and all the other essential characters for success in biomedical engineering entrepreneurism. It is essential that the young biomedical engineers being trained today learn how to mentor and educate the next generation, so that the development of biomedical engineering and entrepreneurism can be sustained and amplified.

19.3. Inter-personal Interactions

No person can live as an island . The need for interactions with other people is particularly important for biomedical engineering entrepreneurs, who work in a team environment in the generation and delivery of products . The importance of the relations with family members and mentors has already been mentioned. Engineers with excellent managerial skills and superior business acumen, in addition to their superb technical capabilities, are needed to lead Corporate America to turn technological innovations into profitability. A study by the National Science Foundation estimated that almost one half of engineers or scientists will be engaged in managing people, projects, teams, technology and other resources to add value to their companies.

In industrial companies, the biomedical entrepreneur works with other engineers, the management, technical and supporting staff, and field representatives . In delivering the products, he/she works with physicians, other health professionals, and the patients (though mostly indirectly). Positive and effective interactions with all of them are critical. In the design and manufacture of products, and in marketing and advertising, it is essential to have the spirit of "customer first". In the final analysis, the aim of these products is to improve the health of the patient and treat their illness. The positive outcome in patients drives the passion of the entrepreneur, the productivity of the company, and the success of the business. It is always the patients first.

19.4. Roles of the Government and the Private Sector

The funding support by the National Institutes of Health (NIH), National Science Foundation, and the other government agencies for research and training has played an important role in fostering the creation of novel ideas, development of new products, and educ ation of the next generation of biomedical engineers. The Small Business Innovation Research (SBIR) and Small Business Technology Transfer (STTR) programs are especially valuable in fostering the establishment and development of small business, with a sign ificant number related to biomedical engineering.

The unprecedented, strong, and dedicated support of biomedical engineering by The Whitaker Foundation has made a major impact on the development of the discipline from 1976 to 2006 . The Foundation helped to establish the research careers of over 1,000 faculty members, and to triple the number of biomedical engineering departments. The fostering of the education of a new generation of biomedical engineers has brought about strong and long -term benefits. They have not only excelled in the science of biomedical engineering, but also contributed importantly to entrepreneurism, through the design of devices, materials and processes that solve biomedical problems, filing of over 300 patents, and making possible th e formation of over 100 new companies. Most recently, the Wallace H. Coulter Foundation has initiated Translation Research Partnership Awards to promote translational research by enhancing collaborations between biomedical engineers and clinicians, supporting the movement of promising technologies to clinical applications, and developing sustainable processes. The Thomas Siebel Scholars Foundation has extended its Siebel Scholars Program to Biomedical Engineering Ph.D. students who have outstanding academic achievements, a track record of distinguished research, and excellence in leadership qualities. The Howard Hughes Medical Research Institute (HHMI) and other foundations and institutes have also begun to support biomedical engineering education, including   translation to clinical medicine and industrial products. Professional Societies such as the Biomedical Engineering Society (BMES), IEEE/Engineering in Medicine and Biology, and many others have been playing significant roles in fostering entrepreneurism for students and other members.

While the funding for research and education in the United States is at the top of the world, its rate of change is rather alarming   . For example, the annual increase in NIH funding is barely in keeping with inflation. The recent stimulus funding provides a large infusion of funds, but its effectiveness remains to be determined, and the post   -stimulus cliff effect, unless countered by a measure for sustaining, could be devastating. In comparison to some other countries, e.g., China, the rate of % change of U.S. funding support is markedly behind. There is an urgent need to enhance funding support for research and training from the government and the private sector in order to sustain and enhance the engines of discovery in universities and research institutions.

19.5. Public Policy and Healthcare Delivery

The convergence of the remarkable advances in biology with the rapid
developments in novel engineering technologies has impacted
healthcare, e.g., the emergence of combinati on products (e.g., biologic
and device or drug and device) offer new therapeutic possibilities . The
use of various types of stem cells in regenerative medicine provides the
opportunity to develop cell   -based and other novel therapies for the
treatment of di seases heretofore not possible. As new therapeutic and
diagnostic procedures become increasingly available, there is the
important question of rising healthcare expenditures; therefore, it is
important to develop policies to assess comparative cost-effectiveness in
order to curtail spending and enhance value. This is particularly
important in the U.S. because of the growing number of people without
health insurance.

With the rapid advances in healthcare approaches, it is important
that our regulatory proced ures can adapt to these increasing demands by
making the best cost -effective therapeutic modalities available to the
public while protecting them from potential risks of untoward effects.

Intellectual property is the primary asset for the innovative
entrepreneurs, and we should be diligent in maximizing the effectiveness
for protecting their discoveries. Risk capital is the fuel of innovation,
and we must develop new and sustainable models to fund innovation.

The important role of federal funding in fueli   ng and translating
novel discovery has already been mentioned . Organizations such as the
Federation of American Societies for Experimental Biology (FASEB),
Research!America, American Medical Association, AIMBE and others
have been active in providing inputs for federal funding and other public
policy matters. It is important that individual biomedical engineers join
in these efforts to enhance our voice from the biomedical engineering
community and our communication with our legislators and our society.

19.6. Global Nature of Biomedical Engineering Entrepreneurism

Science and engineering have become increasingly global with
vanishing national boundaries, and this is also the case for biomedical
engineering entrepreneurism. Global economy also requires enh   anced
partnership to reach out nationally and internationally and share our
contacts. We need to interact with and learn from each other on the

various matters mentioned above. An example is the adoption of policies that curtail spending and enhance value, e.g., assessment of comparative cost-effectiveness of therapeutic procedures, implementation of information technology, easy access to primary care, role of government in negotiating payment for care, and payment systems that reward preventive care, manag ement of chronic conditions, care coordination, and health outcomes.

As a result of the global nature of our society, biomedical engineering must address health problems in not only the developed, but also the developing, countries. We must view every huma n life as equal in worth and their saving . Inequality in access to education and economic opportunities by disadvantaged people across the world leads to intractable health problems and inequality in healthcare. Public health should be used to improve peop le's health and lives. We should develop healthcare technologies that are not only effective, but also cost - effective and easy to deliver. Public health can be advanced by using biomedical technologies from discovery to development, and to therapeutical delivery.

19.7. Conclusions

In order to be a successful biomedical engineering entrepreneur, the individual must have the basic core values and characters, including passion and dedication for the work, but these must be balanced with other priorities in life: health and family.

The development of a biomedical engineer entrepreneur requires an excellent interdisciplinary background and education, with the abilities to identify important problems and to convert ideas into innovative products for clinical a pplication. It is important to have outstanding mentors or role models in career development.

Biomedical engineering entrepreneurs need to interact with other engineers, the management, technical and supporting staff, field representatives, physicians, other health professionals, and patients, with the final aim of improving the health of patients and treat their illness. Managerial and inter -personal skills are particularly important for those who would take a managerial position.

The funding support by go vernment agencies for research and training has played an important role in fostering the creation of novel ideas, development of new products, and education of biomedical engineers. The unprecedented, strong, and dedicated support of biomedical engineering by The Whitaker Foundation has made a major impact on the development of the discipline. There is an urgent need to increase research and training funding by governmental agencies and foundations to sustain and enhance the fountain of innovation and engine of discovery.

The convergence of the remarkable advances in biology with the rapid developments in novel engineering technologies has impacted healthcare, and there is the possibility of concurrent rise in healthcare expenditures. It is important to dev elop policies to assess comparative cost-effectiveness and to adapt our regulatory procedures. It is also important to develop models for intellectual property and risk capital. Biomedical engineers should enhance our voice regarding funding and other matters, and increase communications with our legislators and our society.

Biomedical engineering entrepreneurism has become increasingly global. Global economy requires enhanced partnership to reach out and share our contacts. We need to interact with and lea rn from each other on the various matters mentioned above related to healthcare delivery and health policy. Biomedical engineering must address health problems in developing countries and value every human life as equal in worth.

The various topics discus   sed above can be summarized in a diagrammatic form in the next page (Fig. 19.1).

Acknowledgments: Many of the passages and ideas were taken from the excellent comments in Chapter 18 of this book by Earl E. Bakken, C. M. Chang, Karen Davis, Bill Gates, Bill Hawkins, R obert Jarvik, Peter G. Katona, Michael Khoo, Robert Nerem, President Barack Obama, Duane Roth, and Harold Varmus. Because several of the thoughts were common to several contributors, the author apologizes that there are no clear identifications of the specific sources.

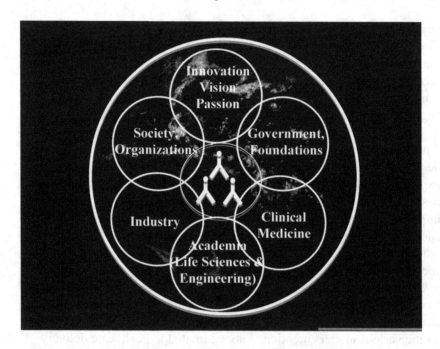

Figure 19.1. A schematic diagram to illustrate the thoughts presented in this Chapter. In the center of the diagram, each of the three lambda   -like figures represents symbolically a person: It is the Ch inese character for a person 人. Each person must have the core values and be able to balance his/her life, as mentioned in the text. It is essential for the person to have ideas for innovation, a clear vision, and a strong passion for his work and for other people, especially the pati ents. In the Chinese language, the combination of three such person symbols becomes a group of persons, or people 众. Thus, people are in the center of everything, and it is essential to have interactions among people, including that between entrepreneur s and colleagues, physicians, and patients, that between mentor and mentee, and many others.

The bottom part indicates the importance of having a strong interaction among academia (including life science and engineering), clinical medicine, and industry. The biomedical engineering enterprise needs the support of government and foundation, and it is essential to have effective professional organization and to interaction with the society. The large round background indicates the global nature of these activities and objectives.

Index